Winifred Foley was born in 1914 in a mining community in the Forest of Dean. She was married for over fifty years and had three sons and a daughter, as well as ten grandchildren and twelve great-grandchildren. After living and working in London, Winifred and her husband moved back to south-west England when their children were young. Winifred stayed in the area until her death in 2009. Her first volume of autobiography, *Full Hearts and Empty Bellies*, is also available in paperback from Abacus.

Also by Winifred Foley

Full Hearts and Empty Bellies

SHINY PENNIES
AND
GRUBBY PINAFORES

How We Overcame Hardship to Raise
a Happy Family in the 1950s

Winifred Foley

ABACUS

Book 1 first published in Great Britain with the title *Back to the Forest* in
1981 by Macdonald & Co, copyright © Winifred Foley, 1981

Book 2 first published in Great Britain with the title *No Pipe Dreams for Father*
in 1977 by Douglas McLean and in 1978 with additional material
by Futura Publications, a division of Macdonald & Co,
copyright © Winifred Foley, 1977, 1978

This edition published in 2011 for Index Books Ltd.

The moral right of the author has been asserted.

A CIP catalogue record for this book
is available from the British Library.

ISBN 978-0-349-12293-9

Typeset in Goudy by M Rules
Printed and bound in Great Britain by
Clays Ltd, St Ives plc

Papers used by Abacus are from well-managed forests
and other responsible sources.

MIX
Paper from
responsible sources
FSC
www.fsc.org   FSC® C104740

Abacus
An imprint of
Little, Brown Book Group
100 Victoria Embankment
London EC4Y 0DY

An Hachette UK Company
www.hachette.co.uk

www.littlebrown.co.uk

To my friends

CONTENTS

BOOK 1

Back to the Forest

PART I

Now we had come past Gloucester I began to believe it. I really was coming back to the Forest; not quite back to the heart of the Dean, where I had spent my childhood, with its unique landscape and miles of woodland paths to roam at will, but to a good second-best. This was an isolated cottage on a country estate of farmland, woods, and orchards only a few miles from the Forest's edge.

Over the back flap of the huge removal van I watched the landscape pass; cottages, farms and homesteads that had become so familiar in my many journeys home for the holidays when I was a domestic servant in London.

Syd had moved up into the cab now to act as guide, and sat squashed between the driver, his mate and the gearstick. Our three sons, aged fifteen, eleven, and nine, were perched as comfortably as the driver could arrange us, with Jenny, aged six, on my lap. Between Syd and the children and me were packed all our worldly goods.

Now, one hundred miles from London, I began to think more objectively about our situation. It seemed odd that one human being, a middle-aged, dumpy, homely-looking little woman at that, had driven us to make this momentous decision. I pondered on the power of one human being to affect the lives of others. Two outstanding examples came to mind, Jesus Christ and Hitler. Millions of lives had been changed by their opposing influences. Our experience was microscopic, but all-important to us just the same.

For the umpteenth time I wondered what the cottage would be like. Syd had seen it briefly when he had come for his interview at the sawmill, but all he could tell me was that the surrounding countryside was beautiful, and the interior of the cottage a bit rough and primitive. I hoped we were not again jumping out of the frying-pan into the fire! Never, I thought! No matter what the place was like, it would have the wonderful compensation we needed above all; the freedom to live as a family, not afraid to make a bit of noise, away from the dangers of traffic, and above all, from 'Her downstairs'. Anyway, my curiosity would soon be satisfied.

Then thoughts of our finances took over. After we had paid the driver and his mate we would have only a few pounds left to last us till Syd drew his first wages. I had already decided to double the tip for the driver's mate; coming down the notorious Birdlip Hill must have added five years to his age, and he was already getting on a bit. The driver, who was also the owner, had ignored Syd's warning to take a longer route to avoid Birdlip; he had lived to regret it, but only just.

Nowadays traffic is diverted to a new and gentler slope, but then there was no alternative. Faced with this unexpected challenge, driver and van went at it manfully. The huge pantechnicon, already past retirement age and overloaded, swayed and groaned its way down, exploding with fury at such treatment. Brakes and steering had a terrible job negotiating the headlong descent. On reaching flat ground at the bottom the driver stopped. You could feel the relief; even the old van, still hissing with indignation, cooled off and put on a brave face again.

The children and I clambered out to stretch our legs. I could see the faces of the three men were putty-coloured, with beads of sweat oozing out of their foreheads. I was feeling a bit sick myself, and I told them that the boys and I had been pressing hard against the flap to slow it down. This brought tiny smiles to their wan faces but it was obvious my fear had not been groundless; it could have been a near thing. We all had a little rest, the driver and his mate shared a few swigs from a brandy flask, Syd assured them there were no more hills like that, and we re-started.

A few more miles, and we turned off at the end of a village and drove down a hedgerowed lane, and then up between two lodge houses, the entrance to the private drive of a manor house. It was like a royal welcome, between banks of glorious multi-hued rhododendrons in their full majesty, for this was the latter end of June. The manor, built in the style of a French chateau, was fronted by spacious well-kept lawns. The wide tarmac drive ended at the stables, but forking sharply off was a narrow cobbled road winding steeply up for about three hundred yards between a wild woodland copse and grazing meadows. After climbing a sharp little crest under a huge old chestnut tree, the road gently flattened and came to a peaceful end in a wide stone-pillared gateless entrance. Inside, surrounded by old stone barns, was an area of tangled nettles, thistles, couchgrass and brambles, with a little footpath trodden through. To my city-saturated eyes, even this weedy undergrowth was not objectionable.

The old barns were beautiful; the weathered tiles were

patchily patinaed with yellow-green moss, and the stones had delicately absorbed all the colours of the rainbow. This is not at first obvious to the naked eye, but look long enough and the porous surfaces reveal they are not simply grey but are stained with the blended dyes of nature. Standing forlornly in dusty archways beneath the barns were old farmcarts made redundant by the tractors. They conjured up pictures of the stalwart carthorses that would never again stand harnessed to their cobwebbed shafts. The place had an air of abandoned, beautiful, peaceful sadness.

The pathway led to a little wooden gate under a crumbling rustic arch that was held together with rambler roses. Here I gave a little squeal of delight. 'Look, kids! It's even nicer than Little Grey Rabbit's house!' In London, to keep the children as quiet as the proverbial mice before bedtime, we used to indulge in our favourite daydream, looking through the 'Little Grey Rabbit' books. 'One day maybe we'll have a cottage in the country with woods and fields for you to play in, and you'll all be able to make a noise indoors, and if Mummy nags you, then you can hit me on the head with a hammer.' The way the boys' faces lit up at the thought of bashing me revealed the torture I was putting them through by perpetually hissing to them to Be Quiet.

The gate opened on to a small, stone-paved courtyard flanked by a one-storeyed extension to the cottage proper. There was a pump for our water supply with a stone trough in the front; a pink rambler rose climbed up the cottage wall; winter jasmine had sent its hardy roots under the flagstones and almost covered the low extension; a few weeds grew in a narrow flower bed under the rose; the small picturesque windows were latticed. All this far exceeded my anticipatory dreams.

The original door of the cottage had been boarded up and

replaced with one in the extension. I was charmed by the small octagonal lattice window let into it. The key had been left under a brick by the door. I had the privilege of turning it in the lock. Then I let out another squeal of surprise, this time of disappointment. I suppose one could say that the 'room' it revealed was full of character. A black miserable character it was too, for black seemed to be the predominant colour in it.

'I warned you it was a bit rough,' said Syd, looking at me warily. I was speechless at this understatement. The entrance wall was of normal height, with a 'ceiling' going up to a peak of about fourteen feet which then sloped down to a back wall about five feet high. This wall was of rough stone covered with patches of mildew, and the floor was a rubble of dirt and loose dry bits of concrete. The other three walls were a mixture of brick, stone, and small rough concrete patches, covered, where it could adhere, with flaking smoke-blackened yellow-ochre distemper.

Cobwebs hung from the flaking ceiling, and the doors, once dark green, were now almost black with age and smoke. This 'room' had one surprisingly agreeable feature, a charming, hand-made brick fireplace. The front of this, too, was blackened and sooty, and there was no basket to light a fire in. A rough stone archway led into the rest of the extension, a small square room. Here the floor was not so bad; there were only a couple of rubbledy holes, and whoever had mixed the concrete had made a better job of it. This room was graced with a ceiling of a sort, plasterboard with the joints pasted over with paper. Here and there the paper had cracked open enough to allow dirt-encrusted cobwebs to hang down like stalactites. The walls were unplastered rough brick, and the room was bare of fitments of any sort.

A false wall ran across it to form a narrow cell at the back, the door to which was at the side of the brick fireplace. 'Oh, no!' I gasped, when I saw what was housed in there. But oh, yes, it was; a bucket toilet, which would have to be carried through the 'living-room' for emptying, because there was no back door. The bucket was empty but the odour lingered still. There was a tiny window, but the earth at the back had encroached up beyond the bottom of it and rampant weeds and brambles let but little light filter through.

Bewildered and depressed, I hastened to see the rest of my new home. The door into it was wide enough to let a milk-float through, but it opened easily enough, and my spirits rose a little. Now there was a small proper room, with a staircase going up from it, there was a good window, there was a boxed-in fireplace, and the walls were smooth and nicely distempered in cream. Big enough for a single bed for our Chris, I thought. On my left a door opened into a large larder. Here, too, the ceiling went up to a fourteen-foot apex, but there was a reasonable window and ample storage shelves of sound wood. It was well hung with cobwebs and flakes of whitewash fell everywhere, but it was a very handy storeroom.

Another door, another room, a good square room, big enough for two single beds for Richard and Nick. This had actually been papered, but the damp from outside had bulged it well away from the walls. The floor was of red tiles thick with mildew, there was a tiny, usable grate, and the remains of bacon hooks were hammered deep into the ceiling. This was better; I began to feel I could live here after all. I went upstairs; two rooms, one very small, had been recently papered and painted. There were not many damp patches on the walls, and though the ceilings sloped down in each room and were veined with cracks and slight malformations, they felt sound enough to the touch. This was an improvement.

But what about that shambles downstairs? I could not help feeling very depressed about it all, so sharp a contrast as it was to the modern streamlined flat we had left behind. However, the cottage was wired for electricity, if only for lighting, and that was a marvel considering its isolation. In the 1950s, electric cookers, washers, and fridges had not become part of estate workers' lives. In his efforts to enlarge and modernise his living-space the previous tenant had removed the old cooking range and wash-copper. Being a skilled carpenter and earning extra money outside his regular job, he had bought calor-gas appliances to replace them. He had taken them all away when he moved, and also the fire-basket from the brick fireplace. Oh, well! At least we had a kettle, so I went into the fuel shed to see what I could scrounge to light a fire. There was a small pile of sawdust, a few dry twigs, and a pile of rubbish from which I removed a couple of half-perished gas-masks. I also found some pieces of old brick to balance the kettle on. The chimney had a fit of the sulks; for every wisp of smoke it accepted it belched back acrid clouds into my face as I tried to blow some flame under the kettle.

Syd, the children, and the removal men were busy carrying all our things into the yard. I put out a good spread of the sandwiches and home-made cake I had brought with me. 'Sorry, no tea,' I told the men, 'it'll take till Christmas to boil that kettle,' which was still sitting on some desultory puffs of evil-smelling smoke. We slaked our thirsts with cups of pump water that came up icy-cold and very limey from its source eighty feet below the yard. When they had eaten, we paid the removal men and expected them to go on their way. 'No, no,' they insisted, 'we'll help you upstairs with the beds and wardrobes first.'

We had recently become a 'two-wardrobe family', which gave me a sense of real affluence. One was a double, a utility model, paid for by many hours of charring. The other we bought cheap from a friend's employers. The fact that a budding film starlet had hung her clothes in it gave it a glamour, and it was something to swank about. Syd had wheeled it home from the West End on a barrow borrowed from a street trader.

Looking at the narrow staircase with a right turn at the bottom the driver looked a bit dubious, as well he might. There was just no way either wardrobe was going to be winkled round that bend. And they never were. The same applied to the base of our double bed, metal springs on a stout steel frame. No matter how we turned and twisted, screwed and unscrewed, sweated and cursed, it was not going up. It looked easy enough, and you could start it all right, but you were soon baulked. The bedroom window would have to come out, frame and all; meanwhile Syd and I would have to manage on the mattress.

Our two frustrated helpers said goodbye. Cockneys born and bred, it had been obvious since our arrival that they pitied us as a lot of lunatics for leaving the Smoke for such uncivilised remoteness. 'A place for everything, and everything in its place,' had been a favourite saying of one of my employers in service. Our new home still looked depressing and chaotic when I had done my best to follow her advice. At last we got the children bedded down, the boys too full of curiosity and excitement to feel upset, Jenny cuddling her doll to comfort it. Very soon they fell asleep.

It was late evening, but still light, when Syd and I flopped down into a chair on either side of the obstinate fireplace. None of us had been able to have a warm wash; the pump water was too hard to lather, and soap just turned into a floating grey scum. How on earth could I cope with bringing up a family under these conditions, I asked myself wretchedly. It was no good nagging Syd; I was the one most responsible for bringing us all here. It was all very well for him to come back from his interview raving about the beautiful countryside and the views from the cottage! He *should* have noticed there was not so much as a hob to put a saucepan on, and no means of heating water for washing.

The sawmill had allowed him a day off from work to help us settle in, so I began to plan what he was going to do with it.

'You'll have to go to Gloucester tomorrow and order me an electric cooker and wash-copper.'

'What with?'

'You'll have to get it on the never-never, from the Electricity Board. Get them for the lowest deposit they'll take, with four years to pay.'

'What about the deposit, and the cost of installation?'

'Well, I've got five pound and threepence-ha'penny. I've brought some groceries with us and enough bread for a couple of days. How much have you got?'

'My 'bacca money and two-and-elevenpence. Don't forget this firm keeps a week in hand, so it's a fortnight before I get any money.'

'Can't be helped, you'll have to ask for a sub when we're right broke, and I shall write to the estate manager. It's their responsibility to pay for the installation.'

We sat on, not speaking, gloomily chewing over our problems. The night gloom gathered, too, outside and inside. Neither of us got up to switch on the light until a scratching scuffling noise started above the kitchen ceiling. Mice! Or, worse still, rats! I had suffered from an irrational fear of these creatures since a mouse had run up my skirt as I sat on the mat in the fireglow of a darkened room.

I jumped up to switch on the light, and at that same moment a mouse (or was it a *rat*?) missed its footing and fell through a papered-over crack in the kitchen ceiling.

'Now don't you start screaming or having hysterics, you'll scare Jenny,' warned Syd as I panicked up on to a chair. The mouse (or *rat*?) panicked too, as Syd poked it out from under the sideboard with the broom. Much as I detested them, I could not have borne for Syd to bash it to death, and Syd has no killer instinct either. At last it ran out through the gap under the front door. Well, it had been a long day, but I did not feel tired any more. How could I go to sleep in a house over-run by rodents?

'Come on, let's go to bed; there won't be any mice up there.' Syd was fed up and tired. He is a good husband, but when he is fed up and tired his temper is likely to erupt and it can be quite a temper. I had little choice: stop down here alone with more benighted creatures likely to fall through the ceiling, or go upstairs and lie on a mattress on the floor, a floor with mice probably running about under it and even over it. Holding my nose, I made Syd come in with me to the bucket privy.

'I shall have to have the light on all night,' I said. Syd was too tired to argue; in five minutes he was fast asleep. I lay with my shoulders against the wall, tense, and getting tenser, with horror at every creak and sigh, endemic in the structure of old cottages.

Now I had plenty of time to review the situation. Who was it, I reminded myself, that had kept on about moving? Who would not care where we lived so long as it had four walls and a roof and no-one living underneath? Could we go back to that flat, if we phoned quickly in the morning? Would I, I asked myself, would I go back to that flat with 'Her downstairs'? I was not sure; deep down in me was a feeling that the boats had been burned, and we were going to stay. No, no, I cried, and I *was* sure that I wished myself back in our tenement house in Lisson Grove, where we had lived before the flat.

Lisson Grove, that unsalubrious corner of London; Lisson Grove and the patched-up corner tenement; Lisson Grove and our friends and neighbours. It is said you can live in London and never know your neighbours, but that certainly did not apply in our case.

Six tenancies occupied three floors. Each had two rooms and a big kitchen. We shared two landing lavatories, the front door, the stairs, and most of the ins and outs and ups and downs of each other's lives. The ground floor, the basement, and the back yard were occupied by a firm of cabinet-makers.

The other flat on our landing on the second floor was occupied by Lally and her three little girls. From a childhood spent among an amoral family she had blossomed into a full-blown nymphomaniac. Unhealthily pale, she had become an expert in make-up; slight and bony of build she atoned for her lack of nubility by the open lust in her eyes at the sight of a pair of trousers. She was married to a regular soldier who regularly left her pregnant on his infrequent leaves, but never physically deprived.

Nevertheless Lally continued to assuage her loneliness with a variety of war-time soldiers, thick on the ground just then. If nature insisted that we had to creep across the landing in the small hours, there was a likely chance of bumping into a soldier stealthily leaving or approaching Lally's door. She did it all for lust, not money; I often knew her send one of her children up the road to cadge half a fag off her sister. 'Tell 'er I'm gaspin' for a puff,' she would say.

She often left me gasping with her uninhibited accounts of the ways of a woman with a man. For convention's sake she attributed these to her life with her husband, but even he could not have been that much of a Don Juan. She certainly showed up my own shortcomings in the nuptial field; I had not even passed my 'Oh!' levels. Lally gave me some shock therapy treatment; poor Syd, I had been a dull bed partner. When we had moved there I was pregnant with our second child. We had been married six years, but I was still basically an inhibited prude, due to the childhood influence of a well-meaning but un-enlightened mother.

I am a one-man woman and Lally's generous distribution of her favours held no appeal for me. But just as most women would like to be a Cordon Bleu cook, recipes for cooking a husband's goose are also very handy. Our marriage improved no end.

Lally's family also provided us with our Saturday night 'viewing', not on a TV screen, which had not then become part of life, but through our kitchen window. Every Saturday evening her seventeen-year-old sister baby-sat for Lally so that she could join her large family for their weekly booze-up in the pub opposite. They gathered at the pub entrance in a mood of great affection and camaraderie. Around closing time they either came out or were thrown out, all their pent-up aggros and grievances now released by alcohol. Soon they were shouting a Kinsey-type report of their sexual behaviour, moral lapses, thieving habits, cross couplings, and who's-whose accounts of paternity. Nudgings and pushings turned into challenges, and then fights, joined by fringe enemies or supporters.

Heads crashed against fists, walls, and even pavements. This weekly boil-up of their dirty habits was forgotten and forgiven in time for the next booze-up, even if a couple of heads still sported plasters.

The widening of my sex education, initiated by Lally, was continued, as chance would have it, by Annabelle. Annabelle was a glamorous woman living in the block of flats opposite, and I did a bit of charring for her. She too was prone to entertaining soldiers, mostly from the officer classes, American preferably, but unlike Lally she charged heavily for her services. In exchange for my clothes coupons, which I could not afford to use, she gave me some of her left-off clothing. Tarty tight skirts, high-heeled shoes and underwear! Phew! Nothing to help me keep warm but enough to send the steam out of Syd's earholes! I learned, not without the loss of my romantic idealism, that love is one thing and sex another. Entwined, they are the nearest we can reach towards the stars.

Mr and Mrs B. lived upstairs, and the rest of us considered that they gave a bit of a social status to our tenement. They both worked in an office, and set off each morning smartly dressed and carrying rolled umbrellas. She was decidedly snooty, and had a job to crack her face into a smile if she passed any of us on the stairs. They did not mix at all, which left the rest of us free to gossip and conjecture about where she went every week-end. Mr B. was always left on his own from Friday evening to Monday morning. He was the nicer of the two. A rather delicate man, he was allowed a war-time ration of an extra pint of milk a day because of a stomach ulcer. At weekends he always left this daily pinta unobtrusively by Lally's door for her children.

One evening, as I laid the table for Syd's home-coming meal, I heard the B.s' radiogram playing rather loudly, and I could tell they were dancing to the music. I joined in and picked up a rather puzzled Chris into my arms to waltz around the room. We were happy in the midst of life.

Suddenly I heard footsteps running down the stairs and there was an urgent banging on our door. Mrs B. stood there, wild-eyed and trembling. 'Quick, quick! Please come up! Jeremy is having a dreadful turn. I'm frightened.' I put Chris down and called Lally to keep an eye on him. Then I ran upstairs, relieved to hear Syd coming in at the same time.

Upstairs the radiogram was still playing. Mr B. lay on the settee. I had never seen a dying person before, but my instincts told me he was breathing his last breaths and every one was an agony. Gently I put my arm around his shoulders and talked to him soothingly as to a baby, but I did not think he could hear. His thin pale ascetic face was now swollen and purple, his unseeing eyes bulging almost out of it. I prayed he was not suffering, and almost at once the swollen features subsided and the colour began to go. His breathing stopped, and though he still felt warm in my arms I knew he had died. Mrs B. had turned the radiogram off, and was now having near-hysterics. She too could see he had gone.

'Oh, my God!' she moaned. 'What shall I do? How *could* he die on me like this? We're not married, you see, not married. If my husband ever found out! He's away travelling for his firm all the week. That's why I stay here in London with Jeremy. My God, what can I do now?'

As these revelations tumbled out in her panic I was too surprised to comment. 'Half this furniture is mine,' she went on. At this point I lost sympathy with her; her concern was entirely for herself.

Just then Syd came up and looked at Mr B. He told me to go downstairs with Chris and though he knew little about it, tried to massage life and breath back into the lungs of the dead man.

Meanwhile, Meg from downstairs had got wind that something was amiss. Nosey, but practical and sensible, she sent Syd to ring for the doctor, and took 'Mrs B.' downstairs with her to give her some tea and stop her helpless snivelling. After the doctor had pronounced Mr B. dead, she helped 'Mrs B.' collect and pack her things, called a taxi, saw her into it and watched her disappear from the scene.

A few days later a hearse drew up outside, and some men carried a coffin upstairs. After a while they brought it down. Lally and Meg and I stood by our doors for a moment paying our last respects to our lonely unwanted neighbour who could be such a gentleman. They handed him over the banisters as if he was a piece of furniture. There were no flowers, no mourners, just Mr B.'s last solitary quiet descent down our stairs.

His weekday 'wife' came back just once, to arrange the sale of his furniture to a second-hand dealer. We were not sorry to see the back of her; superior class indeed!

Meg lived in the rooms directly below ours. Many years in London had hardly watered down her Welsh accent, nor diminished her passion, surely shared by the majority of Welsh ladies, for a nice clean doorstep and entrance. With a bunch of young children playing a great deal on the doorsteps, achieving this ambition was a sore trial to Meg. She would chivvy and scold them for the mess they all too frequently made, and then destroy the whole effect by handing out to the miscreants sweets, and toys and crayons, etc., that she got from her charring jobs in the West End.

Some years before, Meg had discarded an erring husband, and now kept herself by being a daily treasure to a variety of people. Many of these were household names at the time, connected with the entertainment world. For the rest of us, Meg was very often a treasure trove as well. By now, war-time rations had been cut to the bone; but the affluent people Meg worked for were able to patronise the black market. Far from feeling the pinch, their cupboards and larders were over-stocked. Whenever she could, Meg relieved them of small amounts of tea, sugar, fats, or anything she could lay her hands on, sharing her pickings with those of us who had children.

She also shared with us her accounts of the unconventional behaviour of the well-known people she worked for. Gulps of juicy scandal went down with our shared pots of tea. Meg had no inhibitions about listening at, or peeping through, keyholes, and anybody's unlocked correspondence was hers for the reading. Once when she was temporarily cleaning the office of a top West End solicitor, we knew about a forthcoming divorce in royal circles months before the story broke in the papers.

Meg was every bit as generous with her help and advice to these straying sheep, as she was to her neighbours. One famous lady journalist she worked for was a widow who was entertaining high matrimonial hopes from an elderly and wealthy city tycoon. At the time he was tied to an invalid and mentally-handicapped wife, who was incarcerated in a very expensive nursing home.

One night a week he stayed with his unofficial fiancée; most other nights she shared her bed with a handsome TV personality. Meg was no prude about this arrangement, but one morning when she took the two cups of tea in, she found the TV man replaced, on one of his working nights, by a well-known well-married actor. Meg waltzed back out again with the tea, and later gave her employer a good scolding for getting a bit too promiscuous. She did not get the sack, which was just as well.

The city tycoon's unfortunate wife obliged everybody by dying quietly, and he quickly upped and married his young secretary. The betrayed lady journalist, her pride mortally wounded, became hysterically suicidal. A fortune had slipped through her grasp and her reputation as a *femme fatale* had been totally undermined. Now forty years old, almost alone, used and rejected by the men she thought she was using, life seemed to have nothing left for her. There was one final, irreversible way out.

Meg told me everything, and analysing her chatter I felt sure she had saved her employer. Her commonsense lectures, and her ability to make Madam see things in proper perspective, slowly brought her back on to an even keel. During this time Meg neglected her other jobs and stayed all hours to help restore the lady's sanity.

Meg was also the house 'banker' for us penurious tenants. Not a bank that we ever put money in; we only had overdrafts of odd shillings when the week was longer than the housekeeping money. Meg earned her living by long hours of charring, yet she never refused a borrower, never charged any interest, and often had to be persuaded into accepting repayment. She was just simply good-natured, but she was practical too, and dealt with the things life sent her as they came along.

One of the things that came along was her boy-friend. Meg had a boy-friend of her own, a Canadian soldier some fourteen years younger than herself – Meg was nudging forty. She was no glamour girl; she had a pleasant little face, a short dumpy figure, and she was a natty dresser. But the Canadian bowled us over; he was exceptionally handsome with a height and physique to match.

Aware of Meg's generous nature, we sniffed disapproval behind her back, convinced that she was just being used as a convenient free lodging for his leaves, and as a provider of hot meals and free gin.

As the time approached for the birth of our second child, the war was still a terrible curse hanging over us all. Here we are, I would think, a large ecological mass going in orbit round the sun, a planet with a core of still-molten fire, its thin crust covered with countless thousands of species of life, flora and fauna, liquids and chemicals, subject to earthquake and flood, tempests and fires, host to continuous death. Yet we added to our burdens of disaster the man-made holocaust of war! We hang the blame handily on such as Hitler, Napoleon, Genghis Khan, and so on, but one evil being could easily be eliminated in the cause of justice. Why did we kill rather than reason? What was in us that made us love to hate?

When I worked as a maid in a London boarding-house, I had met people of many nationalities and colours. They were all just ordinary people, some nice and some not so nice, just the same as everybody else. It was not logical for a whole nation to be the enemy of a whole nation. It could not be, and I did not believe it. I was puzzled and resentful to find myself part of a war, and as helpless to do anything about it as a leaf carried down a turbulent stream.

I was also a coward, with a strong sense of self-preservation, especially for Chris and the coming baby. When the sirens sounded in the small hours, people poured out of buildings like ants whose nests have been poked with a stick. Hearts in our mouths we ran, hoping to reach the comparative safety of the Underground station before the bombs fell. Heroic street wardens shouted at people to take cover. The blacked-out streets became caverns of Hell lit up by vipers' tongues of streaking red light as the guns and searchlights sought the dark enemy. The Devil's orchestra of the bass rumblings of explosions put wings on our feet.

Though handicapped by the large bump in front of me I ran like the clappers, easily keeping up with Syd who carried a sleepy, bundle-wrapped Chris. When the buzzbombs started, they would come anywhere at any time. Warnings were of little use, sleep was out of the question. So I persuaded Syd that the three of us, almost four, must sleep on the Underground platform every night.

The platforms were packed with people lying right to the edges. The few late-night trains broke up the sleep of any who had found it, and the passengers picked their way daintily among the blankets. Against the wall at the back were a few bunks occupied by the very old and the very young. Sometimes Chris had a bunk, if it were not too far from us. Often the three of us huddled together on the draughty stairs, snatching at sleep, waking again, talking in whispers to strangers whom adversity had turned into friends.

Then Hitler started his rocket attacks. There were no warnings; there could be none, because there was nothing to see or hear. Just an earth-shattering ominous explosion somewhere. Some poor soul had had it; not us, yet! These inexplicable explosions were not explained by the authorities for many weeks, but Cockney wit smelled it out, and dubbed them 'flying gas-mains'.

I was now over eight months pregnant, and one particular dread obsessed me. Supposing that all around us was hit by a rocket, and Chris was buried under the rubble and we could not get at him? After all, it was possible, it was even likely. The thought of it was enough to make me give in to Syd's persuasions, and to the entreaties of my parents, to go back to the Forest to stay with them.

My two younger sisters were living at home. Ironically, the war had saved them from a life of domestic service by bringing plenty of factory work to the locality. My parents were now in their fifties, and it caused a considerable upheaval in their little cottage to fit in a small grandson and a heavily pregnant daughter. My time was coming, and the district nurse arranged for me to have the baby in a municipal nursing home twenty-four miles away. Three weeks later I had a bonny boy almost nine pounds in weight. It was a Nature's miracle, really, for that baby had drawn his sustenance from dry porridge oats, health salts, cider, and surreptitious sniffs of metal polish.

The first four months of my pregnancies have always been a living hell of nausea. My taste buds go mad; all normal food smells and tastes like poison. I cannot tolerate tea, coffee, cocoa, or even plain bread and butter. But after four months I become a real pig for dry porridge oats, dry health salts by the handful, and as much cider as I can get; all items I have no liking for normally. Sniffing the metal polish is a great little luxury. Once they were born, however, I was a failure to all of them as a source of nourishment, and reluctantly had to put them on the bottle.

Meanwhile, the principal cause of these troubles, Syd, stayed in London and went on with his job. His wages were none too grand but he came down to see us pretty often. In our small crowded cottage, the brevity of his visits did not help me to re-adjust our marriage. I was worried, too, about the proximity of his lonely manhood to the lustful Lally.

'Wouldn't touch her with a barge-pole!' he would declare breezily. But that would not cure my jealousy; it was not a barge-pole I was worrying about.

Impulsively, obstinately resisting advice, I decided to return with Syd from one of his visits. It was a mistake. The dread of the children being buried by bombs or rockets took over in my mind more strongly than ever. What joy we had from being together again was quite overcast, and though we renewed the old routines they brought us no contentment.

Lally's philosophy was calm acceptance. 'If your number's on it you'll get it, so meanwhile, while you're waitin' for it, 'ave a good time. Enjoy a fag an' a drop o' booze, gel, an' a bit o' the other.' This did nothing for my jitters; I did not smoke or drink, anyway, and spent my nights tensed up to the point of hysterics waiting for oblivion from a rocket. Lally never even bothered to run for shelter.

Meg was brave too. She no longer went charring, as most of her employers had left London. She now worked at the headquarters where comforts for the troops sent from America and Canada were sorted. Early evening she took herself off to a newly-opened shelter under the Great Central hotel, where she enjoyed the luxury of a bunk bed.

Syd had never thought he was likely to get any special protection from Above. He was working very long hours and needed his sleep, so after taking me and the children to the Underground station he went back to bed in the tenement. Now that the rockets were coming day and night without warning, and the old bombing raids had stopped, people seemed more resigned, and calm in despair. The Underground platforms were almost empty; the normality was abnormal; the night-time fraternity had disbanded. The war was not being lost, nor was it being won in a hurry. Every day we wondered, should I leave again, take the children, and return to the Forest? At least, till the war was over?

PART II

Providence made up our minds. I had a letter from a second cousin in the village who was going to stay in Margate with her soldier husband's friends. I could have her cottage at the top of our village, furnished, for ten shillings a week. I wrote by return, saying yes, please, and thank you, and I told my Mam and Dad we were coming back again. It would be a struggle to find the ten shillings, but it was better than imposing on them.

It was a small and primitive cottage: downstairs, one room and a back-kitchen which also served as a coalhouse; upstairs, two small bedrooms. The bucket privy was at the bottom of a narrow strip of untended garden. There was a cold-water tap in the back-kitchen, but no sink or drainage. Cooking and water heating had to be done on a big open black-leaded grate with an oven at the side. The downstairs floor was stone-flagged, the furniture strictly utilitarian, and not the sort to worry about. But even without the cheery fire lit by a friendly neighbour for our cold evening arrival my heart was full of gratitude for this comparatively safe haven.

Then at three in the morning I faced a new sort of fear. At this awkward time Richard would wake for a bottle. Soft talk, cuddling, or a drink of Government orange juice were not acceptable substitutes, and his whimpers would develop into furious howls of frustration until he got what he wanted. Coming downstairs by candlelight to re-kindle the fire was an eerie business. The unlatchable back-kitchen door moaned creakily on its old hinges, the shadowy corners seemed full of ghosts. On this same sofa under this window an eld-erly relative of mine had been laid out. As a child I had seen her corpse there, for at the time, my shoulder aug-mented the walking stick of our arthritic old great-aunt. Viewing the corpses of her old friends was a social ritual for her. This particular old friend had been a kindly soul, but lying there emaciated by age, with her loose white hair and bony folded hands, she had looked already like a spectre.

I knelt by the fire blowing it into life. The candle flickered in the draughts, this way and that. As the fitful light fell on the sofa I could see it first empty, then in the dark, what shade was lying there? The back-kitchen door moaned open again; the leaky tap was dripping into a zinc bath. Plop, plop. Water, was it? Or maybe blood from the talons of a ghoul? I had to go in there for water to cool the bottle! I felt prickles of fear up the back of my neck, as candle in hand I pushed open the creaking door. Now, save for the firelight, the other room was dark, and the empty sofa waited for the wraith. Oh, come on, I told myself: brave enough by day scoffing at the notion of spirits coming back, yet now expecting an apparition any minute.

My task completed, I hurried back upstairs, courage return-ing with every step. What a comfort it was to hold the fat red-faced screaming little tyrant and put the teat to his lips!

He was comforted immediately, and apart from a few little grunts that might have been scolding or satisfaction, soon fell quiet. Chris had slept through it all in the old iron double bed he shared with me. I knew I would have to face this caper always at this time, for unlike to-day's mothers I had no plug-in gadgets for preparing night feeds. Anyway, I thought, imaginary things that did not really go bump in the night were better than bombs and rockets that did!

Adding to these nocturnal discomforts, we soon found that the roof leaked. When it rained I had to sleep with my knees up so I would not kick over the tin bath I put at the bottom of the bed to catch the regularly plopping drops. In this small room there was no way to place the bed so as to avoid the cascade. The back bedroom was even tinier, and quite unusable.

With two rents to pay out of Syd's modest wages we had to live very frugally. War-time rations were now at their most stringent, and kept the food bills small. Even so, I could not afford to buy coal, and my parents gave me a generous por-tion, though it was ill-spared. Mam needed a fire almost day and night. Dad was on shifts, and there were winter-wet pit clothes to dry. There was the washing for four grown-ups and the drying and airing of it round the fire. Then there was all the cooking. Domestic life revolved around a grate seldom empty.

Dustmen had not been thought of then, in our area, and village housewives tipped their ashes on to rubbish-mixes peppered about on the fringes of the woods. This was lucky for me, and I found it quite delightful going out into the snowy frosty beautiful forest to scrape the cokes from the ashes. Maybe, too, I would pick up some kindling wood, dead twigs sticking up through the snow. Sometimes when we got home a bucket of lump coal, a cabbage, or a few vegetables had been put by my back door. Knowing my inability to repay these kind gestures, the donors never embarrassed me by giving away their identities.

Worry for Syd's safety, and guilty feelings that I had no right to be luckier than those who still battled on in the bombed city, were my biggest headaches. When we could manage the fare, Syd came down for the week-end. He looked thinner every time, and eventually came out in multiple boils on his arms from poor diet and lack of wife's attentions. Once again I began to have doubts as to where my duty lay.

The dark days lengthened into a glorious spring and an early summer. Baby Richard was approaching his first birthday. The Forest was green again underfoot and overhead. It was a glorious place for me to take my two lovely children out walking. Suddenly my problem was solved. The war in Europe was smouldering to a halt; not, alas, because lessons had been drawn from its macabre futility, but because the military power of one side had overwhelmed the other. Just as when a baby is born the relief from pain is too great to comprehend, so it was too wonderful to believe that the war was really over, that we had survived it, and that the tenement house and our neighbours had been spared. The war was over, nothing else mattered, and we went back to London. To be all together again in our ugly little corner made light of my regret at leaving our lovely pastoral surroundings.

Our euphoria soon took a bit of a knock. Syd might have got thin from malnourishment, but he soon proved that he was still in working order. To my great distress, and despite the teachings of Marie Stopes, I was pregnant again and Richard barely a year old! Old wives' remedies, potions magic and absurd, kangaroo jumps, carrying heavy loads, and wishful thinking, all had no effect. It was back to the nausea, back to the cider, the dry oats, the health salts, and the metal polish sniffs again. Never mind, perhaps this time it would be the longed-for girl. I day-dreamed of tying bonnet ribbons instead of popping on round woolly hats, and I tried not to think of our inadequate finances and the escalating laundry problems.

Our rooms had a sink and cold-water tap in the kitchen, and nowhere at all outside to dry the washing; so twice a week I went to the municipal wash-house half a mile away. I had to push two prams, with Chris hanging on to my skirts. The one pram held Richard and all his paraphernalia – orange juice, bottle of feed, biscuits, and rattles to keep him amused – for often there was a queue. In the other pram, big, ancient and hoodless, I put our dirty washing tied up in a sheet like a gargantuan Christmas pudding. Wheeling a pram with each hand, with a protesting little boy hanging on your skirts, takes a bit of doing. Pedestrians had the choice of squeezing up to the shop-fronts or stepping off the pavements to let us through. At the busy crossings I took Richard's pram over first and made sure the brake was on properly, before coming back for the washing. Not once did I ever have to cross over again. Gentlemen abounded in London. Sometimes it was a road sweeper, a road mender, a barrow-boy, or a man in overalls. But gentlemen come in other guises. Once it was a city type, complete with bowler hat, natty striped suit, gold-topped umbrella and all. He made an incongruous picture, wheeling my old pram of dirty washing across the busy road, and raising his hat to me before calling a taxi. The two prams, with Lally's one, were housed under the stairs in the entrance passage.

One afternoon, when I was about seven months pregnant, I was feeling so relieved as I pulled the prams up the front steps, carted the load of clean washing up four flights, and came down again for Richard, to bring him up. Chris clattered up in front ready for his tea. I was just in time to see to Syd's meal. The casserole and rice-pudding had been put in the oven on a low heat, and had cooked to a nicety. I put the kettle on for a longed-for cup of tea. Chris sat to the table, and I put Richard up in his high chair beside him. I stood and looked at them while the kettle sang behind me.

There was a knock on the door, and I stepped happily across to open it. With some surprise, and a little apprehension, I found a telegram boy standing there. He thrust the little envelope into my hand, and hurried away down the stairs. Standing by the open door in a daze I opened it and read it. PLEASE COME HOME FATHER BADLY HURT CISS

Dad badly hurt? Badly hurt! How? Where? Why had Ciss sent the telegram? She was a close friend to all the family, but why was it not from my brother, Dick, or one of my sisters? Shocked and confused, I stood where I was. Only one thought came again and again through the jumble of dear memories and dreadful speculations; I must go home to him at once. Whatever the difficulties, they must be overcome; I must go. Somehow, I and all the family, and all those around him who loved him, would make him better again, no matter how grievous the wound.

Then Meg came up, nosey helpful Meg, curious to know what the telegram was about. Without a word I held it out to her. She took one look at me and ran downstairs, coming back with a glass of brandy. She led me back indoors, pushed me down into a chair in the corner, and gave me the glass.

'Meg, I must go home. *Now*,' I moaned.

She was getting the boys' tea out, and she said calmly, 'Now, Win, you mustn't upset yourself so much, not in your state. It may not be as bad as you think. Anyway, here's Syd coming up the stairs. Good job the kettle's boiling; I'll wet him a cup of tea.'

Syd came in and his eye met mine immediately. 'Whatever's up?' he said, and Meg handed him the telegram. His face paled, for he too dearly loved my Dad. Unable to speak, he sat down, looking at the telegram again and again. Meg put the cup of tea in his hand, and rummaged through her bag for a handful of change. 'Go and phone the policeman in Win's village,' she said in reassuring tones. 'Find out how things are.' He knew there was no policeman, but he phoned the garage on the main road. They would know. He had hurried to the phone box but he came back slowly, his feet dragging, his mind in turmoil as he sought for words and ways to tell me.

There was no need; his stricken face revealed his thoughts; the dismal truth was etched in his drawn cheeks and his downcast eyes. Though muted by time, the mental anguish of that moment lives with me still. The emotional torture swelled into a pain that threatened to burst my head and heart. Father dead. Merciless logic insisted I accept it, but everything else, mind, soul, body, being, emotions, memories, all shouted it down. I screamed out, 'No, no, no.' Then I was broken, and unable to move. Syd stood there with his cap and coat still on, dull, grey, helpless. 'He didn't suffer, Win. It was instantaneous, a fall in the pit.'

I could not take any comfort from his words; there was no

comfort now, nor sense, nor any meaning to life. If Father was dead, why carry on with this cruel joke called existence, where, whatever our merits, our lives and deaths were ruled by a feckless destiny? Where one so good as Dad, so true, so loved, could be destroyed as thoughtlessly as a gnat swatted by a gardener? Yet even the poor gnat has feelings; does it too not suffer pain? The world was full of pain, and by living in it I was contributing to it. Never had I wanted to cause suffering, but it was too late. There at the table sat two little human beings I had brought into the world and another lived inside me. They, too, would suffer, and cause suffering. I was trapped in despair. What was love, where was its power or purpose, if one could not even bid its inspirer the last goodbye?

I picked Richard out of his chair, and sat cuddling him to me, rocking back and forth and moaning, 'I must go home, I must go home.' Syd came to me and said again and again, 'He did not suffer, Win, he did not suffer. How can we go, now, tonight, with you like this? We'll have to go in the morning. What good can you do now?' I took no notice as I sat there in my stunned and helpless dismay.

Meg had fetched Syd's sister, and the two of them were moving about doing what had to be done. To me they were like figures in a dream; everything seemed unreal except the hurt inside me. Syd's sister said, 'All right, dear, all right, Win, you shall go home. Now. Pull yourself together a bit, and we'll get you ready. I'll take Chris and look after him till you come back.' I knew Chris would not mind. Syd got up. 'Oh, come on then,' he said. 'It's no good arguing. Might as well get on with it.'

The two women packed Richard's clothes and nappies and some things for me. We had almost no money, and the shoes

I wore, my only pair, were shabby and downtrodden. Meg fetched up a pair of hers, and one of her smart coats, and helped me into them. She pushed some pound notes into Syd's hand. Syd's sister called and paid for a taxi to take us to Paddington Station. We kissed our Chris goodbye for now. He went off with his auntie, and we got into the cab.

The steam train rushed on its unseeing way through the cold dark. The rhythmic swaying of the carriage, the muffled music of the wheels, the dimness of the light, nothing could make us doze, or even close our eyes. We sat the whole way in miserable silence. One mad ray of hope came again and again to my fevered mind; the man at the garage could be wrong, he was at the far end of the village, and everything got exaggerated. No, Dad was not dead; badly hurt, true, but not dead; it could not be. Yet at the same time my mind was trying to adjust to the thought that I would never see him again. I had often heard the stricken and the crippled talk of life 'before I lost my leg', 'before I lost my hearing'. Now the curtain of bereavement was cutting my life into two.

I had lost my begetter and my life-long friend; my heart would never be whole again. Father had travelled the decades with us, cuddler of babies, interested listener to our childish chatter, widener of our grown-up horizons with his rich mind. How he had loved to spend his holidays with us in London, tasting its culture at the museums and exhibitions, thirsty for knowledge never acquired in his brief schooldays. At the age of eleven he had gone into the pit as hod-boy to his stepfather. Torn away from school, he had never stopped learning since.

Science, in particular, fascinated him, and he loved to dwell on man's discoveries and his inventive ingenuity with the earth's resources. He would ponder on what man had achieved, and discuss the pros and cons of the way he used it.

Dad had a scientific ambition of his own, 'when I 'a' got the time an' the money to do't.' He was convinced that a pedal-powered plane could be achieved. One day Syd and I had taken him and Mam to the West End, and on to Selfridge's roof garden. While Mam marvelled at a garden stuck up so high in the air, Dad looking critically around observed that it would be just the place to land his pedal-plane. 'Just think on't, Mother, thee an' I flyin' in over thic Marble Arch, an' all they crowds o' Cockneys a-gawpin' up at us, an' thee wi' thee best 'at on a-wavin' to 'em.' Mam automatically straightened her shoulders, adjusted her hat, and put on her Sunday chapel face, rehearsing for the occasion.

One of his many talents, buried for lack of time, was an ability to draw and paint. We took him to the National Gallery and watched him shaking his head in reverent bewildered homage at the great master-works. This aura of acute appreciation of so many things transmitted itself strongly to us all. He enriched his world, and asked us into it.

In the process of his logic Father had come to share Macbeth's opinion, that life was a tale told by an idiot, full of sound and fury and signifying nothing. It was a bitter philosophy, yet it had not embittered him one jot. Now his untimely death, crushed deep under the earth, seemed to prove it. But it was too strong a truth for me to take, and all through this sad and silent journey I clung to my illusion that our Dad was still alive.

It was well past midnight when my eldest sister let us in through Mother's cottage door. Her face was grey with grief.

'Oh, Bess, is it true?' She nodded, and took me in her arms. Mam sat beside the fire, for the first time in her life not jumping up to welcome visitors by putting on the kettle. Syd put Richard in her lap, and a lifetime's instincts took over. She chaffed his cold little hands in hers, began to take his woolly wrappings off, and pulled her chair nearer the fire for him. She seemed to have shrunk.

My two younger sisters raised their tear-swollen faces, their eyes sad dulled question marks. My brother sat with drawn white face staring into space. We could find no words to comfort one another. Bess had already drunk the bitterest dregs of bereavement some years before, when her first-born, a lovely little boy only four years old, had died of cancer. It was she who saw to Richard's bottle and put out some food for Syd. In a couple of hours Syd would have to catch the dawn train back to London.

Bess and her husband and five children lived in the next door cottage, so my brother-in-law took him into their place to get a little rest. Presently my brother rose from his chair and went through to the workshop on the other side of the cottage. Ironically, the war had given better wages and plenty of overtime to the miners. With the extra funds, Dad and Dick had fashioned a rough extension, housing a wood-turning lathe and other tools. On a bench by the lathe were some unfinished wooden toys, fire engines, scooters, destined for the grandchildren's Christmas stockings.

They had built in an old range, and Mam had put ready by the fire the tin bath for Father's home-from-pit wash, his change of boots stood on the fender, and his trousers hung from a hook by the mantelpiece to be warm and aired for him. The shape of his knees bulged in the cheap tweed. The poignancy of these reminders was so overwhelming that I felt a scream rising in my throat, but the sound of my brother's indrawn sobs stopped it.

'I wish I'd 'a' bin a better boy to'n,' he wept as I put my arms around him.

The day of the funeral was bitterly cold with a cruel east wind laced with sleet and snow. My brother had ordered cars for the mourners, but there was an overflow. Numbers of Father's pit butties wanted to carry him to his last rest on their shoulders. In times of great emotional stress Nature provides a safety valve for our sanity by surrounding events with an air of un-reality. Ignoring Father's known agnosticism, a little service was held over the coffin outside the cottage, by a local preacher. The little yard, the steps, and the long garden path were crowded with men and women, come to pay their last respects. Bare-headed men with saddened faces, women with tear-filled eyes, huddling together against the bitter wind, singing the beautiful old hymns and finishing with 'Rock of Ages'.

There was no comfort for me in the preacher's words or the sentiment of the hymns; they brought me no visions of a benign Almighty receiving Father's soul. Indeed these man-made notions seemed a betrayal of reality. The sympathy, respect and sense of loss in the singers' faces were beautiful to me, however. I felt grateful and proud that they had held Father in such high esteem. I felt love, too, for the pit-scarred hands holding the coffin, the men's hard shoulders, their brave set faces as they carried their comrade into the teeth of the freezing wind. They carried him in relays, nearly two miles to the church, and every one was glad to take the burden. He was a man.

*

In spite of all the loving kindness shown me by my neighbours and friends when I came back to London, I could not climb out of my misery. I had not the character to take the first long step out of my slough of despair. I went into labour with my third child a month prematurely. I was taken to Paddington Hospital where I was delivered of a fine boy, and we called him Nicholas. He was perfectly formed, but he lacked the flesh he should have put on had he stayed his full time in the womb. Not for him the cooing joyous baby-talk of a happy fulfilled mother; instead, his round little head was constantly christened with my tears.

I became fearful and anxious about the children, and suffered from an obsession when I took them out that holes would suddenly appear in the pavement and swallow them down. Any form of beauty, from a sunray to a snatch of music, would start me weeping because Father's eyes and ears were closed to it. Selfish in my grief, I failed even to be a wife to Syd. One day his sister called and found me listless and abject as usual. She had been very kind and helpful for a long time, but she now risked my displeasure and our affectionate relationship by giving me a little lecture.

'You can't go on like this, Win,' she upbraided me, 'it isn't fair to the children. What kind of mother are you now with all this misery? And what about Syd? And just think how you're letting your Dad down! Would he have carried on like this? How miserable he would feel to be the cause of all this suffering!'

Letting Father down? She spoke the truth; I was, and it was the very last sin I would wish to commit. It was a cruel little jolt, but I felt deeply ashamed, and I realised that she had given me a straw to grasp. From now on, for Father's sake, I would pull myself together.

And so the healing began, but only just in time. How true were the words of my sister-in-law! I was puzzled and distressed to find that as I combed Chris's hair it began to come out in handfuls, leaving two bald patches. I took him to the doctor. 'Have you had a shock recently?' she asked. Still vulnerable, I burst into tears and told her of my loss. 'Your little boy has been grieving about you; that's the cause of the trouble.' The doctor was a Jewish lady, a humanist if ever there was one. Her surgery was always packed, often with a queue outside as well, but she spared the time to help me with her understanding of bereavement. I came out determined to be a more mature person.

This resolve was soon put to the test, for I had not escaped a physical repercussion either. I began to have spasms of feeling strangely ill, but without any particular pains. I felt I was going to die, my stamina would give out completely, and I got palpitations. I noticed a small lump developing in the front of my neck. Again I went to the doctor, and within three days I was admitted to St Mary's Hospital, Paddington, for the removal of a growth on my thyroid gland. Again I was asked if I had suffered a shock, and the tears welled up within me, but this time I contained them.

Never in my life have I been so cosseted and spoiled as during my week in that hospital. The nurses really seemed like angels, and Syd came to visit me every evening after work. His sister took care of the children, our neighbours sent me fruit and flowers, and all these kind attentions began to heal my pain. Back home again after the operation I felt so much better in every way.

With three children it was a struggle to manage on Syd's wages, and it was difficult for me to get charring work, with a baby and a toddler to see to. But a bit of luck turned up, almost literally on our doorstep. Opposite our tenement was a large block of flats called the 'Mansions', stretching from the pub along the street, round the corner, and on again to end by another big pub. These buildings had three communal stone staircases, three large doorsteps, and of course three sets of stairs down to the basement areas where the dustbins were kept. For sweeping down and scrubbing all these stairs and doorsteps, plus sweeping and sluicing the basement areas, I could earn fifteen shillings. This was done once a week; the old woman who used to do it was now unable. I jumped at the chance; fifteen shillings was a welcome boost to my house-keeping money. The blessing of it was that I could do it and keep half an eye on Richard and the baby at the same time, by putting one in each pram, tied for safety to the iron railings surrounding the mansions.

The sweeping was the worst part of the job, especially the areas, for besides the thick coating of dust all sorts of debris blew down and got trapped. Scrubbing down with bucket after bucket of hot soapy water was quite a pleasure by comparison. Resolutely I coughed my way through the dust, for sometimes there were perks to be had. After I had enjoyed myself sluicing down with water laced with Jeyes' fluid, I felt quite justified in beating the dustmen to the first pickings. The more thought-ful tenants would leave little parcels in clean carrier bags round the bins; odd crockery, a rug with plenty of wear left in it, occasionally clothing, and once, a white Grecian-style vase. Certainly this had a crack down one side, but that could be turned to the wall. I put a jam jar inside the water, and filled it with sprays of the greenery growing among the rubble on the bombsites.

When I had finished sluicing down the areas, I usually had

another little area to mop up. Richard, sitting up in his pram, endeared himself to the women passers-by with his beautiful big eyes and ready smile, his mouth open ready for anything they could contribute. I used to check on him every time I fetched water and he always seemed to be eating something. The offerings were varied; a few chips, a chocolate biscuit, a piece of peeled orange, a cold sausage. He must have had a digestion like an ostrich. It all went quite easily down one way, and by gum it came out with no difficulty at the other. 'Tut-tut,' some mothers may be saying as they read this. 'Why on earth didn't she have a notice on his pram asking people not to feed him?' In that part of London such snubs to kind intentions would not have gone down very well. Richard's gannet appetite did him no harm; he was never sick, and because of these attentions he never objected to his sessions of waiting by the railings.

Meantime, Chris had started at the school across the road, and was telling the teachers how to go about their business. 'That ain't like a beetle,' he informed the infant teacher when she drew one on the blackboard. Then he marched out of his desk, picked up a piece of chalk, rubbed hers out and drew one himself. His talents did not match his precociousness, and the class laughed loudly at his inferior effort. Justly punished, thought the astonished teacher, but Chris was not at all pleased. When they lined up at playtime for their daily spoonful of malt he dodged out of the queue and ran home to me. There were many occasions when I had to take him back.

A natural extrovert anyway, Chris suffered from the frustrations of a child bright beyond his years. At four and a half years old, without tuition from anyone, he could read fluently with a vocabulary astonishing for his age. I was too busy to notice the phenomenon; it was Mother who pointed it out to me when she was staying with us.

'D'you know, that boy's reading the paper!' she observed with astonishment as Chris sat with the newspaper in front of him. I thought he was just soliloquising. The paper was the *Daily Telegraph*, no less, brought up by Meg wrapped round some soap that she had nicked for me from one of her jobs.

So I pointed to a paragraph and asked Chris to read it, which he did with very little hesitation or difficulty in pronouncing even the longest words. He had no idea himself how he had learned to read. Syd's theory was that his manual had been advertising posters – for example a picture of a packet of tea identifying the word by the product – and he must have gone on from there.

It is more widely recognised now that children of high intelligence have special problems often channelled through lack of understanding into naughtiness. Poor Chris, as the first-born he suffered most as I struggled for my own maternal education.

I do not suppose I was unique in suffering from the illusion during my first pregnancy that this much-wanted baby would grow into a perfect example of humanity. Would it not have love and care lavished upon it, and all the comfort we could provide? If a girl, then she would be as beautiful as my sisters; if a boy, as wise as my father, and at least as handsome as his. I quite overlooked the fact that Syd and I had at least the average number of flaws in our characters, and that an obstinate streak can be handed down as easily as a fine complexion. I meant well in expecting my children to be infinitely nicer than myself, but what a bad, even cruel, philosophy it was. As the years passed, I realised my mistake and paid for it.

*

About this time I also got a 'posh' job. Although I was beginning again to count my blessings, sleep still did not come easily. I needed to be absolutely exhausted to fight the melancholia that came with time to think. Through one of her employers, Meg recommended me for an evening job as a general help in the Wimpole Street household of a famous surgeon. It meant that Syd would have to mind the children, a task he did quite well and without too much complaint. His hand was firmer than mine but they seemed none the worse for that.

Because of the way that 'resident' staff came and went so capriciously, my work at Wimpole Street was varied. Perhaps one evening I would just have to sit and clean a tableful of silver-ware, and have a good supper brought in by the cook. Another time I assumed the duties of an absconding housemaid. So I became temporary charlady, surrogate butler, deputy cook, and general dogsbody.

One evening I was met at the door by an absolutely distraught mistress. She had no staff at all; the cook and housemaid had taken umbrage and taken themselves off with it. Two guests were coming to dinner: an elderly and famous Belgian actress and her friend. They could not be put off; it was seven o'clock. The mistress had prepared the dinner for cooking herself, and made the sweets, strawberry angel-cake and apricot compote with cream. This still left the vegetables to be cooked, and a dish of partridge to be roasted with all the trimmings.

Could I, would I, do it? And also act as parlour-maid? This would mean putting on a black dress left behind by an ex-maid, covering it with a voluminous white overall for doing the cooking, then removing the same to don a maid's apron and cap, taking the food up in the lift to the dining-room, and serving it as well.

This was a challenge. I said I would do my best, and hurried into the big kitchen in the basement. I do not know what the guests thought of their hostess's frequent disappearances. She was checking me. Had I laid the table properly? Oh, the beautiful cut glass, the solid silver cutlery, the hand-made lace tablecloth, and the bowls of roses! The exquisite bone-china coffee-cups! The gold-embossed dinner-service! It made me a bundle of nerves just to handle it, but I had a lot more than that to do. Luckily there was no time to think.

With enough pushing I can be very competent. The vegetables were easy enough, and with a dash of luck and a sprinkling of judgement the partridges came out just right. On my own initiative I garnished them with sprays of watercress, then took it all up just on time. Straight-faced despite my inward amusement, I remembered to serve from the left and clear from the right (or was it the other way round?). 'Thank you, *thank you*,' said my mistress's eyes as they caught mine during my parlour-maid role. Then I served coffee in the drawing-room, and politely accepted a complimentary message to the cook from the actress guest.

Back down in the kitchen, surrounded by what seemed acres of washing-up, I complimented myself all round, and then started as kitchen-maid at the sink. No slap-dash clatter washing-up with this lot; everything had to be handled with gingerly reverence. By the time all was in order it was well past midnight. My mistress had boosted my energy with a ten-shilling tip for my efforts, but there were no buses and I had to walk a good mile home. I was too tired even to walk straight. Like one drunk I staggered up the tenement stairs, into the bedroom, and without the energy to undress fell across the bottom of the bed and slept like a log.

*

The war was receding into memory, food was becoming more plentiful, and our funds were being boosted by my part-time work. The three little boys were thriving, and we were surrounded by friendly neighbours. Syd was tall and handsome and had put on a bit of weight. In exchange for clothing coupons, the surgeon's wife gave me one of her husband's overcoats and a suit. They fitted Syd well, and he looked a proper toff on Sunday when we all went out together. Now I began to really count my blessings; and little did I know then that another blessing was on the way.

One morning the familiar unmistakable nausea hit me again. It could not be, it just must not be, that I was pregnant again. Nicky, the youngest, was three, our quiver was full, and our tenement rooms stretched to capacity. Dr Marie Stopes could not have let me down again? Thank goodness abortions were almost impossible for the poor in those days, although this pregnancy was the worst, the most nauseous and difficult of them all. This time I did not indulge myself dreaming of bonnet ribbons; it was sure to be a boy. So I just ate my dry oats, and health salts, drank all the cider I could lay hands on, and prayed for the months to go by. I knew the women shook their heads and said, 'Ah, she's a boy-breeder, that one,' as if it was somehow all my fault.

I had become friendly with a young woman in the Mansions, a sweet Yorkshire girl married to a nice Welsh fellow. She often gave me coffee and biscuits when I was cleaning the stairs by her door. Once she had shyly asked me if I would mind accepting some clothes that her only child, a boy, had grown out of. I had accepted with gratitude, and we had become firm friends. Our windows were opposite each other across the narrow street. I promised her that if the baby arrived in the night I would get Syd to put out something blue or pink on the windowsill to let her know at once. 'But it's sure to be blue,' I told her, defying Fate beforehand.

This time I had decided to have the baby at home, and I warned the friendly tenants I should probably wake them all up with my howls if it happened at night. Meg would not mind; she was all agog, and anxious to be in at the birth. My labour pains started about midnight but it was one o'clock before I felt sure enough to poke Syd awake. He got up and dressed at once as he had to go to the nurses' centre two miles away. Hanging on to the back of the big chair doubled up with pain, I gasped to him, 'Go on, go on, get that gas-and-air. Hurry up.' I had been through three births without any form of pain-killer; this time I was demanding something, anything. Giving me a quick peck on the cheek he hurried downstairs.

Marylebone Road was almost empty; what buses were still running were not in sight. A taxi came along heading east and Syd jumped out into the road to stop it. 'Come orf it, mate,' said the driver. 'I've turned it in, ain' I, goin' 'ome.' Hanging on to the door, Syd quickly explained his errand. 'Oh well,' said the cabbie, 'that's different, ennit? Jump in,' and he swung round in the empty road.

Syd asked him to wait outside the nurses' centre while he ran in. The two nurses on duty seemed very calm, gave him the gas-and-air machine in its heavy case, and said they would follow on their bikes in a few minutes. The taxi hurried back and dropped Syd off at the tenement.

'How much do I owe you?' asked Syd.

'Go on, nuffin', mate, nuffin'. Wet the baby's 'ead wiv it. Good luck mate, 'ope it all goes all right fer yer missus,' and he swung away to his doubly-earned rest.

I suppose all was going all right for me, but it was a distressing and very painful sort of all right. As soon as Syd had gone I went into the kitchen. The three boys were sound asleep in their room. The pains were now doubling me up. It was March the eighteenth and bitterly cold; I would make a cup of cocoa for the nurses. Immobilised every other minute by the contractions, I could not seem to get from cupboard to table. Then Syd hurried up the stairs carrying the gas-and-air. He rekindled the fire and sat beside it, cleaning his boots for the morning of all things.

The nurses tip-toed up to our open door, took one look at me, and helped me on to the bed. 'Just in time,' said the elder one. On separate occasions both these nurses had visited me to check up and advise how to prepare the bedroom for the birth. They were friendly nice girls and they knew we had three little boys.

The last stages of labour had begun, but I was too engrossed in the painful procedure to remember the gas-and-air. 'It's a girl, a beautiful girl!' they chorused ecstatically under their breath, as soon as our daughter emerged. Their kind faces were full of pleasure and congratulation. Warm from the womb, and I think still attached to the womb, and to the umbilical cord, they put her straight into my arms; a precious moment, and I loved them for the gesture. The new-born in the animal kingdom gets its immediate welcome from the tongue or nudging of the mother. In hospitals at that time the babies were all too often washed, wrapped up, and taken away without being put in the mother's arms, and not brought to her for hours, a bad breach of primitive instinct when the birth has gone without complications.

When all was done, the baby tucked up and comfy against the pillows, they got their cocoa and cake. Syd had managed that as well as all the hot water, and his boots! Then they left, going down the stairs very quietly. Syd came in to look at his daughter and knelt by the cradle as if afraid to breathe on her. As he got up and turned to me, the look of thanks he gave me was never to be forgotten. 'My two ladies,' he said, kneeling down with one arm round me and one round the cradle. Not a soul could be heard stirring in the rest of the tenement.

Meg left for work in the mornings just before six, to do a little office-cleaning before going on to her regulars. As usual at lunch-time she popped up to me to dish out her daily dollop of news.

'Isn't Win well then?' she asked when Syd opened the door.

'She's fine,' smirked Syd. 'Pop in and have a look at her.'

Poor Meg, her eyes nearly popped out of her head at the sight of the *two* of us. 'It's a girl,' I bragged, 'it really is.'

'But when did you have her?'

'Half-past two this morning.'

'But I never heard a sound, nothing. I can't hardly believe it,' and she looked again into the cradle for verification. She was at a loss. Her expression said it all. How could I do it to her? She had been robbed. All that going on, and she had missed it, slept through it all!

By the evening I was forgiven; up she came with a plate of daintily cooked supper for me.

In our tiny corner the coming of our daughter was treated like a royal birth. Syd had put a pink cloth on the windowsill, and this must have sent my friend in the Mansions post-haste to a toyshop for a doll. She must have spent the rest of the day sewing its glamorous outfit of silk, lace, and ribbons.

By the following evening our baby had acquired eight silk dresses trimmed with pink, bootees and bonnets, and a pink frilled pram-cover. Syd kept answering our door to a conveyor belt of food offerings, and for the first time since I had known him he dashed out and bought me a bunch of flowers. It was almost overwhelming.

The three boys, however, were not unduly impressed. After Syd gave them their breakfast, they were rather taken aback by his lining them up, brushing their hair, making sure their hands and faces were spotless, socks pulled up, shoes shined, before leading them into the royal presence. Standing them round the cradle at a respectful distance he announced proudly, 'This is your new sister.'

'Pooh, she don't look much, ain't got no 'air,' said Richard in a stage whisper after the inspection. Syd, of course, adored his sons, and he had never hinted at the slightest disappointment about my single-sex reproduction system. But fathering a daughter seemed to soften his character at once, and put me a couple of notches up on the wifely pedestal. For me, the choice of her name was no problem. I had read *The Forsyte Saga*, and I felt a profound joy for Soames when his second wife gave birth to his daughter and murmured 'my petite fleur'. There and then I made up my mind that if ever I had a daughter Fleur should be her name. Syd agreed, but he feared that odd names could be a handicap to his children and he liked Jennifer. So she became Jennifer Fleur; 'our Jen' for short.

The problem now was our cramped accommodation and lack of amenities. We put our name down on the council housing list. Two years later a letter arrived inviting us to the housing department at the Town Hall. Here I was handed the keys of a second floor flat in a post-war block three streets away. If the accommodation suited us, it was ours.

Suited us? I could not believe our luck! It was palatial, it was luxurious, far better than many flats I had gone charring in! There was a communal courtyard for the children, each tenant had a brick-built shed, and there was a large modern laundry with the latest facilities for the tenants' use at a token price. The flat had piped hot water, and consisted of a hall, bathroom, separate toilet, good-sized kitchen with plenty of cupboards, a stove and a fridge and a hatchway service to a spacious lounge-diner. Three good bedrooms opened up from a passage fitted with a built-in wardrobe and broom cupboards. There were two small balconies, a roomy airing cupboard always hot, as were the chromium towel rails in bathroom and kitchen. Coal was delivered from the landing through an aperture in the wall into a coal-cupboard just inside the front door. All our rubbish went into a similar aperture on the landing, and slid down a chute. I would bet that Aladdin felt no more gratified when the Genie opened the door to his treasure cave than I did. The rent would be double what we were paying, but now the three boys all went to school and there were plenty of charring jobs about.

Unable to contain my delight, I returned to the housing department, deliriously grateful to accept the flat. The lady at the desk was very nice, 'but I must warn you,' she began. Then she told me we would be living over one of the most difficult of tenants whose behaviour had already affected the three previous occupants of the flat above her so badly that they had asked for transfer. Investigating her complaints, the council had found most of them either quite unjustified or grossly exaggerated. She advised me to ignore this tenant's behaviour, as they now intended to take no notice of her complaints. Feeling full of magnanimity towards the world in general, complainers included, I said I was sure we could manage. To get such accommodation we would bend over backwards to be the quietest and most considerate tenants possible.

*

After moving into our grand new flat I gradually began to understand why slum-dwellers, uprooted and taken to bright new towns, confound well-meaning sociologists by longing to go back. After the first flush of excitement had faded, as I moved about in my streamlined warm kitchen and polished the smooth composition floors of our big new flat, I became aware that something was missing. We had left the tenement behind us, and we had left a community. Nobody was bringing a cup of tea to my door, nobody was having a chat on the landing, there was no smiling face in the opposite window. There was no nosey vital Meg clattering upstairs full of scandal and good humour, no dozy sexy Lally with her pale face and eternal fag. Syd's sister, too, had moved away now.

On these new big clean stairways there was no fellow feeling. Everybody seemed in a hurry, exchanging perhaps a tiny smile or a little nod and sometimes no greeting at all. These fine new glossy doors were always shut. They opened only partly for the inmates to slip through, and then not very often. The old tenement was only half a mile away round a couple of corners, and sometimes Meg came to us and sometimes I saw Lally in the market, but the old feeling never came back. Something had been destroyed and would not revive. Never mind, I thought, this place is so much better for the children.

But I wish I could blot out the memories of my own guilt about the children for what I did to them in the next few months. For a start, I became that most unsuitable creature, an over-house-proud mother. That flat had gone to my head and partly covered my heart. After living in the tenement I never really felt at home in the flat, but more like a daily cleaner. Not a speck or spot of dirt or dust, not any sort of muddle would I tolerate. Our old furniture and second-hand rugs and mats were simply not good enough for our new grandeur, and I was determined to replace them. These resolves and the constant necessity of keeping quiet for the sake of 'Her Downstairs' caused me to make more demands of my children than I should, sometimes more than they could bear. And I was blind to it! Our Nicky, born premature after his grandfather's sudden death, was especially affected. My behaviour made him a highly-strung nervous little boy, and he responded with what we took to be wilful naughtiness. Excessive nagging was the last thing he needed, but Heaven forgive me, that was what he and his siblings got!

As soon as the boys went to school and I had fixed up toddler Jenny in her pram, I was off with her, putting in an hour or two's charring wherever I could get it. On Saturdays Syd had to take them all out whatever the weather so that I could go washing-up in a fish-and-chip shop. One objective filled my thoughts, the purple patterned carpet in Jordan's window. This large store did not oblige its customers with credit but would allow payment for goods in advance. The going rate for charring was half-a-crown an hour. I earned this mostly on my knees, scrubbing and polishing floors, or washing paintwork down. Be it half-a-crown, three and ninepence, or five shillings a stint, I did not keep it in my hand long enough to get warm. I hurried back to Jordan's to knock a bit more off the nine-guinea price of the carpet.

One day when I was eagerly handing in three shillings to the man at the cash desk, I saw him give a very meaningful glance to a male shopwalker looking on. I read the message, and felt a flush of anger and embarrassment come over my face. So that's what they thought! That I was 'on the game', and for such paltry sums as that! I did not know which implication annoyed me the more. After that I saved up my earnings and paid weekly.

Pretty soon, between our new carpet and our rugs and mats, every part of the flat except the tiled kitchen floor was covered, hopefully to reduce still further what noise our shoe-less feet made. Apart from meals, baths, and bedtime, we made every effort to take the children out. On winter Sundays we had the frozen parks almost to ourselves, and I took sandwiches and flasks of soup to warm us up when our aching legs forced a rest. We were banishing ourselves from our new-found comfort for the sake of an anonymous nuisance whom we did not know and had hardly even seen. When we were indoors because we had to be, the monastic atmosphere was almost comical.

Meanwhile the object of all this consideration, 'Her downstairs', never even took her turn at cleaning her part of the stairs. No matter, I scrubbed her flight as well as ours. Not surprisingly, my supine attitude and conciliatory efforts did not appease, but rather made matters worse. She took the offensive and opened her campaign to drive us out.

I was flabbergasted one day, as I passed her door, to see her open it, give me one vicious look of concentrated hatred and then slam it with all her might. She must have sat behind her curtains watching who was coming in, because she treated my women friends from the old tenement to the same door-slamming performance. It was puzzling and hurtful for them and humiliating for me. I was further disheartened when I was doing the washing in the communal laundry and a woman from across the courtyard said, 'What a shame you gotta live over that old cow; she says you're an awful woman. Mind, she said just the same about the people before you. The last one had to go to the hospital with her nerves before the council give her a transfer. Hateful old cow! If I was you I'd ask to be moved. Put the poison in.' I felt sick and near to tears. To be the object of a well-founded dislike is an uncomfortable experience. To be held in contempt without any reason, especially if prepared and anxious to please, is like being locked in a room with no window or door. If we were giving cause for complaint, why did she not approach me and explain what it was? I realised later that that was the last thing she wanted.

One day the two youngest boys came in from school and asked me, 'What's that woman shaking her fist at us for when we come up the stairs, Mum?'

'Were you making a noise?'

'No, Mum, honest. Just walking up quiet.'

So they, too, were being puzzled and hurt by her. Chris came in with the same tale. 'That woman downstairs is a nutter,' he said boldly. 'Shook her fist at me as I came by her door. I made a face at her as though I was mad as well.' He was quite unabashed and a better psychologist than I, but I reprimanded him severely for his reaction. I expect he continued his little vendetta on the quiet. Left alone long enough, he would have driven her out.

Another time I saw our little Jenny coming across the courtyard. I began to think she was a long time coming up, so I went down to investigate. I found her cowering, literally cowering, in a corner of the stairway. Her large brown eyes were filled with fear and she was trembling.

'What's the matter, darling?' I cried. 'Why didn't you come on up?' I took her in my arms, and with a lot of cuddling and coaxing I got it out of her. She was scared to come by that woman's door because she made a face at her like a witch. Oddly enough, just recently, Jenny had worried us two or three times by waking up in the night with nightmares. These had made her delirious for a short while so we had to take her into our bed till morning and by then she had forgotten. Now I put two and two together, and realised that I was dealing with a villainess, a real witch. Looking back, I cannot understand why I did not go down straight away, and, in the local idiom, 'sort 'er aht'. Instead I felt hopeless, and inadequate.

'Her downstairs' wisely ignored Syd's comings and goings, so her behaviour had not perturbed him unduly. After all, the council had warned us and said she should not be taken notice of, and that was his opinion. 'Take no notice at all of the miserable old faggot.' He often became irritable with me because of my perpetual insistence on silence, and did not think she was worth a confrontation. As for her husband, poor little bloke, an inoffensive wraith who came and went and never turned his head to speak or acknowledge anyone, he and his personality had parted long ago.

Syd expected his boys to be tough enough to withstand the eccentric behaviour of a miserable middle-aged woman. So they were, but I knew he would feel differently about his small vulnerable daughter. When the boys escorted Jenny home from school they stayed outside playing until teatime. When Syd came home they were sitting quietly indoors, and while he was eating I told him about Jenny's reaction on the stairs. I regretted it instantly. His face went pale, his eyes darkened with anger, and he put down his knife and fork. Getting up he said quietly, 'I'm going down to sort this out.' It was the way he said it, and the look of him, that reminded me of what sort of temper he had when thoroughly roused. Just then I really feared for the safety of 'Her downstairs'.

'Oh, no, no!' I begged, hanging on to his coat-tails. 'Finish your tea and calm down a bit.' This only added to his exasperation, and the boys too sensed his dangerous mood. I began to cry and the children joined in. His hand was on the doorknob, but the sight of our distress made him pause. 'Syd, Syd,' I cried, 'think how bad it would look if you go assaulting her, you a big strong man. People would not understand. I'll just have to write to the council and complain about her.'

'Look,' he said, 'look, I'm not goin' to hurt her, just frighten her a bit, get this bloody silly stunt stopped for good. She won't slam the door in my face.'

I pleaded with him again and eventually he sat back down to his meal. 'Right,' he said. 'You see to it then. Better not happen again. That's all.' It was lucky for her Syd did not catch sight of her that evening, and from then on I fetched Jenny up the stairs.

The time had come for Syd's annual holiday, two whole weeks off, fourteen days when we could all be together to do just what we liked, go where we wanted! Rather gloomily he ripped open his pay-packet. Taking his tobacco money and a few shillings, he handed me the rest. 'There,' he said, 'a decent week's pay!' Three weeks' money at one go seemed quite a lot to me. Cautiously, providently, I paid three weeks' rent in advance, and three weeks' milk money. Then such affluence went to my head and I bought the four children a pair of winter shoes and wellington boots each. I counted what I had left of the money; I had made a tidy hole in it. Somewhat dismayed, I still felt sure I could manage the three weeks until the next pay with careful budgeting, but it would have to be careful indeed.

Never mind! It was August, and the weather had turned warm and dry. After breakfast Syd took all the children out until lunch-time. This gave me the chance to get the house-work and shopping done, prepare a meal, and pack food and drink for our afternoon and evening out in one of the parks. The first day they came in from their morning walk in high good humour. Chris and Richard smirked at each other across the lunch table; obviously they were enjoying some little secret, but did not intend to tell me.

As soon as I had washed up we set off on our usual free excursion, taking our books, some balls, and a doll for Jenny. We decided to go to Regent's Park, the far end of it near the Zoo and the canal. Here we had one of our special 'places', quiet and lonely, with a little hill to roly-poly down, well away from traffic, and sometimes a barge to look at, its prow barely wrinkling the limpid waters of the tree-lined canal. The children could play in safety, and we could sit on the lush uncut grass and read, and sometimes do nothing at all but stare at the trees that leaned over the water, or watch the slow progress of a chestnut leaf sailing down to a watery grave. The sun shone on us, but its full glare and heat were tempered by the maze of limbs and twigs above. Traffic rumbled in the distance, and sometimes we saw a squirrel. So greedy were we for the sylvan peace we often went the long way round, just to enjoy the tree-lined quiet roads and the mock rusticity of St John's Wood.

This day Chris led us on an unfamiliar detour, and we came across a block of large war-wrecked Victorian houses. In front, alongside their mosaic paths and porticoes, were small gardens strewn with rubble through which were struggling all manner of half-hearted weeds, seeding before their time, desperate for reproduction. Tall wooden gates, mysteriously surviving, led through an enclosed passage to tradesmen's entrances at the back. The boys ran forward and unlatched the first of these gates.

'Come on, Mummy, come and have a look!'

'It was only because Richard couldn't wait to get to the park to have a pee that we found it!'

We followed them through the gate and shut it behind us. I could hardly believe my eyes. There in front of us was an oasis of green stretching the full length behind the ten bombed residences, an acre of long grass, unpruned shrubs, tumbledown walls, a magnificent mulberry tree, and not a single soul in sight! We had found ourselves a country holiday estate, rent-free, right in the heart of London! No park-keepers, no keep-off-the-grass signs, no scouting around for a spare seat! We moved in. I was as ecstatic about their discovery as the children. The boys had trees to climb, walls to crouch behind to shoot the Indians, a jungle to creep through stalking the enemy. Syd and I spread ourselves out on a patch of long grass, and Jenny played mother to her doll in a make-believe house between shrubs. We had books, drinks, and food, and the glorious sun overhead. Jenny had her afternoon nap, and so did Syd, and I had a struggle to keep awake. Syd reached up into the mulberry tree and gathered enough to make a big pot of jam, the boys began to flag, and we made for home. I was thrilled to pluck some sprays of foliage from the shrubs to arrange around our sitting-room.

Had we been the sort of family to say our goodnight prayers we should have prayed that no-one else would discover our paradise. No one did. Right through till the Sunday before Syd went back to work the weather remained gloriously sunny. That holiday in our private elysium acted like a balm on all our nerves. We woke up on the Sunday morning to rain-drenched streets and a sky full of scurrying clouds threatening more rain. At last the weather had broken, and I was broke, too. Apart from Syd's fares to work I had three shillings and ninepence left, very little food in the house, and six days to go before Syd got his next wages. It was my fault; I should not have bought those shoes and wellingtons for all of them in one go. Luckily I had paid the rent and milk in advance.

Well, I would have to borrow off Meg, much as I hated the idea. Now we had moved it did not seem right to go on asking her, and it would have to be a big borrow, thirty shillings or so, however carefully I budgeted. We had no money for bus fares, but this did not worry us. It had stopped raining now, so we decided to go for a walk; up Edgware Road looking in the shop windows, through Hyde Park to the Serpentine, and if we felt like it and could dodge the showers, we could go to the museums. I left it till the last minute to tell Syd of our bankruptcy; not that he would be surprised.

Londoners do not patronise Hyde Park much in wet weather. It was almost empty; anyway I was glad the children had their new wellingtons on in that long wet grass. Hands behind his back, head disconsolately down, Syd walked by my side. Suddenly he bent down and picked something up from the grass; it was a soaking wet, neatly-folded ten-shilling note. Honest moralists might think he should have taken it to a police station; I must confess it never crossed my mind. A good deal of cuddling and kissing goes on in Hyde Park, amateur and professional, but few men get a warmer hug and kiss than I gave Syd there and then when he handed it to me. We were solvent again, at least for a couple of days. Now I felt like a spring lamb again and raced the boys across the grass.

By Tuesday I was broke again. Oh well! After Syd had had his tea I would go round to the tenement and ask Meg for the loan of a pound.

*

Coming home from work Syd used to get off the trolley-bus at Paddington Green and walk through the market. Apart from the sawdust in his hair and down his shirt, the only perk of his job was a daily sack of wood blocks, which we stored to eke out the coal in the winter. We had many a merry fire, a silent comfort that even 'Her downstairs' could not complain about. With a sack on his back a man must perforce bow his head. This day, as he made his way along the market, among the debris in the gutter Syd's eagle eye noticed a piece of paper of a distinctive reddish hue. Putting his sack down he picked up the little piece of paper. Yes, it was, another neatly-folded ten-shilling note. The road sweepers were coming down that side, and no doubt this would have been a little bonus for one of them. 'Sorry, mate,' thought Syd. 'To each according to his needs,' and he brought it home to me. For a moment we both felt a bit awestruck by the coincidence, but I was elated; with care I could manage another couple of days.

However, by Thursday, our cupboard was again nearly as bare as Old Mother Hubbard's. Chris decided to go round knocking on doors asking for old papers and magazines; he could get a few coppers at the rag-shop for a huge bundle of papers, and he would buy us some buns. It was a lovely day and I would have liked to take them out, but I had accumulated a huge pile of washing. Richard was pressing me to let him take Nicky to the park on their own. I gave in eventually, but he had to solemnly promise to ask a lady, and it had to be a lady, to see them across the two busy roads on the way, and that they would only go in the children's playground, and were to ask the lady in charge to tell them when it was half-past three. Then they would be home by four o'clock without fail. Richard promised faithfully to abide by these conditions, nodding eagerly at every one, his brown eyes fixed sincerely on mine. I rustled

up a little food for them, then I took Jenny and my huge
bundle of washing over to the laundry. Our entrepreneur paper
merchant, Chris, could look after himself. Cockney boys of his
age, especially one who had passed for Marylebone Grammar
at eleven years old, had their wits about them.

We were not going to have a very rich stew that evening. A
shilling's worth of scrag end (for the dog!), a few pennies'
worth of potherbs, and two eggs for pancakes, had emptied my
purse again. But worrying about our dinner took second place
when by half-past four none of the boys had come home. The
stew was simmering and so was I, and I kept going with Jenny
to the street corner to see if they were coming. I had forgotten
to tell them which route to come home, and if I went the
wrong way they might come home tired and hungry to an
empty flat.

By the time Syd was due in I was frantic. Chris and he
arrived at the same time, Chris proudly carrying a bag of
penny iced buns. I was too distraught to thank him at the time
as I quickly explained to Syd about Richard and Nicky.

'Seven hours they've been gone, seven hours,' I wailed.

'Keep calm,' said Syd. 'I'll go and find them.' He swallowed
a cup of tea. 'I've got my fare for the morning, but I'll use it
now for a bus to the park and keep an eye out for 'em on the
way. It'll be quicker. Now don't worry, you know how kids
forget the time when they're playing.' Don't worry? I could see
that under his calm front he was worried.

'I'll go and look for 'em the other way,' said Chris.

It was just gone eight when I saw them all plodding their way
homewards. If Chris and Syd had not been with the younger
boys I would hardly have recognised them. They were both covered from top to bottom with soot. I did not care; my four men
were all there safe and sound and the relief was indescribable.

'Little perishers!' said Syd. 'I found them in the park, down that bank near the canal. They'd found a heap of soot dumped there by the barges.' Syd looked tired and unusually pale, but neither of us had the heart to scold them just then.

When the boys had sat down to eat Syd drew me by the hand into the kitchen. Sitting down, he rubbed his brow and said, 'Well, I don't know what to say. You'll never believe this, Win, it's making me feel quite queer. Look what I found again!' He opened his hand and in it was yet another neatly-folded ten-shilling note.

'Where on earth did you find that?'

'Well, I got on top of the bus, you see, to watch each side of the pavement in case I spotted the boys. I was the only one up there. A penny slipped out of my hand down the back of the seat. I had to get it back before the conductor came up, so I squeezed my fingers down there and up came the penny and this little bit of paper, another ten-bob note folded up just like the others. It's weird.'

I began to feel a bit spooky myself. My agnostic convictions were getting a shaking. Was this money manna? Pennies from heaven? A hundred and twenty at a time, sent for convenience in the form of neat little notes?

I did not dwell too long on the matter. After all, it was pay-day tomorrow so there was no need to stint too harshly. While the family sat eating their anaemic stew I popped out for the second course, six fourpennies of fried fish and six-penn'orth of chips.

For weeks after that Syd walked on the kerbs with his eyes on the gutter, but all he ever found was a broken biro and a comb full of dandruff. Eventually I stopped him, but I sometimes wonder what we have missed.

*

With a young family, winter inevitably brings its quota of ills and chills. Nicky had come home from school on the Friday with the sniffles, and by Sunday he was feverish. After an early lunch Syd went out with the other three. I tucked Nicky up in an armchair by the fire in the sitting-room. Then I went into the kitchen to do some ironing and kept an eye on him through the open serving-hatch. We were both very quiet, and at least we were not doing anything to offend 'Her down-stairs', I thought. The ironing finished I made a glass of orange juice to take into my feverish little boy.

As I got to his chair I froze with horror. Suddenly a strange unseeing flash came into his eyes, his body contorted, he went purple and then pale, and his breathing laboured. I had never seen a fit or convulsion before. Panic-stricken, I held the writhing convulsing little body tightly in my arms until the spasm passed. Ignorant, terrified, heartbroken by his distress, holding him tight in the blanket, I ran out across the landing and knocked on the door of the elderly couple at the other end. They were a gentle nice old pair who always had a kind word and a smile for us and the children.

'Oh, please, please help me,' I sobbed. 'My little boy has had a fit. Can you get the doctor for me? I mustn't leave him, I mustn't!'

'All right, my dear,' she answered kindly and calmly. 'Yes, of course, right away,' and she turned to call her husband.

I ran back to the fire, and almost at once she followed me in, carrying a glass. Nicky appeared to be asleep now, so I sat down by the fire with him on my lap. 'Drink this drop of brandy, dear,' she said. 'My husband's gone down to the phone box. Doctor'll be here soon. I'll make you a nice cup of tea; I can see you've had a nasty shock. Where's your hubby?' I told her he had taken the other children out. She sat there with me till the doctor came, and then till Syd returned.

Usually, once a doctor is on the scene nothing seems quite as bad as it did. This time, despite her calmness and efficiency, the tumult inside me was hardly stilled. Yes, Nicky had had a convulsion, she said almost casually, as she examined him. But this sometimes happened to children with high temperatures. Yet Nicky's temperature was not all that high. The doctor confessed herself a bit puzzled and asked if the child had been under any sort of stress lately. She left medicine, and would call again on the morrow.

How incredibly precious we realise our children are when danger threatens them. Nicky, vulnerable and ill and dependent on my care; how bitterly I regretted every reprimand and unjust scolding I had given him. Stress? Of course, of course. The realisation of my guilt was almost more than I could bear; my melancholia at the time of his birth and my selfish indulgence in it afterwards; keeping him quiet because of 'Her downstairs'; this bloody posh flat. How cruelly selfish I had been with my priorities! Nag, nag, nag, that's all I did.

That night I spent at Nicky's bedside, watching his every breath, terrified of another convulsion.

The next day the doctor decided further tests should be done in case Nicky was suffering from a form of epilepsy. I kept him home from school for three months and gave up all my charring jobs. Syd slept in the boys' room so that I could have Nicky in my bed. An appointment was made for an EEG test at St Mary's Hospital, and for regular visits to a neurological specialist at the Children's Hospital. Nothing definite emerged from the investigations, but during these three months Nicky distressed us all with another though milder convulsion. As far as we know that was the last, and he has grown into a strong

well-balanced man, a good husband, and father to three children. During this time of trial I was amazed to discover how
many families had a similar problem to face. I only hope that
in the long run they were as lucky as we.

The strain of bringing up four children in a flat surrounded by
busy dangerous roads; the perpetual worry of 'Her downstairs';
the lack of sleep in case Nicky had a turn; at the same time
struggling to be, for everyone's sake, a calm and kind mum; all
this left me exhausted, with my nerve-ends in tatters.
Gradually the worry of Nicky subsided and I began to think
about going out to work again. Also our rent had risen little by
little till we were now paying twice as much, so I was glad to
accept the chance of a Saturday job washing up in a fish-and-
chip shop.

This meant that Syd would have to cope with the children
most of the day. Quite apart from 'Her downstairs', we had
always taken them out for all the fresh air they could get. So
between breakfast and an early Saturday lunch Syd took them
out, and then again for the afternoon and evening while I was
at work. They always had a fish-and-chip supper to look forward to, bought out of my earnings.

The fish-and-chip shop was in the crowded street-market
that ran along the front of our flats. It was owned by Sam, a
very untypical member of the Jewish fraternity; he did not
believe in pleading or wooing or wheedling for custom, not
Sam. Sam stood his ground and defied the world, customers
included. His fish-and-chips were superb, and his temper
appalling. He sold over the counter, and also to the dozen or
so tables for diners at the back of the shop.

Sam had been there as long as anyone could remember, and
the years of self-incarceration in that atmosphere had taken

their toll. He was beginning to look like a fish, a fish out of water, a lugubrious cod on a slab, a fish with a chip on his shoulder. His pale formless face, the watery blue eyes, the receding close-cut grey hair, the large rubbery toothless mouth, the piscine lack of humour – he bore more than a passing resemblance to the poor creatures that earned him his living. Sam knew that he did the best fried fish in the world, and the world had just better come and buy it or else. When they came too quickly for him, that did not suit and they got a cussing, and when trade was slow the blaspheming was even worse.

His opening hours were elastic. Each Saturday he cooked the same enormous quota of fish; in winter he effed and blinded the queueing customers who were making life hard for him and his assistant fryer; in summer he would still be sitting in his empty shop effing and blinding the occasional passer-by for not coming in to buy the last lone piece displayed in glory in the window. He *would not* leave until everything was sold, but if all his stock went too early he cursed his customers for leaving him hours of idleness to spend at home with a wife he detested.

His fryer had been with him for years; tall and thin, his hair, body, and overall saturated with frying-oil vapour, he was like a piece of greasy string. The flat-footed Cockney waitress must have been nudging seventy. Sam gave her the sack every half-hour or so, insulting her with such epithets as 'an effin' dehydrated ruptured old duck', all of which she was expected to ignore, and did. New customers had been known to run out, and some brave souls ticked him off for his language and behaviour, but never the Cockney women who queued for his succulent wares.

'Christ, Sam, 's cold enough ter freeze them things orf a brass monkey today.'

'Garn, eff off.'

'Wosser matter, Sam? D'yer 'ave ter use a winkle-pin ter get it out 's mornin?'

'Eff off.'

Like his waitress, they ignored his rudeness. His fish was worth it, and they knew that he often shoved half the price back with the fish-and-chips if the customer was old and doddery.

My job was to stand at the sink in front of the window and cope with the piles of washing-up. Right beside me was a boiling urn from which I made pots of tea for the diners and jugfuls for the stallholders to take away. In between, and when I could manage it, I dashed to help old Flossie clear the tables. Nearby, Sam was in charge of the till, the clink of the coins as he flung them in, his heavenly orchestra.

For him, Sam was reasonably polite to me, except when I asked him for soda or washing-up liquid, or dish-cloths. Nothing would persuade him to lay out a farthing on these necessities, and I had to take my own. He paid me half-a-crown an hour, gratefully telling me to bugger-off when nearly all his stock was sold. He knocked nothing at all off the price of the fish-and-chips I bought, but I still got a bargain.

That job, the infinite variety of Sam's insults, matched by the repartee of his Cockney customers, glimpsing the polyglot crowds passing the window, hurrying eagerly home with the warm newspaper-wrapped bundle for our supper, my few shillings' earnings swelling out my lean purse, looking forward to the hot bath that I really needed, my lovely kiddies enjoying the fish; yes, Saturday was quite a day.

Some months later old Sam's frustrations and blasphemies came to an end. Everyone around was shocked and truly sorry to hear that he had suddenly dropped dead. His widow and the fryer carried on the business, but it was never the same without Sam.

One memory of old Sam lives with me still like a photograph. Meg and I, returning from the music-hall at nearly midnight, passed his shop. In the window was the last lone piece of cod, and leaning on the counter above it was old Sam, gazing lugubriously at the dark cold street. I could see his lips moving as he cursed the world for not buying that fish. I knew he could not leave it; I had to put him out of his misery. 'Hold on, Meg,' I said, and I went back and bought it. He could not manage to smile, but he gave me quite a warm grunt.

After Sam's sudden death the job lost its flavour and became just another tiresome job, and a smelly one. Word came through on the charwomen's grapevine of a job that might suit me near Regent's Park. This one, too, turned out to have a rather fishy flavour. It was in a flat in one of the houses in a Nash terrace. The facade of the tall narrow house was indeed architecturally lovely, but the interior was falling into a state of decay. It had recently been bought by a charming lady civil servant. She was a spinster in her forties and planned to live on the rents during her retirement. She shared the basement and ground floor with her recently-widowed Welsh mother.

Two single gentlemen each had a room on the next floor. Above them a small flat was rented by a couple; she a masseuse with the business name of Miss La Monte, and he with no business at all but to live on her earnings. At that time my knowledge of sexual deviations, despite Lally, could have been written on the back of the proverbial stamp, mostly owing to my lack of interest in the subject. I knew hazily about 'queers', but a massage parlour was still an unknown quantity.

I accepted them, and the adverts for colonic irrigation, as a private medical service.

Certainly, on the morning Miss La Monte opened her door to me she wore a starched overall as virginal as any hospital nurse's. Other than that, with a few exotic fruits pinned into her high contorted jet-black coiffure, she would have made a stand-in for Carmen Miranda. Her French accent was as thick as the make-up on her rather coarse lascivious little face. She wore very high-heeled shoes and sheer black stockings. No wonder she had to practise privately, I thought, no self-respecting hospital matron would employ such a common-looking person. Her husband was on the point of going out. Had he stood still, I could have mistaken him for a wax model in a West End store window. He looked too immaculately handsome to be flesh and blood. His dark hair and moustache were flecked with just the right amount of grey to set off his flawless features and his after-shave-lotioned pink and white complexion. He topped six feet, and she just over five feet in her spindly heels. She looked up at him as though he were a god, and by God she was welcome to him, I thought, as he took a long caressing glance at himself in the landing mirror.

The flat had a bedroom, sitting-room, bathroom, toilet and tiny kitchen. It would be my job to clean these rooms and the landing and two flights of carpeted stairs, and answer the front door to her clients during my two hours. An elderly, very respectable-looking widow named Mrs Murphy also came. All she had to do was sit by the phone in the sitting-room. The clients came by appointment about every half-hour. I was surprised that they were all men, and even more surprised that so many were young. They bounded up the stairs so eager, so agile, whatever did the likes of these need a massage for, I wondered. I did become quite concerned, however, for one of her customers, a really old man, in his eighties I thought. He could hardly climb the stairs; I could have carried him up quicker. I thought a vigorous massage would just about finish him off for good, and sometimes I wondered if he would even make it up the stairs. Still, he kept coming, so I presumed she was doing him good.

The walls were rather thin between the rooms, and after a client went into the bedroom I could hear the sound of smacking on bare flesh for a minute or two. It was odd the way Mrs Murphy would suddenly burst into snatches of song when a client began to moan a bit. I found out that she only came in the mornings; Miss La Monte had a young woman assistant in the afternoons and she was a 'foreigner' as well. During (funny) business hours the husband kept out of the way, and just in case a client was still there he used a special ringing code on the doorbell.

My first half-hour was spent cleaning the bedroom before the first client was due. One day I was in there conscientiously hoovering and I opened a cupboard to clean its base. I was immensely surprised to find in there a number of riding-crops and whips and boots. Somehow I could not picture Miss La Monte on a horse!

I began to have my suspicions; this was a very queer set-up. But hypocritically I was reluctant to admit it to my conscience. The work was easy and she often gave me a couple of shillings over the odds. However, one day, the elderly Welsh mother of the landlady approached me as I emptied the rubbish basket into the dustbin. She was nearly as green as I was, poor old dear, but as a dedicated chapel-goer she was perturbed about the constant stream of men going upstairs.

'I shall have to speak to my daughter about it. It looks so

bad, and I don't like the look of that woman either. Indeed she pays a terrible high rent, but I think we'd be better off with someone more respectable for a cheaper rent.'

I was now inclined to agree with her. It did seem rather sad and sordid that men should find relief in such a fashion, especially when I thought of all the lonely girls and women there were about. That this was indeed the set-up here was proved to me the very next morning. Mrs Murphy did not turn up to answer the phone and enliven the morning with her strategic bursts of song, and Miss La Monte herself had to go out somewhere urgently. I was alone in the flat, and the phone rang. I answered it.

The caller was a man, and I told him Miss La Monte was out, I was only the daily cleaner and would he ring later. To my astonishment he immediately suggested that I would do. Could I meet him in his car by Regent's Park and do a special service for him and he would pay me fifteen pounds? Special service? All my special services of that nature were devoted exclusively to Syd! I slammed the phone down.

An unknown voice, coming from someone I had never seen, asking such an intimate thing from someone he had never seen, it was like a mental and emotional rape. My puritanical impulses came to the boil. I got my coat, overlooked the two mornings' wages I had earned, and hurried away out of Miss La Monte's life. I was only a char, and my job was to make things clean, but she was too unclean for me.

My observations had given me a clue to the war of the sexes; a cold war, cold because of woman's attitudes as judged by man. But a true woman likes the path to sex strewn with compliments and flowers, a path that twists and turns and meanders, taking its time to reach its goal while she practises her femininity. The urgent need in the loins of man makes him want to tread rough-shod and unhindered to his ultimate desire. Bridging the gap between these extremes, the Miss La Montes extract their greedy toll-gate fees.

It is no wonder that the rich have town houses and country houses. When I was fourteen and had to leave my beloved Forest of Dean and my cottage home, for a life of service in London, it had seemed my heart was breaking. However, like a baby at the mother's breast, I was gradually weaned to the mixed feeding of our wonderful capital.

At about the half-way point on my journeys home on the long-distance coach during holidays, a certain black-and-white Elizabethan cottage became the frontier of my opposing tastes. 'Dear London,' I mentally promised as I passed this landmark, 'I'll be back'; and 'Dear Forest, I'll be back,' I promised on my return to the city.

After twenty-six years in London, married to a Londoner, with four Cockney offspring, I had begun to consider myself a Londoner. Only occasionally had I felt a pang for my country origins. Now the tables began to turn, and more and more often I felt like an exiled Forester. The strain of living over such a difficult neighbour, the problem of Nicky's nerves, the traffic dangers for the children, the doubts about their future, the claustrophobia of the streets compared with the wild sweet country freedom I had enjoyed, all this brought on a recurring dream. In this dream I ran and ran all the way from a London which had turned into dust. At last I reached the green, grassy, dew-wet bank near the chestnut tree where we used to play houses. In an ecstasy of relief I threw myself down on to the wet grass and buried my face in it, running my hands over its damp clean freshness, adding my tears of thanks to those of Nature. But when I woke it was only my pillow and my cheeks that were damp. There was no green through my window, just the tall grey blocks of flats blotting out the sky. It was time to tip-toe to the bathroom and wash the tell-tale tears away, and square up to another urban day.

Until 'Her downstairs' made me so sensitive to noise the sounds of London had never disturbed my senses. They were the pulse, the heartbeats, the pains and the joys of this wonderful old capital. One Saturday morning I was alone in our flat rushing through the washing-up. The porridge saucepan slipped from my hand and fell, not on the mat by the sink but with a clatter on the bare tiles. Oh, my God! 'Her downstairs' would think I had done it on purpose! By then the sound of a dropped saucepan had assumed the importance of the crack of doom. I started to tremble. I felt trapped; trapped in a purgatory of noise: the automatic dust-cart clanging in the yard; the yelling and shouting of the children playing round it; the bawling of the street traders exhorting customers to buy; the rumbling hum of the customers' voices; a pneumatic drill just down the street repairing the drains of the public lavatories; and, trying to fight the din with a loudspeaker-van, the voice of Sir Wavell Wakefield asking us to vote him in as our next MP.

Hands to my head I cowered against the wall of the passage that ran through the flat. Was I going mad? I wanted to scream my own neuroses into the din. I heard the letter-box open and went to see if it was the postman. On the carpet was a post-card of a picture taken in the Forest of Dean. Sunlight filtered through the branches of the oaks on green ferns and foxgloves, and a woodland path led peacefully through this pastoral beauty. The pent-up tears broke; I sobbed and sobbed for the green peaceful aura of my childhood years. Oh, if only I could summon a magic carpet to take us all there! I pictured our children running as I did, arms outstretched to the wind and the sun, with no-one to say them nay.

I took paper, envelope, and stamp, and there and then wrote to my mother, asking her to let us know if any place turned up at home that we could rent cheaply. So long as it had four walls and a roof, and was in the country, that would do. That evening, after we had got the children to bed, Syd and I sat and had a long talk about it. It seemed a momentous decision, but the more we pondered it the easier and more attractive it became. Anyway, no harm could be done by posting the letter, so we did, and with our minds full of pictures of sunlit fields and floral glades we went happily to bed.

After that, everything happened with surprising speed, as if it had been meant. I checked with the Children's Hospital whether such a move would be better for Nicky and they approved. Within a few days my mother wrote back and enclosed a cutting from her local paper; an advert offering a job as a sawyer in an estate sawmill eight miles from Gloucester, cottage available. Syd applied, they seemed keen on him, and he went down on his own to have a look at it. So, in less than a month, the question had been mooted, the decision taken, the move made, and a new life opened up for the family. And here I was, none too pleased yet at the return of the native, lying awake on the creaking bedroom floor, in fear of the mice, casting my mind back over my life in London, marriage and children, joys and sorrows.

The summer dawn came early, greeted by a rapturous chorus of birdsong. As its grey light struggled through the dusty lattice I snuggled down by Syd's back and fell into the sleep that I had so justly earned.

*

'Wake up, wake up, Win! Just come and have a look through this window.'

I struggled back from my oblivion and on to my feet to join Syd who was standing at the open window. Puffing out his chest, stretching his arms wide, breathing deeply, he looked like an emperor surveying his domain. On this summer morning the outlook was rich indeed; golden sunshine on a field of golden corn sloping up behind the barns; the berries of the rowan branches that almost touched the back roof beginning to turn a brilliant red. And who would long for caskets of emeralds when there are such trees to behold? The cherry orchard. The copse of oak and ash and chestnut and pine complementing each other with their differing shades and shapes. The mellowed old barns, and the pale pink rambler rose that covered the rustic arch at the yard entrance. All set against the perfect backdrop of a cloudless blue sky.

'That's what I call a heavenly outlook!' enthused Syd.

'Yes, so it is,' I said. 'But what about that hell-hole of a living-room and kitchen downstairs? The Crumbles, that's what this place ought to be called.' Of course he could look on the bright side, he had had a good sleep. He hadn't lain awake all night for fear of a mouse running over his face.

The children slept on, so we tip-toed downstairs into the living-room. Putting her house in order is a satisfying job for most women, but I felt defeated about achieving it here. The two wardrobes looked incongruous and overpowering against the wall, and added to the claustrophobia brought on by the sloping ceiling and the small dirty window. Above all, I needed a cup of tea to lift my downcast spirits. I had not been born a child in the Forest for nothing. Telling Syd to scrounge up our newspaper packaging I hurried round the house to the copse at the back and returned with an apronful of twigs. It took a lot of paper, a lot of blowing, and a lot of patience, but when eventually the kettle began to sing, so did I.

The children woke up in high good humour, but Syd lost some of his when I pointed out that he would have to go at once to the Electricity Board in Gloucester. After a cup of tea and very little else he dashed off to trot the mile to the bus-stop, his ears still ringing with my exhortations. 'Mind and emphasise how urgently we need a cooker and a boiler, and mind and buy some bread, because till I get a cooker that's all you're having, bread and eggs.' Boiled eggs was all I could hope to achieve on that fire, at least until the chimney was swept.

Jenny pottered about with me, putting our clothes, crocks and oddments into some sort of order. The boys, being boys, disappeared to investigate the surroundings. They came home somewhat chastened, having had a lecture on estate discip-lines from the bailiff. Boys did not go into the orchards. They did not go into fenced woods because they might disturb the pheasants. They kept to the footpaths through fields with sheep, cows and horses in them. They left gates as they found them and in general behaved like civilised human beings. It was asking a lot, but it was his duty. They recovered from their little depression probably quicker than he did. Meanwhile there was plenty of scope for their surplus energies right here, and for a start they could go into 'our' copse and gather twigs and fallen dead wood for the fire.

Syd came home with some welcome news. For a two-pound deposit with four years to pay he had been able to order an electric cooker and a boiler, and they would be delivered within four days. Heartened no end, I thought we could strug-gle through till then. At the end of the four days nothing had been delivered. Never mind, they would be sure to come any minute. At the end of a week, with the washing piling up, and no hot meals, I wrote a polite but urgent reminder to the Electricity Board. A week later, another one, more urgent and less polite. By the end of a month, my sore-tried temper was reaching boiling point much quicker than the old black kettle on its heap of twigs. Camping-out is fun, but not in your own home.

Well, I had given them long enough. Taking the four children I walked the mile to the phone box in the village. In those pre-automated days one could put twopence in the box and natter on ad infinitum. Just as well, I thought, as I got through to the electricity showrooms, because I was choked up with anger, frustration and self-pity. I demanded to speak to the manager. Yes, I could hang on, it was an urgent matter; only the manager would do. Eventually I told the male voice at the other end that if the promised cooker and boiler had not arrived on the morrow, four hungry unwashed kids and their hungry unwashed mother would come and squat in his showroom until they did.

There was no need for us to hurry home. The weather was lovely, and we took the footpath across the meadows to the tiny stream in the dipple where the children had a paddle. Up the other side into Sawpit Meadow and we stopped again to see how the blackberries were coming on in the hedges. A friendly cottager's wife was by her door, so we paused for a chat and were rewarded with an armful of juicy rhubarb. Eventually we emerged one at a time through a little swing-gate right opposite the drive.

Now we had to climb, but the step was in the chestnut's shade and we were nearly home. We had just got past the big old chestnut and in sight of our entrance, when the electricity van passed us. The sight of it gave me the energy to run up the last bit, rancour now forgotten. I could have hugged the driver and his mate. I was already visualising golden-crusted rhubarb pies. But I felt like walloping the pair of them when they told me they had not got the gear with them to install the cooker and the boiler.

'Right,' I warned them. 'If you're not here first thing in the morning to get the job done, I shall carry out my threat, and you can see what a lot of gypsies we look like already, thanks to you lot.' Suitably chastened, they left full of promises, and returned the next morning and fixed it all up. I spent the whole afternoon up to my elbows in flour and fat. We were making progress.

We had a lot of relatives and friends in the Forest, and they began to call on us, many of them on our very first day. So did some of our Londoners; it was amazing how some who were too busy to walk round the block to see us in town were now ready to drive over a hundred miles for the same dubious pleasure. 'Such a lovely day!' they would announce blandly as they got out of their cars dressed in their Sunday best, the women with their hair done. 'Such a lovely day, we thought we'd come and see you. What a place, aren't you lucky?' Standing there being nice, in my dirty old trousers, my uncombed hair full of soot and smuts, I sometimes had doubts. Never mind, throw some more twigs on the hearth, and bang on the poor old kettle again. We had no warning from those on foot, but the sound of a car coming up the hill raised cries of 'Bucket, bucket!' Chris, or Syd if available, or if not it had to be me, had to run into the cubby-hole and grab the privy bucket. In 'our' copse round the back Syd and the boys had dug holes for emptying it, but more often than not we met the

visitors head on as we were hurrying round with it. They made
no comment on this quaint old country custom, and the har-
dier souls even managed a rather brief handshake. Everybody
meant well, bless them, but they did add a few complications
to an already complicated existence.

The beauty of this place has always drawn people to it, and
as we gradually got it civilised we enjoyed their company
properly. They may have got some entertainment from our
antics in those early days, but they provided some for us. All
the men fell into the wardrobe trap. All the women said at
once, 'But what about the wardrobes? You can't leave 'em
here, surely?' I shrugged. 'Can't get 'em upstairs, not yet.
Doing something about it later.' The men, who had probably
not even noticed them, perked up their ears. 'Why not? Let's
have a look.' Away they went, looking up the stairs, measuring
with arms outspread. 'Reckon we can, you know. Give us a
hand.'

We got quite blase watching them heaving and sweating, to
me, to you, whoa, back a bit, up a bit, down a bit, sideways a
bit, try him the other way round. We knew there was just no
way. Eventually the bedroom window had to be removed, and
it was still an awkward feat getting them in. We got them in at
last, but how we shall ever get them out I do not know.
Perhaps we shall have a lot of visitors.

Jenny was more entertained by the kitten Mother got us to
keep the mice out of the house. It quickly grew into her
beloved fat pet cat, and sure enough it kept the mice out of
our rooms but not out of the cottage structures. Those mice
had been there for generations but they did not mind our
moving into their house. In fact they were quite curious
about us and used to come to the hole in the wall by the
beam and look down at us as we ate. They were healthy

sturdy mice, and once battle was joined they went down with flags flying.

Between getting up in the morning and going to bed at night Syd is far the more patient of us two. But night disturbances, be they from crying offspring, wailing tomcats, or mice scrabbling behind the skirting board near his head, bring out the black side of his character. He had no aversion to quiet mice; if they napped peacefully on the bottom of our bed it would not worry him. But after many nights of their persistent scrabbling behind the skirting board Syd's temper reached explosion point. He came to the irrational conclusion that the mice were deliberately picking that spot for their nocturnal skirmishing in order to drive him nuts. One night, after banging the skirting board and revealing an unsuspected streak of sadism in his threats to the so-and-so perishers, he was reduced to banging his own head on the wall in his frenzy. I could not help it; I started to giggle.

'That bloody useless cat,' he moaned. 'What's *he* doing all day?'

'It's not the cat's fault. He can't get inside the walls any more than you can.'

'It's your fault. You overfeed the lazy sod.'

I humped myself over to the extreme edge of our bed. 'You're a bigger nuisance than the perishing mice, keeping me awake all night with your temper.'

It was a relief to get up in the morning. 'I've got the answer,' said Syd through his toast. 'I'll put the cat up in the loft over the kitchen before I go to work. That's where their run is, straight in from the barn where it meets the kitchen roof. Mind you leave him up there; I'll get him down when I come home from work.'

I called the cat, and under Syd's eagle eye I gave him a

stingy bit of breakfast. We dragged the table out, put a chair on top, and Syd lifted the protesting cat up through the trap-door. We turned a deaf ear to his disgusted miaowings.

I was glad that evening the boys had been invited to the Scout party; after his tea Syd could indulge in a nap and make up his loss of sleep. He looked tired when he came in from his eight-hour day of manual work and the uphill mile-long walk home. He had just swallowed his first cup of tea and started on his cooked meal, when he suddenly remembered the cat. We dragged the table with a chair on top under the ceiling hatch. Syd clambered up out of sight, but no cat came down.

'Hand me up the torch. I can't see or hear him.' It was quite dark up there. Jenny climbed up with the torch, and I lit a candle in a jam jar. There was no cat to be seen, but the dim light did reveal a broken disused chimney in the far wall that had once served as a fireplace for farmworkers.

'Oh dear, oh dear!' cried a contrite Syd. 'I think I know what's happened. That poor cat must have fallen down this hole in the old chimney. He could never have got up, it's too tall and straight. He must have gone down. Poor little devil, he's probably lying injured down at the bottom. But I can't see him down there.'

Jenny had been scolding us for putting the cat up there in the first place, and now she burst into tears.

I had more faith in feline agility than they. 'Don't worry, darling, I'm sure that cat climbed out. You go out and call him. I expect he's asleep in the hay-barn.'

Her call got no response. Syd poked about in the attic, and his dinner congealed on the plate. 'Tell you what we'll do,' he shouted from the gloom above. 'Tie some meat off my plate on a long string, and I'll lower it down the chimney. He must be hungry by now. If he takes it, we'll know he's alive.'

Jenny climbed up with it herself, and they took turns hanging it down the chimney, peering down into the murky cobwebbed depths, calling, 'Puss, puss.' All in vain, the bait was ignored. Finally they pulled the dusty meat back and got down in despair.

'Well,' said Syd, 'I'm going to knock a hole in the wall. He must be down there somewhere. Now where do I start?' All he had for the task was a small hammer and a cold chisel, and the centuries-old cottage has stone walls about two feet thick. The sweat was dropping off him before he managed to prise out the first stone. By the time he had made a hole a couple of feet square we seemed to have half-a-ton of rubble and stone piled up on the kitchen floor. It was just unbelievable that all that had come from that small hole. At ten o'clock I put a tired and reluctant Jenny to bed, bolstering up her hopes as best I could. When the boys came home it was nearly eleven, and they reckoned pragmatically that the cat must have snuffed it anyway, if it was under all that rubble. I gave them a milky drink and biscuits and hustled them off to bed.

At one a.m. Syd was still pulling out stones and rubble. 'Well, I must have knocked the hole in the wrong place. There's no chimney shaft there, but it looks right. Just have to knock a hole further along.' He put the hammer down and filled his pipe. All the evening I had been falling in love with this overtired worried man so concerned for the cat and his little daughter's feelings.

'Go and sit down,' I ordered him, and as he did I kissed the top of his balding head, and banked my love for a later date. 'I'm going to warm up your food, and while you're eating it I'll go round the barns calling the cat. You're *not* going to make another hole in that wall tonight. You're beaten, and you've got to be up at half-past six to go to work.' He ate his food, while I went around calling in vain; now I too was convinced that the cat was a corpse in that wall. It took all my persuasion to stop Syd making a fresh start. By two a.m. he was washed ready for bed, and then made a last abortive stroll round the cottage calling, 'Puss, puss.'

'Win, Win, listen! I can hear the cat miaowing!'

I struggled awake to Syd's excited voice as he jumped out of bed and ran downstairs. The alarm clock said four o'clock. In a few minutes Syd came back beaming like a lighthouse, with the cat in his arms. Before I could stop him he went into Jenny's room.

'Darling, wake up, look, look what Daddy's got, the puss! There now, he can stop on your bed with you till the morning; he's not hurt at all; he was outside all the time.'

'Why on earth did you wake her up this time of night?'

'Well, I thought she might have a nightmare over him.'

'He'd have had my toe up his behind and gone for another mystery trip if I'd got hold of him,' was my grumpy retort. I did my bit, though. My maiden name was not Mason for nothing. I got hold of some cement, and during the day I reconstructed the wall. I must have done it with remarkable economy, because when I had finished it took me ages to carry away the left-over stones and rubble.

The cat went up a few more times and earned his keep. The mice decided upon a tactical retreat into the barns after they had lost a few bold scouts, and we never heard them behind the skirting boards again.

*

Now the problem was – was I a timid mouse or a woman? I decided I was a woman, and no woman could be expected to put up with that living-room floor, and not having a back door to take the privy bucket out. I wrote to the estate manager asking him to call at his earliest convenience, an apt word, and he kindly came within a couple of days.

Old cottages can be a headache to their owners; they are always needing repairs which are in no way covered by the token rent. However, he agreed for us to have a back door installed, and a floor laid in the living-room. The work would be done at week-ends by Fritz, with Syd offering his own labour free. Fritz came up by the same evening. He was a German, an ex-prisoner who had chosen to become a British subject, and worked in the same sawmill as Syd. He put me in mind of a human pneumatic drill, there was so much energy exuding from his wiry frame. His blue eyes were like a pair of laser beams, and they cut a way through the most difficult problems at once. For a few minutes he sized the job up, looking at the back wall, and then at the living-room floor.

'Ve manage,' he said, and somehow I knew he would. 'Ve manage. I tell zem get the stuff 'ere by Sunday. I come seven o'clock.'

'I suppose the floor will just be concrete?' I said with a little sigh. 'Wouldn't it be lovely if the estate would let you do it in red quarry tiles to match the grate?' I thought I might as well push my luck; nothing ventured nothing gained.

He bit at once. 'OK. Ve manage,' he said with reassuring conviction, and he was gone.

Sunday morning he reappeared sharp on seven, looking as keen as a razor blade, while we were still rubbing the sleep from our eyes. Immoveable objects meant little to this irresistible force. Bash, bang, wallop, the huge stones fell out of the back wall, and he soon had a door-hole. This alone was a wonderful start: no more carrying the privy bucket through the living-room! By the end of the third Sunday the new door was hung, a perfect fit. The lowness of the back roof meant that the door was only five feet high, and for weeks afterwards Syd, Chris and I sported a variety of lumps on our heads! By the time he had laid our new red-tiled floor, I had put Fritz on a pedestal. He went up a few more notches when he decided to build on some more courses of bricks atop our chimney to stop the down-draught – and it worked! It was hard to say whether all this was from innate generosity or for the pure joy of doing the job. Fritz tactfully shrugged off our thanks, and marched away to destroy the next problem. Once or twice Syd quietly made it known to me that he, too, had helped; Fritz could not have quite all the credit!

Our living-room now had a nice brick grate that worked properly, and a tiled floor that gave me joy to scrub, but the rough and grubby walls still made it depressing to live in. Syd, as usual, willing to put up with almost anything for a bit of peace, wanted to put the matter off till we could do 'a proper job'. Privately I told myself something was going to be done before that, an improper job if necessary, as soon as I could earn a few pounds of my own.

Towards the end of August, Chris and Richard started at their new grammar school, a five-mile bus ride away. Nicky and Jenny I took to be registered at the tiny school next to the church, a half-mile walk. An inconvenient distance in wet or icy weather, but a beautiful walk at all seasons: down the hill to the back of the Manor; then up a wandering pathway through a kissing gate; along the top of the 'seedbeds', where a dozen or so men and women were busy hoeing and weeding seedling trees; on to the Park, a wide stretch of grass dotted with a few magnificent oaks and grazing sheep. The Park was overlooked by dense woodlands that climbed over the foothills, and pushed back into their lee stood the game-keeper's black-and-white Elizabethan cottage. Its terraced garden paced down the slope and tumbled over with vivid scarlet and gold nasturtiums, a sight that stopped us in our tracks. If Snow White and the Seven Dwarfs had come troop-ing out of the door we would not have been surprised. Nicky and Jenny soon discovered that the gamekeeper's wife had magic pockets which produced sweets for any child that crossed her path.

At the end of the Park a stile led into the Nursery where an enormous variety of shrubs, roses and decorative trees was raised for sale. Many were in bloom, and some were heavy with perfume on the still summer air. Our earthly Eden. But Eden's end came suddenly at the churchyard gate. The flower-decked little monuments of the common folk were dotted at random down the grassy slope, while up at the top wall under the mourning yews stood the damp grey tombs of their mas-ters. Distant and distinct in death as they were in life; the worms mocked their folly. How many laid beneath this turf had once run chattering over it to school? One day – how soon – but I closed my mind.

The infant children were gathering at the old school door. The ancient church and the little school, built in the same Norman style, snuggled together under the wooded hillocks, and delighted the eye. The school had only one classroom, shared by all the pupils and the two teachers. They were suit-ably named: Miss Bird and Miss Sparrow. Miss Bird, the headmistress, was a middle-aged lady from the north of England, who had come to the school as a 'temporary' and was still there thirty years on. A shrewd and kindly woman, she summed me up: four children, coming to live in a tied cottage, well, well. So during our conversation she tactfully let me know that there was often casual work to be got on the estate. Quite probably, she said, they still needed pickers in the plum orchards.

I left Jenny and Nicky in her capable charge. I could only guess at what scholastic standard they might achieve in that tiny one-room school, but just the abiding memory of its heavenly environs would be an asset beyond price.

One of my primeval ancestors must have fallen out of a tree; at any rate I have no head for heights. Nevertheless, on the way home from the school I made enquiries about the plum job and was relieved to hear that there was some work left picking up off the ground. Most of the orchards had already been picked and marketed; the two as yet unpicked were for the jam factory and would be shaken down. The pay was half-a-crown for each half-hundredweight box you could fill, and I could start the very next day! Not only would the extra money be a godsend, but what a relief to get away from the rough-hewn living-room!

It was half-a-mile to the orchard and I had to be there by nine o'clock. I do not know how Dr Spock would have coped with getting my brood out of bed in the mornings. It reduced me to bad temper, frayed nerves, and threatenings, and it brought home to me how my mother had suffered from my own slug-a-bed nature. I was sure that growing children needed a good breakfast, and I often ran after one or another screaming like a banshee for them to stop for the sandwich of congealed egg in toast that I was carrying. With work to go to myself, I too had to hurry. Once, in desperation, I threatened them with the ultimate: I would leave home and go back to the comparative luxury of domestic service! This left them apparently unmoved, and seemed even to encourage their tardiness. What a blow to my mother-ego! What would Dr Spock have made of that?

'Right,' I screamed. 'Any of you not up, washed, and at the table in four minutes flat, gets no breakfast *nor* anything to drink.'

'That doesn't apply to me,' called out a grumpy Nicky, "cos I'm still asleep and can't hear you.'

Somehow I got them all out of the door by quarter to nine. I threw their leavings into a paper bag, put it in my pocket, and made a dash for it across the fields to the plum orchard. The other four women pickers were already there. Two elderly farm men had just started shaking the branches with long hooked wooden poles. A pair of dear old codgers they were, and well past retirement age, but work was an ingrained habit necessary to these men who had started odd-jobbing on the estate as children. Wizened old apples they were, still ruddy of cheek, and their talk full of the flavour of the fields.

Before they moved to the next tree they left a purple circle of juicy plums for us to start on. Piles of wooden boxes were placed strategically between the rows of trees, and we pickers were each supplied with a basket and told to work from the outside towards the tree-trunk. The weather was perfect, and the company of the other women a welcome change. Between them, my four companions seemed to have most of the traits commonly associated with our sex.

I was surprised to see a type like Moira doing this job. A woman of middle age she still had the remains of what must have been ravishing good looks. She clung to her fading glamour with lipstick, powder, and eyebrow pencil. She wore rubber gloves to protect her hands and her varnished nails were the colour of the plums. I soon found that whatever sweetness had illumined her nature had faded with her youth. Red in tooth and claw, with a conspiratorial drawling hiss of a voice, she was a real cat. As I picked at her side she gave me a running commentary on the other three, their indiscretions, failings, and faults. While she criticised them icily behind their backs, she spoke with the oiliest of tongues to their faces.

I had enough sense to be tactful and kept my tongue still and my hands busy. Gradually I sidled away from her and worked my way nearer to Rona. It was difficult to tell Rona's age, but not difficult to see that she was a true child of the earth. Plenty of it clung to her ragged old jacket, to her shabby wellington boots, and to her person. The undermost layer looked as though it had been clinging for some time. She was as thin as a bean pole and round-shouldered, and what you could see of her face was quite plain. It was lit up now and again with a companionable grin from ear to ear, a lopsided grin enabling her to keep the everlasting fag going in the corner of her mouth. Her bony fingers picked up the plums with the speed of a chameleon's tongue after a fly. She looked like a downtrodden waif. Probably, I conjectured, she had an out-of-work lazy husband and a brood of offspring at home. I thought that it was greatly to her credit that she grinned so much and occasionally hummed the latest songs. Moira had told me how Rona and her husband lived like pigs in a hovel. By the end of the day I had learned that Rona was only twenty-four, and that she lived in happy squalor with a husband as hard-working as herself. They both worked on the land, planting, weeding, and garnering the fruits of the earth without a grumble for the parsimonious pay it brought them.

On Saturdays they washed off the top layers of the week's accumulation of sweat and earth, and took themselves and the best part of their wages off to the pub. When they had got their skinfuls they entertained the customers with Rona's version of the conga and their own interpretation of the latest songs. They brought in a good deal of custom for the landlord. Years of practice had taught them to hold their drink with proper dignity as they walked the dark mile-and-a-half home. But once even Rona was temporarily overcome by the strong local 'stun-'em' cider. They held each other up till the top of the steep-sloping lane which led to their cottage. Then Rona fell down, still singing. Her husband could not get her up so he did the next best thing. Gathering up her long hair in his strong right hand he dragged her in true caveman style the rest of the way home to their cottage by the stream.

They had no children; they were never known to quarrel; they contributed greatly to society, and demanded very little in return. As the day progressed and the boxes filled and the tidal wave of plums receded, I warmed more and more to Rona.

Minnie reminded me irresistibly of Mole in *The Wind in the Willows*. In her little woolly hat gathered into a point at the top, with her nose to the ground – and it did not have far to go for she was very short of stature – and with her completely domesticated outlook on life, she gave off an aura of cosiness. Her talk was all of domestic bliss:

'So I thought to meself I'll turn round an' make Sam a nice dumplin' stew for 'is tea'; 'That back-kitchen could do with a bit o' whitewash, I thought, so I turned round an' done it'; 'It's no good, I shall 'ave to sort that muddle in the cupboard drawers out, so I turned round an' done 'em'; 'It blowed up that nice an' windy I might as well do me bit o' washin' so I turned round an' done it *and* got it all dry by teatime'; 'I shall put some o' these plums in the bottom of me bag; then I shall turn round after tea an' make a bit o' jam.'

I tried to picture this miniature whirling dervish at home. When later I called at her tiny cosy overcrowded cottage I wondered how she managed to get all that turning round done!

Dolly had brought her four-year-old son with her, a handsome sturdy little boy who ran ahead with the two old men. She too was handsome, tall and Junoesque, but though, as they say, well-preserved, obviously in her forties. She must have read my thoughts.

'Yeah, I'm a bit long in the tooth to have a kid that age,' she laughed. 'I'd already got five, two of 'em married, and me a grannie, my poor chap was still alive then, hale and hearty, too bloody hale and hearty. We had a nice piece of rented land of our own them days, but we had to work dawn till dark to make a livin' off it. 'Twas gone eleven one night when we just finished bringin' our hay in before a spell of rain broke that might 'a' ruined it. I was that tired I hardly had the strength to wash meself and climb into bed. But him; he was that pleased we'd got it all under cover, he came up to bed like a young colt. '"Ow about a bit, then?" he said when he got into bed. I can tell you I wasn't interested, but anything for a quiet life, so I opened me legs and said help your bloody self and he did. And that's the result, and me forty-four year old!' She looked fondly at the fruit of her generosity. 'Poor Bill,' she went on, 'he never lived to see that 'un. Had a stroke in the cowshed and was gone before the doctor could get to us, and 'im only fifty-two. 'Course I couldn't keep up with the rent o' the land, but d'you know, I don't seem to work so hard these days as I did when us worked for ourselves.'

Maybe her work-load had lessened, but I thought this fine full-blooded woman must find her nights lonely. Meanwhile I pressed on; my ears were open but my hands were full. The novelty of the job, the sunshine, and the beautiful pastoral surroundings more than made up for the ache in my back. The thought of that half-a-crown for each filled box made me a very nifty picker indeed.

'Just look at the galloping manger!' cried Minnie as they noted I had filled the most boxes. Unaware of it herself, Minnie mispronounced something in every sentence; she had hyder-angles in her garden, and summed it up by often singing 'I'm just a little peculiar in an onion bed'. Her feathers got very ruffled if any iggerant listener dared to correct her, and she was always ready to turn round and give them a good lecture.

The two old men whistled to let us know it was one o'clock. I had popped a fair few of the juicy plums in my mouth but by now I had a raging thirst. We all sat down on the grass near a hedge. I jumped up very quickly when Moira languidly observed she thought I had sat on a grass-snake. 'Won't hurt you, silly,' she said tartly in response to my ignorant panic. My scraps of toast were going down very dry indeed; if there had been any moisture left in my mouth I would have drooled at the sight of the tea they poured from their flasks.

I tried to look indifferent. 'Didn't you bring nothing to drink?' asked Rona. I shook my head in what I hoped was an offhand manner. The stained, dirt-encrusted cup on the top of her flask was as black as the brew she poured out of it. A bit of ash dropped into it from her fag-end, but she drank it with gusto, poured out a second cup, and handed it to me. In my hurry to get off to work I had not even had a cup of tea and by now my thirst was unendurable. I am not a very fastidious person, but still I was daunted. There were hours more to go, for Rona worked till six whereas I was leaving to get home for the children, so it was a most generous gesture. There was concern and kindness in her face. Eventually I took the cup, shut my eyes, and gulped down half the contents. 'That's plenty; thank you *very* much.' She had no qualms about drinking after me.

The other four had all brought their 'bait' in generous-sized bags, and before they started picking again they carefully filled the bottoms of these bags with the firmest plums they could find. I was learning. Tomorrow I would bring my food in a shopping-bag with plenty to drink. I was learning too that a stomach needed time to get used to a sudden excess of plums! Sharp at four o'clock I bade them a hasty cheerio, and had to do a galloping manger sprint across the fields for a dash into our privy, and just in time.

At the end of three weeks' plum picking I had earned quite a few pounds. The biggest percentage of it went into the house-keeping but I kept some back for an idea that had been fermenting in my mind. I was going to have a go at papering our living-room. The new Polycell paste had just come on to the market, and unlike the old flour and water, this stuff stuck the paper to bulges and dips. I had a good testing-ground for it. To help camouflage the uneven walls I decided it would have to be a patterned paper, a quiet pattern in pastel shades of grey or mushroom. I had it all worked out and could practically see it, but I kept the idea to myself to give the family a lovely surprise by doing the job all in one day.

That day came. I could hardly wait to get the children off to school. It was late September and a sunny balmy morning.

I had the choice of walking down the tarmacked lane to the village, or taking the short cut across the fields. Though time was precious I had a good look across the fields first to make sure there were no cattle or horses there. I have an irrational fear of animals great and small since a childhood experience of being in a field with a charging bull. They seemed to be all clear. Happy as a lark I hurried on past the small tenant farmstead and down the sloping field to the plank bridge across the tiny stream, and then up the grassy slopes on the other side.

Now I could see the police station, the first house in the village, and something else! I got a nasty shock when I saw the corner of the last field was enclosed in barbed wire, and in it a bovine animal raging at his confinement. It had no udders so I knew it was not a cow; I did not bother to inspect whatever else it had! I found the energy to run like the clappers over the stile that led to the snicket path into the village. The bus passed me about a hundred yards before the stop, but in the manner of country buses it waited for my breathless arrival.

A seven-mile ride through the country is very pleasant with so many individual types of cottages and gardens peppered along the way. At the next stop the driver waited again for two familiar travellers, a pair of jolly red-faced women. They settled down in the seat behind me.

'No need for me to come in the mornin', but the old man give me such a treat last night,' one said with a roguish giggle, 'I thought I'd give *'im* a treat wi' 'is tea – 'e do love the individual fruit pies from Lyons's.'

'No wonder thy old man 'a' got to 'ave a nap in 'is bait time! I be getting some wellington boots for meself; 'twill be tater pickin' soon an' my old 'uns 'a' got a great split in one on 'em.' Mentally I took note that potato picking would be in the offing soon.

Right opposite the bus stop at the entrance to the city was a wallpaper shop, and I planned to nip over to it, make my purchases, and catch the same bus on its way back. In the shop doorway there were some bargain sale offers stuck up in large cardboard boxes. Among them were eight rolls of excellent quality Regency-stripe paper, one side ready trimmed, at a real knock-down price. As far as I could see, there was nothing wrong with it, and it had a pattern of close red, gold, and white stripes. My ideas on decor took an instant about turn. Of course, Regency stripes, very posh, just what the room was crying out for, and good thick quality too! I should have enough money left to get a tin of gold paint for our knick-knacks and picture frames to set it off. With two parcels of four rolls each, a tin of gold paint, and a large packet of paste, I still had enough change for some chocolate to treat the kids. I felt full of the milk of human kindness. A two-minute wait and I was on the bus again, wishing it would not dawdle so much on the homeward journey. Time was of the essence to get it all done in a matter of hours.

When I got off at the village I was in a dilemma. I could save at least ten invaluable minutes by going across the fields, but this would mean passing the enclosure with the bull again. Impatiently throwing caution to the winds I decided to risk it. After all, how could it get out? If it could, why had it not? And why should it choose this moment? Full of dutch courage I marched boldly through the snicket, and though hampered by my purchases I began to run across the field. I could see the animal, and it was now in a proper frenzy, stampeding up and down inside its barbed enclosure. Running must have been my mistake, for just as I got opposite him and he could see me, he charged his way out.

I know what the expression 'rooted to the spot' means. He

came running right in my direction. Frozen with horror, I could just imagine headlines in the local paper: 'Woman gored to death by bull only yards from police station.' There was no sense in running, he had a bull's strength and four legs: I only had two. I threw my parcels headlong and waited for a horrible death. When I could almost feel his breath I stood aside in a manner that would have brought the house down at a Spanish bull-ring. The animal rushed past me apparently indifferent to my presence; no wonder, in a distant field separated by two hedges were a herd of similar bovines. I did not wait for him to do a U-turn when he met the next hedge.

Picking up my parcels I ran somehow on legs turned to rubber and scrambled over the hedge bordering the lane, throwing the long-suffering wallpaper on to the road. A four-foot thick hawthorn hedge takes some scrambling over, but it is amazing how athletic sharing a field with a bull makes one.

Scratched, torn, and breathless I still had enough inspiration left to hurry along the lane and up the hill to home. It was a bit of an anti-climax to find out later that it was only a bullock isolated from the herd with an eye infection.

With one hand I mixed a bowl of paste, and with the other made a pot of tea. There was no time to eat. Then I realised that I had not got the pasting-brush. No matter, Syd had a large and splendid shaving-brush given him for last Christmas; that would have to do.

Papering by oneself a fourteen-foot wall that reaches up to a peak is quite a feat. I measured, cut, and pasted. I had to stand on a chair atop a table with extra height provided by Syd's precious thick volumes of Shakespeare. He was going to kill me when he came in and found out, but I had already escaped death by inches, and as soon as he saw the new-papered room he would forgive me. I had achieved two walls before I stood back to admire the result. Well actually, I reeled back; the effect was psychedelic. Over the peaks and into the valleys of the uneven walls the stripes had run into each other, and away, and back again in the most alarming clashes. I began to feel a bit giddy, and a headache started up like a first cousin to a migraine. I was in no mood to believe the evidence of my own eyes, and pig-headedly put my symptoms down to the encounter with the bull. Anyway, I was forty-one years old; perhaps this was a sudden start to the 'change of life'. I hoped it would not be as drastic as the change that was coming over our living-room!

Never mind, when the other two walls were done and the room more unified, there would be a better effect. So I hurried on, earning a medal for speed if not for skill. Finishing, I felt a bit cross-eyed, and my head was worse, so I was glad to escape into the kitchen. I still had fifteen minutes before my hungry brood came charging in. As a child in the twenties I had once seen a miner's wife making some hurried 'workhouse gallop' for her husband's dinner. Into a saucepan of salted water she put some thinly sliced onions and potatoes. They cooked in minutes, and then she added a knob of dripping and thick-ened it all with well-peppered flour. I could do better than that; I could throw in a tin of corned beef and a tin of peas, and for dessert the old standby, the remains of a plum pie. This would fill them up, and perhaps take their minds off the wall-paper.

Long-legged Chris arrived first. Fifth-form grammar-school boys consider themselves a rather shockproof lot. However, as he came in he did not quite hide his stagger before quietly commenting, 'Mum, it's time you were certified.' Richard followed closely on his heels, and let out quite an oath before saying, 'Sorry, Mum, it was the shock.' Nicky – well, for the first time in his life he was struck speechless. Six-year-old Jenny, whose vocabulary had been somewhat coarsened by her three brothers, put her hands on her hips, her budding feminine instincts outraged by my taste. 'Mummy,' she scolded, 'Mummy! It looks bloody awfuller than it did before!'

Poor Syd, after a long day in the sawmill and a tiring walk home, had to come in at the best of times to four lively extroverts and an unpredictable spouse. Now this! As he opened the door he reeled back, shading his eyes with his hands. 'God help me,' he cried and it was a prayer from the heart. We all shaded our eyes, eating our meal with hanging heads.

While I was washing up, one of Syd's mates called to offer him the chance of a week-end fencing job. I asked him in and proffered a chair. He sat for a while looking out of the window rather pointedly and acting very fidgety, and then said, 'D'you mind 'avin' the door open till I go, missus? I've got a bit of 'eadache comin' on.'

Well, they would all just have to get used to it, I thought, but when my brother-in-law called and sat through his visit with his sunglasses on I knew I was defeated.

That night I went to bed knowing that I had murdered good taste; it ran in blood-red wavy stripes down our bumpy walls. It took me two days and several coats of cream emulsion to bury my mistake.

Luckily there was now plenty to lure me out of the house. For a start there were the ripening blackberries. Down through the woods at the back of the cottage the gamekeeper had cut rough paths ready for the pheasant-shooting season. Brambles heavy with ripening fruit grew profusely on each side and spread under the trees fighting for survival in the wild under-growth that made such excellent cover for the beautiful doomed birds. Each year the gamekeeper's busy sickle pruned the vigorous plants and they responded with strong young shoots and fine big fruit.

A lovely mixture of flora and fauna; teeming insect life that would bring joy to the heart of the entomologist; sinuous grey squirrels making lightning forays among the branches. What a feast for the eye in the myriad shapes and hues of the foliage. The graceful languid tendrils of delicate parasite plants drooped gently from those sturdier growths whom they caressed and climbed for their share of the sun. Summer's bold colours still blazed, although the margins of the woods were touched with autumn's soberer hues. Hardly a soul went into these woods. Instead of the human voice there was the busy hum of the insects, the sudden secret rustlings in the bracken, the singing, whistling and twittering of the birds. What a strange and beautiful world to walk through all alone! In the gloaming this was the haunt of the ghostly barn owl that swooped and glided through the trees as white and silent as a spectre, while his lesser brethren called him names from wood to wood as the sun sank over the hill and the gardeners cleaned their spades and thought about their suppers.

I picked my colander full of berries in a very short time, spotting as I did so plenty of tinder-dry wood felled by wintry gales. I gathered a load under my arm and made my way out. Emerging from the wood I could see in the field above it a patch of whitish round things of varied size, showing brightly in the grass. Mushrooms? Could it be? I put down my wood and blackberries and climbed over the wire fence to find out. Yes, the fine-pleated pale pink undersides confirmed my hopes. What treasure, more than a couple of pounds to tie up in my pinny! Awkwardly but richly laden with wood, blackberries and mushrooms, and glowing with some primitive satisfaction, I went indoors. I would give the family a meal fit for a king to come home to! Blackberry tart, and mushrooms, figured largely on the menu for the next three weeks, and in the larder, next to the jewel-red jars of plum jam I soon added a store of dark purply-red blackberry jam.

Too soon the days grew short, the autumn sun gave way to rain and damp cold mists. Now it was time for potato picking, and I got myself a job. Potato picking is one of the hardest and most unpleasant jobs I have done on the land. A potato field is usually a cold and muddy place, squelchy mud and reddish clay, mud that clings. It clings to your boots so that every step is a slippery misery, and every time you pick your foot up you are lifting several pounds' weight of mother earth. It clings to the bottom of the boxes which are cumbersome enough when clean and empty. It clings thickly to your hands, caking and shaping the gloves you wear to protect your freezing fingers.

Perhaps the method is more mechanised these days. Twenty years ago, a contraption on the back of a tractor lifted the hoed-up rows of potatoes into the large wooden boxes. These boxes were heavy in themselves but they had to be dragged along until they were filled. By that time the outsides were caked in wet mud, and with their insides filled to the brim with big muddy potatoes, they nearly dragged my arms out of their sockets. The perpetual bending was back-breaking, and how we all longed for our one o'clock bait-time.

We made sure we took a perch on a box with potatoes in it, and a few went into the bottom of our dinner-bags. We could not afford to have scruples about these perks, not at the two shillings an hour we were being paid for our non-stop labour. We had to work at the double to keep up with the tractor.

Even so, we were getting paid something, which was a change-about from what had been the Squire's perks a few decades beforehand. There were still some old hands about who could remember those times. The farm bailiff would go into the village school and pick out the strongest boys who were sons of his tenants. Out they had to go, into the clammy fields, to pick the Squire's potatoes for nothing. They had no dinner-bags to take some home to their mums. Some of the old men said it did them good, but it seemed no bad thing for the Squire either.

By knocking-off time on the first day I felt I would never be able to stand up straight again, and I nearly went up the last steep bit of hill to home on all fours.

When the picking-up was finished, a few of the regular farmhands bagged the potatoes for market, delivered plenty to the tenants at a special price of ten shillings a hundredweight, and stored the surplus in huge clamps. Potatoes, potatoes, mashed, chipped, boiled or roasted, we seemed to eat little else.

Meanwhile other farmhands had been in the apple orchards hand-picking the best of the fine crop of Bramley cookers. The rest of the apples were shaken from the trees and fell among the windfalls to be picked up for the cider makers. Now accepted as a member of 'the casuals', I was glad of this extra job, especially with Christmas not so far away.

This was much nicer work, with no noisy beast of a tractor breathing down our necks. There were just eight pickers-up, all women. We divided into two groups, each taking a row of trees at a time. We put the apples into large round wicker baskets, and then took turns holding the sacks open, tipping in the apples till there was barely room to tie the tops with baling string. Then we left the sacks holding each other up in rings round the tree trunks.

Some mornings the apples were frozen to the grass until the sun was out long enough to melt the ice. We were kept warm enough meanwhile, not only by the work but by the patches of tall nettles under the trees. They stung our faces and hands liberally before we could tread them down. Everything went into the baskets, even the bad apples, even those that had dropped in the cow manure. 'Help it ferment,' they said, 'do it good; give it some flavour.'

Woolly gloves were soon soaked by the frost and had to be discarded; the experienced pickers wore rubber ones over theirs. Putting these on warmed up the tongue of one of our number, a conversational sex maniac, who did her best to keep our blood on the boil. Any initial disgust at her professionally rampant sexual appetites was soon dispelled by her comical ability to find a carnal innuendo in every innocent remark. Scolding her for shame's sake only acted as an inspiration, and even the prim among us were often reduced to helpless laughter by her genuinely funny crudities. For her, sex had to be sublimated by ribaldry, for she was married to a limp-handed soft-voiced effeminate sort of man, who was as good as gold to her everywhere but in bed.

For our half-hour bait-time we sheltered between bags of apples. Chilled through and through we were glad to start again and shiver away the short and shady afternoon. It was uphill walking all the way home, and I got as warm as toast. My pockets, and the bottom of my capacious 'dinner-bag', filled with the firmest of the windfall apples, weighed me down, but it was a welcome burden. We pickers pooled our culinary methods of using them. We saved on toothpaste by eating them raw. They went into tarts, pies, and fritters. We had them plainly stewed. We added them to jams, grated them into fruit-cake mixture, pushed them into chutney, used them liberally in the Christmas pudding and mincemeat. That first year the apple picking-up lasted into early December.

After the apple picking came the winter proper and our long evenings were confined to the fireside, at least those of us who could get round it. Our thick stone walls had tempered the summer's heat and now kept out a good deal of the cold. Nevertheless, our living-room had four doors and an open archway into an unheated kitchen, and there was no porch. Sometimes with luck we might roast our knees, but there was always plenty of icy draught to cool our backs. The fire became a god, our smoke-stained grate his altar, and we his worshippers sat in a sacred semi-circle round him.

During the Christmas holidays we were joined by our fourteen-year-old nephew from London. Accustomed to central heating he was an ardent devotee of our 'real' fire, watching it so intently that he never remembered to make it up. He and our three boys manoeuvred and competed for the warmest place right in the front. Let one vacate his chair, perhaps for a quick trip to the frozen privy that he could no longer postpone, or to fetch a book from a satchel, and there would be a scuffle among the other three to fill his seat. Jenny was assured of her own perch on a stool by the hearth. Syd and I, well, we had to finish the odd jobs and the chores, and then we took a back seat till the younger two were prised out to get ready for bed.

We had no television but we all had long tongues and individual opinions on matters great and small. Discussions flared into arguments, and arguments subsided into discussions. I learned quite a lot in the process. Supper was usually toast and cocoa. I would put a pile of sliced bread on a plate on the mantelpiece and the butter-dish and some plates among the assorted feet on the hearth. Starting with Jenny, each took his turn with the long-handled toasting fork, getting his own supper.

There were quiet lulls for games of chess and 'I spy', for reading and for anagrams, but there was plenty of noisy grumbling when I made bedtime preparations. We had acquired an antiquated oil-stove to warm up the little space next to the privy that we graced with the name of bathroom. In here we washed for bed; the water was heated in the copper and carried in through the living-room. Each shivering victim returned quickly to the fire for a last few minutes' warm-up before the arctic trip to bed. Jenny was no problem, but I suspect that my stern admonitions to the boys 'mind and wash all over' were largely ignored.

In the winter holidays when there was no need for them to get up early for school, it was often quite late before Syd and I had the dying fire to ourselves. With our chairs pulled close to the hearth we soon dozed off, to be awakened by the cramping cold as the untended fire turned to the dead powder of ashes.

That winter followed an old-fashioned summer, and was itself of the same vintage. By the end of February our winter's store of coal was down to the last few knobs, and Syd's wages would not stretch to buying any more. Being the depth of winter, there was no casual work for me. Every day Syd carried home a small bag of firewood on his back, but this gave us a blaze for only an hour or so. Doing my housework during the day I kept warm, or almost, with Syd's old woolly socks over my own, a woolly hat pulled over my ears, and an old dressing-gown tied on round my peculiar assortment of clothes. I looked like the proverbial sack of manure. A re-filled hot water bottle tied round my waist kept my hands thawed. Thus I could endure the day without a fire and only lit it just before the children came home from school.

March did not come in like a lion, more like a polar bear. Freezing winds as vicious as a snarling vixen's bared teeth heralded a blanket of snow as soft as her tail. A flawlessly pure covering and ornament to the lifeless scenery of winter, it turned coats, scarves, caps and boots to soggy suffering dampness, and melted into little puddles all over the kitchen floor. There was no adequate means of drying the damp clothes, let alone the forlorn washing, dripping from the clothes-horse on to sheets of newspaper. When we went to bed I arranged it hopefully in front of the lukewarm grate. I had no spin-drier, and not even an airing cupboard. The fire had become more and more the very hub of our existence and we were running into a crisis.

Then Syd came home with some good news. Behind the Manor was a tree-clad hill, and at the bottom the woodsmen were thinning out. After the usable timber was trimmed, and pulled out by the patient old horse, they burned the brushwood. There were plenty of small limbs and pieces still lying around, and we should do no harm if we helped ourselves to them. Besides, we would get warmed three times – carying it home, sawing it up, and burning it. After a hurried tea we parcelled ourselves up in old scarves and woollies and set out. The robin on our pump gave us an asthmatic wheeze as we passed. No blithe spirit he, but he had had his few crumbs.

The hushed world seemed even quieter. A thin cold mist had come from nowhere and divided the landscape into sections. One landmark disappeared before we caught sight of the next. Crossing the clumsy humps of the ploughed field we entered the secretive wood. We had never really set foot here before, for these were the real coverts, keeper's country, and the powers-that-be frowned upon entry. Now the shooting was over. Away on the edge of the mist we could see two hen pheasants busily doing nothing, and one lucky surviving cock bird croaked dismally from afar. Gingerly we negotiated our way down the steep narrow icy path cut by the gamekeeper between the trees. Sometimes we slid on our feet, sometimes on our behinds. From time to time we clutched at a tree to get our balance back. Masses of brambles under the trees impeded progress and caused more tumbles. All of us except Syd came some sort of a cropper.

'Not much good taking you lot for a skiing holiday,' he observed loftily as we approached the bottom, and promptly lost his own footing and made an undignified sprawling descent right the way down. As he went, his pipe flew out of his mouth. 'My pipe, my pipe,' he wailed piteously. He got no pity from us; we were all doubled up in laughter, although we knew that without his pipe we would be living with a bear with a sore head. Nobody had a clue where it had flown to, but more by luck than judgement Chris found it for him. Putting it safely in his pocket, and ramming his cap squarely back on, Syd resumed his role of captain. 'Right,' he said, 'let's get on then.'

We found plenty of small branches and pieces of brush, and each carrying as much as we could, we laughed ourselves silly, slipping falling and struggling with them to the top of the hill. By this time we were all as warm as toast, not exactly sweating but definitely glowing, and the evening light held out long enough for a second foray. On our return our fire had gone out. While I tried to start it Syd and the boys worked in the yard by the lighted window, breaking, sawing and chopping. All I could get for my puffing and coaxing were spitty froths of melting snow, and sap boiling out of the twig ends from the heat of the paper I had lit under them. We did not indulge in a daily paper, and the little store I had was almost gone, and still there was no spark. Jenny and I were beginning to shiver.

'Tell you what,' shouted Syd from the yard, 'tell you what. We're going to have us a real fire tonight! One bloody great blaze! I'll make you lot sit back, I'll roast your legs!' He sounded desperately cheerful; a good job he could not see the dismal failure in the hearth.

In the middle of the kitchen floor I had a small square of lino. It was in a bad way, dying of old age and cracked in several places. It would have to go! I tore it up into pieces small enough to push between the twigs. After a moment's hesitation it caught and a glorious blaze filled the grate, and the chimney. 'Look at that!' I yelled jubilantly.

'Look at that!' echoed Syd as showers of soot and black-caked lumps came down everywhere, especially on to my new-born fire.

'The roof's on fire,' shouted Richard. From under and between the tiles, smoke was billowing out into the yard. While I ran in and out like a hen in a panic Syd brought in shovels of snow and mud to put out the fire in the grate. Chris and Richard pumped buckets of water to throw over the low roof. Climbing on a chair Syd got up through the hatch in the ramshackle home-made kitchen ceiling to have a look round. The timbers were not alight and the smoke was pouring from a crack in the chimney. Nevertheless, the fire would have to remain out for the evening so we could check up again to-morrow. The relief gave me strength to face mopping up the puddles of sooty muddy water overflowing from the hearth and all over the floor. Syd shovelled up the soot. The chimney, at least, had had a good clean. 'Oh well,' I thought hopefully, 'lighting that lino has cleaned our chimney, and there's enough left for me to start the fire tomorrow.'

We simply had to look for some little consolation. What a fiasco! All that work, all those high hopes and expectations! Syd had had his bloody great blaze all right, but not quite as he had expected. When we stopped running about, the arctic cold hit us again as we looked at our dismal empty grate. We huddled round the paraffin heater with our cocoa mugs between our palms, then we made somewhat reluctantly for the warmest places, our beds.

Underneath the ice and snow the dormant roots began to stir and make ready for the spring. In their burrows and their warrens the little hibernators rolled over in their sleep and opened one eye to the light of promise. As the sun broke through in short but glorious bursts, transient samples of what was soon to come, my own inherited gardening senses began to itch.

'A garden is a lovesome thing, God wot', and God, what a lot of work goes into making one from scratch. In our case we would have to start well behind scratch, for ours was a large piece of rough overgrown earth at the back of the cottage, heavily populated with tree saplings, brambles, nettles, thistles and docks. Country-born, I knew the value of a garden, and with six mouths to fill on a small income I began to wish my husband was more of a man of the soil. Syd had grown up in a London back-street slum without as much as a bulb in a flower-pot. His only interest in vegetables had been where to get the best pennyworth of potherbs for his mother's stews. He and Chris had become quite handy with a spade, however, because they regularly dug deep holes in the copse at the back for emptying the privy bucket.

One autumn Saturday afternoon when we were shopping in the old Woolworth's in Gloucester, Syd's eye had been caught by the display of roses on sale. The truncated, leafless, barren bundles of thorn were packed in cartons that gaily illustrated the glory that was to come the following summer. Uncharacteristically, Syd sorted them over in his deliberate manner, then counting up his pocket-money took out half-a-crown and actually bought one. Next morning he had dug and weeded a tiny square of earth by the yard gate and pushed the root somehow between the stones beneath. Stamping the ground down with his heel, he turned away, and apparently forgot it. During its long dormant winter he never mentioned it, and I felt he was convinced he had wasted half-a-crown. No light matter.

In the spring, when it began to sprout its tiny leaves, if he could have crowed he would have cock-a-doodle-dooed his achievement to the whole world. In early June the first bud began to open.

Through our kitchen window I saw him coming in through what would one day be our front garden. He looked tired from his uphill walk home. Coming to the rose, he dropped his bag of firewood and straightened his back. He removed his shabby cap, as a gentleman should in front of a beautiful lady, and stood there in admiration. It was no wonder; her flawless creamy pink complexion, her perfect form and subtle perfume had turned his head. He bent down as if to touch her, changed his mind, picked up his bag and came in.

In deference to my country upbringing he damped down his pride and allowed himself only, 'That rose I planted seems to be doing well enough, so far.'

'Yes, it's smashing,' I enthused, 'and there's quite a few more buds on it.'

I could see that, with luck, Nature had sent me an ally, a

seductive guide to lure Syd up the garden path. My plans for that jungly patch at the back of the house took more definite shape. If only we could get started! Until now, my horticulturally ignorant husband had snorted at the idea, and put me off as usual with his 'Later on, later on, one day we'll make a proper job of it.' Now Rose, it seemed, had hooked him. With considerably fewer charms, it was my task to lure him out into the wilderness round the back.

It worked. There was no sudden conversion, but he did agree to come with me and try just a tiny piece for a sample. Tiny it was, just one square yard the first day, but weakening resolution was reinforced by pride. The weeds were not going to have it back now! So we went on. What we did not know was that the roots had insinuated themselves between the hardcore and the big flat stones of what had once been a rickyard. No spade or garden fork would pierce that ground, but we had a secret weapon, a heavy old pick-axe; out came the stones, in went the spade, over went the earth, and out came the weeds. The whole thing was an ecologist's paradise, sheltering every weed, insect and pest in the book.

It brought out in us a streak of mad obstinacy as we laboured on, and it also brought our antics to the notice of some of the local old codgers, whose evening jars of cider were enlivened by talking of our predicament.

'What's thee think o' they nogmens o' Londoners? They be tryin' to make a gyarden where thic old stone rickyard used to be!' Ignoring advice, and despite obstacles and good-humoured ridicule, we battled on – I was going to say in our spare time. We just fitted it in with everything else. We had no wheelbarrow, but the boys helped to carry the stones away in old buckets and tipped them helpfully into the tractor ruts in the path to the cherry orchard.

In my childhood our Mam had spent plenty of her energy nagging me to do some weeding, or to carry a spare bucket when she followed the horse tracks for their precious droppings. Grancher lived next door at the time; he was a good old gardener, and there was a good-natured, sharp but unspoken rivalry between them. Oh, the smirk on her face when she bestowed on him one of her monster cabbages, or a couple of gargantuan parsnips! He was a man of the strong silent sort, and made little comment except a mumbled thanks. But he knew what she meant, and got his own back. One thing I learned from it, that manure is excellent for the garden. If horses and cows and sheep had been sent to us just to convert grass into dung, that alone would justify them. Manure contains the very elixir of life. It drives plants mad with joy. Sucking up the lovely, lively stuff, they reach up for the sun like oak trees. Determined to colonise the world, they throw out their blooms and seed with profligate vigour. Stuffed full of beneficial bacteria, they defy disease and pests. And we had an absolute treasure trove of it handy! A mine of muck!

On the cobbled floor of the biggest barn was a two-feet deep coating of well-rotted straw and manure; residue of the days of horses and carts. It was so old it did not smell, and so dry I could pick it up without soiling my fingers. We could cut it into little blocks like peat, and we did, and carried it round the back to smother our new-born garden. I was not content till all was gone, and I could sweep up the last crumbs off the cobbles. By then, hundreds of bucket-shaped mounds of it peppered our ground. When we got that ground finally dug, manured and planted, it still looked as humpy as a battlefield, but there, we had put up a fight!

*

The results of our efforts gradually brought us enrolment into one of the finest organisations in the world – the gardeners' club. 'Could you do wi' a feow cabbage plants, missus?' ''Ere's a couple o' rows o' early taters, me own grown, I 'a' got these over an' you be welcome to 'em.' 'Try these kidney bean seed. My brother give me a yup on 'em, a new sart 'im sent away for' – and so on ad infinitum. Gardeners are interested in anybody's garden, even ours, and more than once we had expert spectators leaning on our rickety fence. Some who had come at first to jeer remained, not to cheer perhaps, but to give faint praise, then non-committal encouragement, and eventually even compliments. We also got advice, enough to fill a gardening encyclopaedia, and often contradictory. We learned the valuable lore, unwritten, handed down the generations from cottage gardeners who had never heard of ICI or aerosols or artificial fertilisers. They knew the value of compost and manure, bonfire ash, soot, leafmould, and the planting and digging-in of green humus crops like mustard, turnips, and lupin. To them a spade was a spade and dung was dung; phosphates, iron, potassium, and trace elements were things for the new-fangled breed of gardeners to worry about and mess with.

At first we could hardly tell the weed seedlings from our germinating seeds, but oh, the never-diminishing thrill of recognising embryo lettuce, the tiny carrot, the pushful pea! No wonder our Mam had used to nag us for help, the prolific weeds got a head start on everything. Raw students though we were in Nature's university, before the year was out we gave ourselves several honours degrees for our achievements.

Who would envy the lady of the manor who goes into the kitchen to plan the menu with the cook, who then instructs the gardener what fruit and vegetables she requires for the

day? How sad in comparison to walking up the garden yourself, gathering the crops of your own labour, and planning the
menu accordingly. Then to sit outside in our sunny courtyard
shelling our own peas, hulling our own strawberries, top-and-
tailing our own gooseberries, and getting a suntan and a rest at
the same time! My sweet little forays into summer's paradise.

All the seasons have their magic. The excitements of
spring, the spade going into the thawed earth, and the first
rows of early seeds lovingly patted down; body and mind in
tune with Nature's timely start. Smug autumn feelings, admiring the strings of fat brown onions and the straw-covered
boxes of home-grown potatoes, tipping the carrots into dry
earth to store in the shed, snatching the odd half-hour to
gather sacks of chestnut leaves for the compost heap. Time
to stand awhile and pay homage to the last tints of autumn
as the first winds of winter blow them victoriously away.
Now we must wrap every apple and pear, each in its separate
paper, ready for the winter pies, jams and pickles, gold and red
and yellow, far better than useless jewels, they gleam on the
pantry shelves. At last the winter darkness comes and forces
rest upon us, as we hibernate cosily round the roaring fire.
Now for a short spell only, we can wag our tongues and work
our brains and give our muscles ease.

That first year the stones made our carrots stump-rooted,
and we had corkscrew parsnips, but we also had potatoes
almost as big as our heads. On one root I counted thirty! Not
all big ones of course; but thirty! The blackfly sneaked up on
our broad beans, and they went into mourning overnight. We
also gathered a little crop of advice.

'Allus plant yer broad beans in the autumn, missus; that
road they be ready to pick afore them dattlin' peskies be
about.'

We were shown how to grow hydrangeas and other plants from cuttings and how to economise by saving our own seeds, and which of them to save, and how to encourage fertility, for which purpose apparently 'a sheep's fart were better than a 'oss's turd.' These old gardeners never tempered the seriousness of their advice with squeamish misgivings about their candour of expression.

Our four long rows of peas began to drip with pods. I had not bought the expensive packets of seeds, but just planted the cheap dried cooking peas. I reckoned that the mass producers of this vegetable would use the hardiest and most prolific strain.

Just when the tiny green pearls were beginning to form the green-finches and the blue-tits had moved in, stripping one side of each pod for the tiny succulent immature peas. The birds, the birds! What friends, what foes! In spring these little gluttons, sprucely uniformed in greens and blues and yellows, had made an enchanting living picture as they played hide-and-seek in the sunlit pink blossoms of the American currant thriving in the shelter of the barn. Thrush and blackbird sang their pastoral symphony to accompany the ballet of the tits. Now these blithe spirits that had sung and danced with joy turned into brigands and pirates who sought their booty with ruthless determination and fiendish ingenuity. The labourer was worthy of his hire; any blackbird that scratched a slug from our garden was welcome to it, and a crust for his whistling. But not our peas, they were not going to have our peas!

I made a scarecrow, and the birds used him for a staging post. I festooned the peas with strings of milk-bottle tops, and they swung on them in the wind. I threaded cotton over and around like a web until it was almost impossible to get between the rows; the birds coped better, they found a way in, and a quick way out. They did not leave us so much as one picking of peas! I suppose those little blighters did not count their chicks before they were hatched. I was learning that a gardener does not count his crops until they are gathered, and then he must protect them from the mice!

Fortunately birds and pests are capricious in their onslaughts; some years they will leave the peas alone but help themselves to most of the soft fruit!

Men of the land have a dignity in their mien and their gait, in their steady eye and their horny hands. It is no wonder; they work for the Earth, man's greatest and all-important benefactor. They deal with high-ranking aides and enemies, the sun, the rain, the winds, the snows and frosts. Urban sophisticates may patronise, but their sneers run off the country labourers like water off a duck's back. They know they work hard with poor pay for a 'simple' life, but to them the environment of bricks and mortar and tube trains and rush hours and traffic jams – that is where the true simpletons live. Technology or turnips; it is all a matter of taste.

PART III

After Christmas the two spiteful months January and February had to be endured. A handful of scraps scattered on the snowy yard produced a good cross-section of native English birds. Bundles of nerves they were; for each other and for any cats that might be lurking about. The robins were the exception. Conscious of their special status in the bird world, they perched on the frozen pump handle in front of the kitchen window, demanding of me, beady-eyed, that I open the window of our chilly unheated kitchen for them to dine in style on the sill inside.

The pheasants were not so lucky; occasional ones strayed in from the woods to eat our Brussels sprouts in the back garden. Poor victims, I did not shoo them off. Their fate hung close about them; come Saturday the beaters and guns would arrive, scaring them out of their ground shelters to shoot them on the wing and bring them thudding forlornly down to earth. A primitive exercise for the rich, 'our betters'. When Saturdays were wet, cold and stormy and they had to plod among the trees in the mud, I thought 'serve 'em right'.

Soon afterwards the golden trumpeters arrived; battalions

of them on grassy banks, in woodland clearings, and dotting the sides of the Forest paths; brave soldiers against the biting winds, to announce that summer was once again on the way. Many thousands of them fell to the estate workers' children; a golden treasure trove to bring them pocket-money for Easter eggs, and a treat or two. Basketfuls and bucketfuls were gathered and taken down to the main road where the children offered them in bunches to the passing drivers.

Our tight budget left only the occasional copper to give our children their spasmodic bits of pocket-money. When they announced their intention of going into the daffodil business I offered to help them pick and bunch. Nicky had been told by a school chum where the best pickings were, nearest to us. Nicky led the way along the bridle path bordered by copses to the wide wooden gates at the bottom of the cherry orchard, gates that were only kept closed in the picking season. These led into thick woods going steeply down into a valley with a small stream in the bottom. We walked in the rutted path made by the timber tractor.

'Oh look, Mummy, here's some primroses,' called Jenny, rushing ahead of me. I love primroses; they look up at you with such sweet and guileless faces from the decayed vegetation around them. When a clump peeps up at the base of a tree, the accidental artistry of their delicate cream-and-yellow flowers against the rough grey bark forms a picture to be carried always in the mind's gallery. We came across so many that I decided to gather some on the way back for bunching, impressing on the children as we went never to disturb the roots of wild flowers or pick too many of their leaves, because as they died back the plant gathered nutriment from them.

The wood we were stumbling down was called Castle

Wood. It was said that in mediaeval times, a castle had dominated the hill opposite it, and the stream had once been the moat that kept enemies at bay. You could well believe it. In that lonely thickly-wooded area it only needed a few wild boars and a couple of peasants with bows and arrows to step back into the Middle Ages. Nothing much had changed.

The stream was now narrow enough for us to jump across, and there they were, the daffodils. In the bottom of the valley was a large clearing, and it was absolutely crammed with them. 'Must be millions here!' enthused Nicky, and he could have been right, though nobody stopped to count. We started at the edges, and by the time we had packed our odd assortment of containers you could hardly notice the difference. I removed my pinafore to put the primroses in, and we started back.

When we got indoors, cups of hot cocoa went cold, and sandwiches were half-heartedly bitten, as we turned the living-room into a 'Covent Garden'.

'Being that we got them free,' said Richard, 'let's give the customers real big bunches, and charge 'em tuppence a time.'

'Can't do that. It wouldn't be fair on the other kids. They charge fourpence a bunch, an' they don't make 'em very big; we should be undercutting them.'

Oh dear, the problems of the business world! We compromised at threepence a bunch, and no stint with numbers, and the same for the primroses which Jenny should carry in her basket. ''Course, if nobody wants 'em at threepence, we'll let 'em go for a penny, Mum.' Pennies were riches for our children in those days.

Warning them that it would be much colder standing by the road than scrambling about picking I insisted on what extra scarves and wrappings I could muster. I arranged the few broken-stemmed flowers left behind in a vase on the table, and I set about doing my housework and making a hot tea-time meal for Syd and our flower-sellers.

They had left home just before noon. Poor kids! They could not be having any luck, and they must be freezing by now, I worried, as five o'clock came, and they were not back. Then they all came bursting in, cherry-nosed, cheeks mottled purple with the cold, eyes shining, like a lot of pools' winners. Pockets rattled with their earnings.

'We sold the lot.'

'We nearly gave up.'

'We're famished.'

'We're freezin'.'

'We'll go again tomorrow.'

After hours of standing in the bitter cold, and with almost all their stock left, they had decided to wait until six more vehicles had passed and then come home. The fifth vehicle had been a crowded coach-load of Welsh day-trippers, mostly elderly ladies. Whether from patriotism aroused by their country's emblem, or from the sight of four red-nosed children all looking alike and stamping their feet to keep warm, they had bought every bunch. 'They would have had more primroses off Jenny if she'd had them.'

Every day of the Easter school holidays we picked and bunched, and they went to the roadside with their wares. Trade was unpredictable. Sometimes every container I could muster, including jam jars, was filled with unsold stock, for unlike most of the children, Jenny could not bear to throw the unsold daffodils over the hedges to die. Not until she pronounced the death sentence was I allowed to put the withered blooms on the compost heap. By the time the Easter holidays finished, my appreciation of Wordsworth's famous poem was considerably diminished.

The day before they started back to school they made an important announcement; they were going to take me to the pictures.

'Don't worry, Mum, it won't cost you anything. We'll pay your bus fare and the money to go in, and treat you to an ice-cream. You can leave Daddy's food in the oven, and we can go to the first house in the evening. It's a smashing picture, Mum; all the kids are talking about it; it's called *The King and I*.'

Apart from my delight at their suggestion, I felt it would be a real treat to go the pictures. In their chattering company, the mile walk to the bus was no problem, and a seven-mile bus-ride through the countryside is a treat in itself. The bus terminus was quite near the picture palace, and as we alighted we could see the beginning of a queue. It was quite a walk to get to the end of it, and I felt dismayed as we tagged on to it. 'Must be a smashing picture to have a queue this long,' enthused Chris. 'I'll go and see what time this house comes out.' We had a twenty-minute wait.

More people came and added to the queue. Shifting my weight from one foot to the other, and listening to the cheerful magpie chatter of the children, the twenty minutes went by quite quickly. We could not see the cinema entrance, but word came down the line, 'They're coming out,' and a lot of people streamed past us, all enthusing about the programme. Our queue began to move forward, and I happily envisaged lowering myself into a comfortable seat for the three hours of escapism.

We were still about three yards from the pay-box when the 'House Full' notice was put up by a commissionaire who informed us we would have to queue another three hours for the last house, unless enough stragglers came out to let us in.

Three more hours of standing, and my ankles already beginning to puff up! 'Let's buy some fish and chips and go back home,' I suggested.

'Oh, Mummy, no,' they groaned. We played 'I spy'. We had guesses how many people would pass the queue whilst I counted a hundred. We thought of all the girls' names from A to Z, and then the boys'. Two long hours went by.

By choice, I would not have stayed another five minutes if the stars of the film had been coming to greet us in person, but the children were in a mood of patient anticipation. My feet were killing me. 'Shan't be a couple of minutes,' said Chris, and he came back with twopence worth of chips for each of us. Warm, salted, and vinegared, they tasted like manna from heaven. His example was soon followed by more people from the ever-growing queue. Still fifty minutes to go. Daffodils! It was all very well for Wordsworth lying in pensive mood on his couch! I could have done with a couch, or anything to put my swollen burning feet up. Some treat this was!

At last, at last, the cinema doors were opened. The crowds streamed out and we streamed in. It was heaven to relax in the warmth and comfort. Even the trailers, the adverts and the cartoons seemed wonderfully entertaining, but they were only the appetiser for the strutting dominating King figure of Yul Brynner, the charming Deborah Kerr, the enchanting Siamese children, the music and the colour; all sent over our heads and on to the screen by the man in the magic box at the back. As well as our chips Chris had bought an ounce of tobacco for his Dad, and Jenny, Richard and Nicky paid for our ice-creams and something towards the tobacco.

After three hours of euphoria, the chill and the dark hit us as we hurried to the comfort of the bus-ride. As we stepped it out sharply on our mile walk at the other end through the lanes the children drowned the hooting of the owls with their rendering of the show's songs. 'Shall we dance?' they carolled and skipped, but I could not, not even for Yul Brynner. My legs were getting heavier with every step up the hill. I felt like the pious little boy who fell behind in the school races, and looking skywards beseeched, 'Oh Lord, if you pick me feet up, I'll put 'em down.'

Syd had a lovely blazing fire and our cocoa cups ready, and a ready ear for our praises of the film, and a proud Dad's beam when he was presented with his extra baccy.

Young seedlings rarely wilt for long when transplanted. Even fifteen-year-old Chris appeared to find more distractions than regrets in our new environment. It is older plants that find difficulty re-establishing; some of my roots had become pot-bound in the cracks of London's pavements. Much of my insignificant identity had been moulded by the sights, sounds, colour and culture of city life, and the friends I had left behind. I missed them all. I had got used to the strident extrovert bustle of packed humanity. Nevertheless it is true that when life has battered us about a bit we dream of the solace and balm to be found in the quiet countryside, a peace for the spirit.

Such a mood came over me one day in early summer. After a night and morning of much-needed gentle rain the sky cleared and the sun came out warm enough for it visibly to coax back some moisture from the soaked earth. The birds began to sing and whistle about their business again. In narrow flower beds round the courtyard we had planted scented stocks, sweet williams and pansies. Having drunk deep, they perked up and seemed to turn their beautiful faces upward to say thank you to the heavens, and sent out their perfume for added measure. Back from their enforced break, the impatient bees resumed their nectar-gathering; a fat bumble-bee kept a precarious hold on the blossoms that bent under his weight.

As I stood leaning against our open doorway the cat brushed by my legs, rubbing his head good-naturedly against them, before relaxing on a sun-warmed flagstone in the court-yard. From the cottage down the field I heard the proud cackle of one of Mrs Saunders' Rhode Island Reds, and I pictured the big warm brown egg lying in the straw of the nest-box. I knew now that the faint mewing sounds I could hear from above did not come from some distressed cat in one of the barns but from a pair of buzzards way up there in the sky, two circling airborne acrobats giving their graceful display and looking like dots against the boundless backcloth of blue.

There was water to be pumped, salad from the garden to be washed for tea, and gardening and housework to get on with, but I could not break this idyllic spell. Like the flowers I was about to raise my face to the sun, when a sudden pouncing movement of the cat showed he had scooped up a mouse between his paws. I knew we kept the cat to keep the mice away, but I was also aware of the sadistic ritual with which this warm-blooded little creature would be worried to its death. The mouse appeared to be still unharmed as I picked up the disgusted cat and shut him indoors.

That taloned paw had pierced my mood of self-delusion. In my heart I knew those buzzards were up there as birds of prey waiting to swoop down and take some living creature for their dinner. I remembered the writhing worm I had accidentally cut in half with my spade only yesterday, and how many more of them were casually consumed alive by moles and birds and other enemies. What was it the poet had written, great fleas have little fleas upon their backs to bite 'em, and little fleas have lesser fleas and so ad infinitum. That was Nature's pattern right enough, but not just to bite, but to kill and devour, red in tooth and claw. From microbe to mammoth we are all links in the chain of prey. My train of thought almost put me off washing the lettuce in salt water in case I tortured the little predators it harboured. Not your fault, I comforted myself, let Nature carry her own cans.

It was quite a relief to hang the bucket under the pump and give the iron pump-handle a good bashing up and down. A few heave-hos and the pure ice-cold water gushed up from its source eighty feet below the yard. As I pumped water I was often reminded of a song my Granny used to hum to herself, 'Ah, you never miss the water till the stream runs dry'. It was water from a tap I was missing. Despite all the family taking turns at the pump, the large white enamel bucket on the kitchen table needed perpetual replenishing, and oh, the slop-overs, as kettle and saucepans were filled with a jug that stood on the tray next to the bucket. Damn it! I groaned as I caught the bottom rim of the bucket on the table as I heaved it up, spilling most of its contents.

'Mrs Mop', that about summed up my role in life, I thought angrily. For some time my patience, never Job-like at its best, had been running dry from every little aggravation. I put it down to the dyspeptic symptoms that had been plaguing me lately. In moments of truth I put my dyspepsia down to my lack of patience. Either way it gave me continual burps and sessions of sharp pain in the stomach. My tendency to hypochondria and secret morbid diagnosis of my own or anyone else's symptoms had been sublimated in the past by worrying over the children's illnesses. They had now all been through the usual childhood infections, Nicky's nerve trouble was almost a thing of the past, the family were hale and hearty. So I had begun to concentrate on my own aches and pains.

I had one genuine grumble, a slipped disc, and here fellow-sufferers will surely sympathise. The agony when the offending discs press on the spinal nerve can be fairly equated with the last stages of childbirth, and can keep one immobilised from a few days to a couple of weeks. I was free of trouble for long periods but once experienced, a little cloud of dread hangs permanently in the back of the mind.

What with this and my indigestion, I was not the most cheerful of hostesses to my young nephew from London who always joined us for the school summer holidays.

Five children in a household always attract more, even though at such times Chris used to find a temporary job on the estate. By mid-morning, Jenny's special school-friend Julie had arrived with a carrier-bag of her toys for them to play with. The two set up house in one of the smaller barns. Provided with dustpan and broom and odds and ends from the house they were little trouble. Boys, however, will be boys. By the time friends Roy and Graham had joined the four already on my hands I was as jumpy as a cat on a hot tin roof. With so much of the estate out of bounds to boys I tried to keep them within eye- and earshot. Boys thrive on challenge and they are full of curiosity; these traits got man to the moon. If there was nothing else about, they would challenge each other, going into three-a-side rugby scrums at the drop of a hat. It was too much of a challenge for one of our two fireside chairs; when they went into attack upon it, it collapsed.

'Get out, you perishers! Can't turn my back on you two minutes before you behave like a pack of wild animals. Take that broken chair with you; put it in the woodshed until your Dad can have a look at it, and you'd better have a good look for that hammer you took out yesterday, which you were supposed to be making a rabbit-hutch with. Your Dad'll do his nut if he can't find it! And one of you pump me a bucket of water.'

'Get down off that barn roof, Leslie, you'll break your neck. Don't be silly; of course the hammer's not up there.'

'I said pump me a bucket of water, not break the handle swinging on it like that.'

'Stop swiping that ball in the courtyard; you'll break a window next.'

'Give the girls that sweeping-brush back. I can't help it if you are trying to balance it on your finger; they asked for it to play houses with.'

On average they drove me to hysterics twice a week, when I would go and sit in the woodshed and have an hour's nervous breakdown. My performances fascinated them. They watched my oncoming bouts of madness with the detached interest of playgoers watching Ophelia going crazy.

'Hungry already? It won't be dinner time for more than an hour yet. Oh well, if you're famished, just you all come inside and sit dead quiet and I'll make you all some toast and cocoa. Ask Jenny and Julie to come in for some too.'

Better do twelve slices at least. Oh, Lord, here's young Micky turned up now; better make it the loaf, and put it on this meat dish. Before I could put the dish of toast down on the table their outstretched hands had cleared the lot. Our income was stretched to feed our own brood, let alone their friends, but remembrance of my own often hungry childhood, and the bliss of getting the unexpected piece of bread and jam, made me love to give food to children. Especially ever-hungry growing boys, even well-fed ones.

Keeping them out of mischief was not so much to my taste. Then I thought of a way to kill two birds with one stone. While they drank their cocoa I got them all enthused with the idea of setting up a camp on the rough ground at the top of the back garden. If they would gather some of the old bricks lying about I would help them build a barbecue. A couple could go down to the rubbish hole by the chestnut tree to find some old iron for a grid to put the frying-pan and saucepan on. Nicky and Graham could gather some kindling wood for their fire. I would contribute a few knobs of coal, a frying-pan, a saucepan, enamel plates, a tin of baked beans, potatoes, an onion or two, two cold sausages to cut up in the fried onions, and some Cornish pasties I had made the day before. They would have to pump and carry their own water. I would supply them with soda and bowl to do their own washing-up afterwards. After all, real cowboys did not cart their mothers round with them.

The gypsy in me got quite carried away with the idea, and the boys were enthusiastic too. The two little girls were happy to keep out of the arrangement. I turned them outside for their argumentative pow-wow about the delegation of chores, and I insisted on the role of safety officer regarding the construction of the barbecue. I would have liked to have mucked in with them really, but I was glad of my ploy to keep them busy. By the time I had handed over all the supplies my cowboys demanded, my kitchen utensil cupboard was looking quite bare. They promised me a plate of chips to share with the girls, and how about a bottle of sauce, and what had I got for their pudding? They made enough fuss, bustle and noise to mount an assault on Everest, but eventually the barbecue was lit. They had fashioned seats from bricks and scraps of wood.

Thankful to be able to get on with my own jobs, I left them

to it. After a few arguments about who should be the cooks, the rest settled down to make themselves some pipes of peace from the hollow-stemmed old man's beard fixed into pieces of wild cherry wood burned out with a hot poker to hold their 'bacca, coltsfoot leaves dried by their fire. I peeped through the back door now and again; it was comical to see them all aping the way Syd sat, held his pipe, and puffed away. But coltsfoot 'bacca soon separates the men from the boys. When I called for one of them to fetch a jug of squash and some cups, only Richard was able to stand up straight and make a wobbly green-faced totter to the back door. Just in time, I thought, as I saw Leslie make a quick dash into the trees. None of them was willing to lose face by putting his pipe out first.

Their nausea must have been short-lived, for soon afterwards I was presented with a thumb-blackened plate of greasy chips. My faulty digestion baulked at the prospect, but I fried them to a crisp brown, and Julie and Jenny accepted them enthusiastically to boost their picnic lunch. My own stomach felt sort of sore inside and could only manage some bread and butter and cups of tea.

After giving the bedrooms a clean and a tidy-up I opened the back door to check on the cowboys. The camp was deserted, and piled up on the back doorstep was all their unwashed cooking paraphernalia, fire-blackened, burned, and covered with grass, dirt and congealed grease. I caught a glimpse of the last back sneaking off round the barn. 'Come back, you rotters,' I yelled, but I knew my screams fell on deaf ears. I stopped worrying about where the young blighters had got to, as I tackled the mess from my bright idea. I could not leave it for them to do because I needed the utensils to cook our evening meal. As I suspected, they kept out of my sight until hunger drove them home, all carrying bundles of firewood for peace-offerings. Washing-up dodgers, embryo chauvinists, hobbledehoys all, yet I still loved them and my love was not misplaced.

By evening the sore feeling in my stomach had become a sharp residual pain, brought on, I supposed, by my all-day mood of irritability. I got them all off to bed a bit sharpish and earlier than usual. Chris was no trouble; he had done a hard day's work hoeing a tree plantation, and he sat out the evening reading, chuckling at the antics of Bertie Wooster and Jeeves. Syd was glad to escape from my general air of the miseries by doing some weeding. At bedtime I took a good dose of stomach powder and hoped that sleep would provide the cure, as it so often had. This was a case of putting a calm mind over a hysterical stomach, I thought, but by two in the morning my stomach had not given in. I crept downstairs for another dose of stomach powder, then sat on the edge of the bed rubbing my fist between my ribs, trying to soothe the pain.

'What on earth are you doing?' grumbled a sleepy Syd.

'Dying!'

'Not again! Well, go downstairs and do it quietly. You're keeping me awake.' I am still giving him the benefit of the doubt when he said he must have been dreaming.

I felt even worse in the morning; Syd and Chris had to get themselves off to work. When I heard the others stirring I tried to get up, but I doubled up with pain. I told Richard they would have to get their own breakfast, and to please behave until I felt well enough to come down. Meanwhile I tossed and turned trying to find a position to make the pain more bearable. This was by far my worst bout of indigestion.

Later in the morning I heard them answering the door to Julie, Roy, and Graham. Oh God, I thought, what sort of mess should I get up to? It was gone eleven before I felt fit enough to crawl downstairs, and I opened the living-room door on to an army of little Mrs Mops, and kindly persuasions to 'Go back to bed, Mum; we can manage.' I felt like hugging the lot of them, bless their hearts. It showed they really did care for me, even if none of them had thought to bring me up a cup of tea.

'What's the matter with Mummy?' asked worried Jenny.

'Nothing much, darling; just the stomach ache.' I did not know then that my gall bladder had been packing itself with stones, and one had decided to emigrate down through the tiny tube leading to the liver.

By the next morning I was free from pain, and so grateful for that and for the children's helpful behaviour that I determined to be very patient and tolerant for the rest of the school holidays until I could go back to work.

Countless books have been written by people who have attempted to opt out of the rat-race and live in primitive isolated cottages far from the madding crowd. They usually reckon to have spent all their capital on some tumbledown dwelling, but in no time at all they manage to install an Aga cooker, and a Heath Robinson contraption to provide some sort of electric power. Good luck to them for their efforts, I say.

It is all very well to live in primitive conditions if one is not expected to maintain modern standards of hygiene. After nine years of pumping water, and the difficulties of drying and airing clothes round the one fire we could afford fuel for, I had begun to reckon that prehistoric women did not have it so bad. No weekly shampoos or baths, no constant changes of underwear for their families! What got me down the most was drying our washing in wet, frosty or snowy weather. Urgently required things had to be put one at a time on the guard in front of the fire. All our underwear and the children's school sports vests and shorts had brown singe marks, often in embarrassing places. How I envied the women with airing cupboards!

Over the years I had become friendly with Helen, the gamekeeper's wife. Like me, she suffers from a complexity of aches and pains. On a couple of occasions she had called and found me lying on the hard floor with my back 'out', and hoping and sometimes praying that promptly stretching out flat would bring a quick cure. She called on me between jobs, and over cups of tea we oozed sympathy for each other's long lists of symptoms. She still has a lovely soft Scots accent, a dry wit, and is much more conversant with estate matters than I. So I can always enjoy her reminiscences of the local characters.

We usually greet each other with long self-pitying expressions, but during the afternoon we get more and more cosy and comfortable. It was her kidneys and blood pressure in particular that had been playing her up on one occasion. Tea and sympathy and free-ranging chat helped us to forget all about them, and about my suspected peptic ulcer, as she enlivened the time with interesting and amusing anecdotes garnered during thirty years on the estate. Laughter is infectious, especially Helen's; smiles became grins, grins chuckles, and soon we were giggling out loud.

As she took her leave across the courtyard I reminded her she *must* go to the doctor about her troubles. Her sweet bonny face, still smiling, broke again into laughter.

'I feel a lot better now,' she said. 'I feel fine after our little chat!'

'So do I,' I giggled. 'That's funny!' which set her off again.

But I added, 'Do be careful; they say you can die o' laughing!'
We both fairly doubled up now, the tensions from our 'ail-
ments' released till her next call, and as she walked through
the old yard I could see her shoulders still shaking.

She always brought a little gift with her; a few new-laid
eggs, a bunch of flowers, some of her gooseberry tartlets, or a
plastic bag of specially luscious blackberries picked on her way
up. One day she brought some wonderful news, so wonderful
that I kept expressing doubt of its truth just to hear her repeat-
ing it. *Our cottage was going to be put on the mains water!*

Was she sure? Yes, she was quite sure. The digger was
already in operation, a good way further up the hill, making
trenches to other out-lying cottages.

'But it's such a long way down to here! The expense! Surely
the estate would never bother?'

'Ah, but it will be for the animals as well; there are going to
be cattle troughs installed at intervals on the way down.'

A tap in the kitchen! A tap that one had only to turn with
thumb and forefinger to get all the clean running water one
wanted! The very thought made me feel better than a visit to
the finest health spa. My aches and pains, real and imaginary,
took a back seat. The only celebration I could manage just
then was to make a dish of toffee for the children, and that
was part ploy – 'Three lumps each, if you'll go up the hill after
tea to see if you can see a digger!'

With toffee-bulging cheeks, Nicky and Jen hurried up the
fields, and came back with the wonderful news. Yes, there *was*
a digger up there, though it was still a long way off.

Chris by now had left home. Lucky Chris, he was going steady
with a delightful girl, now one of our treasured daughters-in-
law. Family circumstances had made it necessary for Carole's

mother to move to Dorset, and she was not well at the time.
Torn between love and loyalty to mother and boyfriend,
Carole unselfishly put her mother first. Chris could not bear
the separation, and left his job as reporter on the local paper
to follow her. With his talents he had been a round peg in a
round hole there. Now, with his impulsive move to Dorset he
was working as a baker's roundsman in the mornings, and as a
cafe counter-hand in the evenings; temporarily the only work
he could get. It was obvious from his letters that he felt
enriched by the sheer beauty of the Dorsetshire coast, and by
the charm of the cottages where he delivered bread. 'In places
it's more beautiful than round home' – and for Chris that was
praise indeed.

As it was vacation time Richard was at home. He had got
a County Major award and was taking economic geography at
Sussex University. He was working as a builder's labourer,
partly on the principle that he ought to put some hard work
into society, and partly to earn some money to boost his grant.
Not only did he cover the cost of his keep whilst at home
but he also delighted Syd and me with presents, gardening
tools and much-needed crockery.

I was all agog waiting for our well-spring of riches to arrive. At
last, one day when I got home from work, I could see the
digger against the skyline only one-and-a half fields away. I ran
in and made a jug of hot sweet tea, put a piece of home-made
cake on a saucer on top, and hurried up the hill to proffer it to
the driver. It was warm weather and I had never known a
manual worker who could not down a jug of tea. No handsome film star had ever received a more idolatrous smile than
the one I gave that driver as I offered him the tea. He was not
a bit handsome; in fact he was downright ugly, a bit long in

the tooth, rusty of physique and dusty of boots and trousers and jacket. A good match for the great dirty unwieldy contraption he was driving, but handsomer to me than St George on his charger. I stroked the rusty side of the giant digger, and I felt like stroking the driver as well, for between them they were making a dream come true.

Some dozen jugs of tea later the driver drank one at last in the old farmyard that had now become our front garden. His part of the project was finished, and the pipe-layers and ditch-fillers were coming behind him. Then builder's workmen would put a standpipe in the barns and lay a pipe across the courtyard into our kitchen. As he drank his tea and ate his cake he revealed that he was a keen gardener who now had only a pocket-handkerchief piece in town. He walked around admiring Syd's giant pansies that edged our colourful flower beds. He left with some pansy roots and a bulging bag of vegetables, herbs and soft fruit from the back garden.

If patience is not one of my virtues, at least anticipation is one of my joys. My spirits soared and slumped in turn, waiting first for the pipes to be laid down the fields, and then for the builder's workmen to arrive. It actually took less than a month, although it did seem like a year, before we could turn our tap on.

A year later the ingrate in me had grown quite blasé about water on tap. Now it seemed such a pity that we still had to empty the privy bucket and could never indulge in a proper bath.

Except for a few weeks in the depth of winter, I was now a regular worker on the seedbeds, and a good speedy one at that. Syd worked conscientiously in the sawmill. Nicky and Jenny did holiday work on the estate lands, for they too were now at the grammar school. Adding it all up, I reckoned we were worth some mod cons, and once again I wrote to the estate office for this request to be considered.

Our benign elderly squire had died the previous year. He was almost eighty, and on his feet to the last. His son and heir from his first marriage had been tragically killed in an air accident during service in the Second World War. Handsome, affable, and capable, he had been struck down by fate just after his twenty-first birthday. We can only imagine what his parents suffered, but there was worse to come. Three months later the Squire was a widower; maybe the heartbreak had accelerated his wife's death.

Politically and morally it seems to me very wrong that large areas of our beautiful country should be owned by wealthy private families. No man or woman, however hard they work in a whole lifetime, or whatever their skills, can ever earn such a reward. Therefore there is a parasitical element in the situation, and some stealing of other human birthrights. Yet I understand the unquestioning acceptance of it. In my present circumstances, here in our tied cottage with its large productive garden and a pantry full of food, with power and light, I do not often compare my lot with that of half-starved natives in other lands, living in tin shacks, watching their children die of malnutrition and disease.

Another thing: although our squire lived in a manor house, he lived in it simply, and even when he was in his seventies he would go out spade in hand to dig out overgrown ditches.

At sixty-two years old, left quite alone without a wife or heir, administering a large estate and lands elsewhere, a lesser man would have broken. But the Squire shouldered his burden and earned the respect and often the affection of his tenants by the way he carried on his duties. Behind his back, the old hands always called him 'father', and I did not think the nickname would have offended him. It was considered a blessing when he married a young war widow, herself with two young daughters, who soon produced for him not a son and heir but two beautiful girls. Soon she too had died, the one girl only a toddler and the other a baby in a pram. Now he was indeed a father, to a brood of four.

One day I was working with another estate wife, weeding seedling trees near the manor gardens. His youngest girl was about nine years old and she came out to talk to us.

'And how are you and your sister getting on?' asked my workmate.

'Oh, my sister is in the study with Daddy now. He's been looking at our school reports.'

'Did you have a good one?'

'Well, I had good marks for ballet and swimming and riding, but not very good for the other subjects. Daddy's just given me a wigging and says I must do better next term. But he gave me some chocolate afterwards. Would you like a piece?'

A few short years later, in awed whispers, the word went round the estate that the Squire was dead. He had suffered a seizure late one evening as he prepared himself a bedtime cup of cocoa. A couple of days before, when I was gathering wood, I had seen him getting out of his Land-Rover. He was in his eightieth year. I saw him get down from the driver's seat a little bent, but he had stood erect, squared his shoulders, and strode on as though defying Time to take him from his land.

I thought of his two younger daughters. There was no Mummy, and now there was no Daddy. No Daddy to call them

into his study for a wigging about their school reports. I wept
for them, and so I am sure did many other mothers on the
estate. Yet the warm arms of sympathy could not break through
the cool barrier of social class. The two children were materi-
ally wealthy, and endowed with outstanding good looks, but
we all sighed deeply and often on their behalf.

The administration of the estate was left in the hands of
excellent trustees and a close friend of the Squire's. It was this
gentleman who came up to our cottage to discuss my request.
Scrupulously conscientious for his charges' interests, he still had
to admit that our cottage left much to be desired. He promised
us a bathroom, a flush toilet, and that the kitchen walls and
ceiling should be plastered. The work would be started without delay.

A couple of weeks later a bath and toilet fittings were delivered and stored ready in one of the barns. I almost trod a path
to the barn door to keep peeping through the crack to make
sure I was not dreaming. When the three workmen arrived the
next week I was beside myself with excitement. To live in
such pastoral splendour, *and* have all mod cons: my cup run-
neth over! I kept those men's energy levels at top pitch by
running to them at intervals with hot cups of tea and coffee,
and samples of my best baking.

When all was done I let the rest of the family have first
bath. Then at last I had a wallow, a long wallow, in a bath, a
bath I could lie down in, a bath where I could turn on hot
water with the push of a toe.

'You all right, dear?' called Syd anxiously, when he noticed
how long I'd been missing.

'Mm – m – m – mm.'

'You old soak! Come on, it's time for bed.'

*

It was wonderful! No more digging holes in the copse to empy the privy bucket! A streamlined kitchen that was a pleasure to cook in! Warm baths on tap! A real airing cupboard built around an immersion tank! But there was a snag: the size of the electricity bill at the end of each quarter.

However, there was plenty of work for me on the land. At apple-picking time, one other woman and myself were put to bag up cider apples in a small orchard on the side of a bank. She was a pleasant companion and we worked well and happily together. The setting was elysian, and the autumn weather, as often, the best of the year. She was holding the sack open for me to tip my basket in; it was a bit awkward on the slope; as I picked up the heavy basket, tilting backwards a little as I did so, the now familiar agonising pain shot through my back. It had come out yet again. It was impossible to lift anything now. Even trying to bend brought the sweat to my forehead. I could not walk straight, but shambled with undignified gait, legs apart like a little boy who has messed his pants. I had to go home.

Home was three-quarters of a mile away, and every dragging reluctant step hurt more and more and exacerbated the trouble, as I forced myself over the stony paths and bumpy meadows. I begged my companion not to leave her work to come with me. Her own way home was a mile uphill in the opposite direction, and having a young family she needed to put in the working hours. My own family came home to find me lying on the floor in front of the fireplace and hardly able to bear the discomfort of lifting my head for their quickly-brewed cup of tea.

By early evening I had to try to get to the toilet, and luckily for me it was downstairs. When I came out, Nicky had decided to run the mile to the nearest phone box to call in the doctor. He came and gave me a pain-killing injection. He advised Syd to make me up a bed on boards, and said that this time he would arrange for an X-ray. It was a miserable eight days before I was able to get on my feet again – an eight days made even more uncomfortable by bouts of severe indigestion.

By the time that my X-ray appointment was due I was feeling fine again. I hurried to the bus-stop feeling slightly guilty that I was wasting the hospital's time. After the X-rays I waited my turn to see the consultant.

He sat back in his chair, and asked, 'How is your general health, Mrs Foley?'

'Very good, doctor, apart from this back trouble, and bouts of indigestion.'

'Indigestion! My goodness! D'you know, you need a plumber's job doing on you. Just look at your X-rays. Your gall bladder is packed with stones! I'm afraid you have some back trouble too, but Nature has been trying to help you. See here how you have grown two extra bits of bone that are helping your vertebrae to adjust. We can fix you up with a surgical corset for your back, and you will have to have your gall bladder out. I'll write to your doctor.'

So I must face another operation! Despite the wonderful kindness I had received in St Mary's Hospital, Paddington, when I had my throat operation, and despite my rapid recovery, I am still a morbid coward where surgery is concerned. And I have a morbid egotistical imagination to go with it. I, of course, would be the rare one who dies under the anaesthetic. The unimportance of my life in the scheme of things bears no relation to my fears. I cannot help it; I only have one life, and I am besottedly fond of it.

This life, I really believe, is my only one. Logic will not allow me to indulge in the notion that I am worth reincarnation, or that I am any more worthy of it than the humblest living creature on the Earth. Nor can I believe that a just and omnipotent Presence is keeping an eye on me. I would love to enjoy that comfort. Myriads find it by calling themselves Christians, Muslims, Catholics, Jews, etc., yet these labels depend on circumstance or place or the people surrounding one at birth.

Man's scientific quest in search of his origins has revealed beyond doubt some incredible facts of evolution. But in so doing he has destroyed many of the myths that comforted humanity. Most religions are based on Man's desire to improve himself, to seek some spiritual comfort to reassure him there is a meaning to his existence. But it seems that it is from his own mind's resources, rather than from facts, that he has tried to solve the mystery of the Universe and create his gods. Religion is like a soap bubble; it has some beautiful facets but it dissolves as soon as it touches hard reality. For this opiate to work Man must have faith in it. Religions other than his own are a dangerous threat to his beliefs, and he will oppose them and all too often kill the 'enemies' who practise them.

Yet biologists reveal that the shape colour and perfume of beautiful flowers were created to attract insects necessary to their survival, and only incidentally to delight the eye of Man. On the television screen we can see the embryo of Man's beginnings in the lowest forms of life. We cannot comprehend Time in millions of years, but we can begin to comprehend the incredible limitless ingenuity of that life force we call Nature; its adaptability, its magic, its all-powerful creative drive, and its total indifference to the individual and to the suffering wreaked by one species on another.

We all bear the cross of our mortality, and we live on an Earth rich with material pickings for the greedy and unscrupulous. So, in general, we back ourselves both ways. I am cursed with the sort of ego that cries out against my knowing why I exist, and I cling to the idea that perhaps in the act of dying the answer will come. It is only a faint hope, but meanwhile I am grateful for every day I remain among those I love and who love me.

In my bewilderment I could not commit my fate into the hands of any particular god, but into the skilled hands of fellow human beings, the surgeons and staff of Gloucester Infirmary. Even as I did so I still threw out a tiny plea for mercy to the Unknown.

That year it looked as though Syd and I were going to have a quiet Christmas to ourselves, a great change for us. His sister was adamant that this time Richard and Nicky must spend Christmas in London with her family. They accepted with alacrity. She and her husband were lavish hosts and there would be visits to shows and pantomimes. Chris was going to stay down in Dorset for Christmas with his fiancée's family. Jenny was now fifteen and had got a Christmas holiday job some twelve miles away looking after two young children from boarding school, while their mother pursued her riding activities with the local Hunt.

Then only ten days before Christmas, I had my admittance card from the Infirmary. With only twenty-four hours' notice it was a mad rush for me to pack the children's things and prepare what food I could for Syd. Jenny offered to forgo her job, but I would not hear of it. It was too late now, and like any teenager she was longing to buy some new clothes with her wages.

My own wardrobe at the time was very sparse. That was no deprivation for me; I am a slummuck by nature, and can manage to look untidy in anything. However, I did have a posh winter cover-up, an ankle-length Jaeger woollen topcoat, a throw-out from one of Meg's charring jobs. I rummaged around for the tidiest things I could wear under it, and packed my hospital case. Richard came in with me for company. In the ward I undressed behind the screens, re-packed my case, and told him to put it under the bed at home, where it would be (hopefully) ready for Syd to bring in when he fetched me home. Poor old Syd! He would have to get his own meals, walk the mile to work and back again, and then run to the bus-stop to visit me most evenings.

The almost forgotten luxury of lying for most of the day in bed, the novelty of being an object for the skilled attentions of the doctors, of having kindly nurses fussing around me, of talking and listening to the other patients, a bunch of women varied in age and character; all this was marred and saddened for me by the plight of an old lady in the bed opposite. At the age of seventy-eight her left leg had been amputated at the top of her thigh! In mind and spirit she was tired out, and all she wanted was to die. Her still-beating heart was her enemy. She would turn her mouth away from the nourishing drinks and messes. The young nurses would persist, 'Come on now, Gran, we shall stay here till you get it down.' Helpless against their cajoling she would at length give in and swallow, and then weep hopelessly in protest at their ministrations.

Mind you, the sister in charge of the ward would have taken it as a personal affront if anyone had dared to die on her. A highly skilled martinet, she was one hundred per cent devoted to the mending of the human body. But God help you if you showed her the slightest sign of enjoying life while she was in charge of it. Patients, nurses and staff were as nervous as jumping beans as soon as she breezed in like a shaft of icy east wind through the ward doors. Knees straightened out, locker tops were hastily tidied, and teeth were gritted ready

not to sigh or tremble as her hypodermic jabs went in. She
still managed to find a fault at every bedside, with every nurse,
and with the cleaners.

But she met her match, a dark-haired, dark-browed
Spanish girl who could not speak a word of English. Oh that
crowded minute of glorious life when Sister came on duty and
the girl was polishing the ward. She had not noticed the water
spilled near a patient's locker, but Sister had, of course. Her
icy reprimands were no match for boiling-over of fiery tem-
perament. 'Whoof' went the polisher, spinning across the
ward and bumping into the bed of a newly-removed appendix.
A torrent of screaming Spanish, accompanied by a frenzy of
gesticulating arms and threatening fists, left little need for
an interpreter to tell us the wardmaid's opinion of the sister.
But the starched Presence kept her cool, while a lava of angry
tears ran down the cheeks of the erupting volcano. Though
her muttered rumblings continued, she resumed her polishing.
There was no relief for us until Sister's lunch hour; then all of
us, nurses and patients, turned into a ward of helpless gigglers.

My operation went well; there were no complications. I had
two small glass jars of gallstones for a memento. I had been on
a non-fat diet for some months, and did not need to have a
tube inserted in my side. I was a very slim eight-and-a-half
stone. When the doctors and the elderly surgeon came on
their rounds he told me playfully that I was a good girl to be so
slim. It had been a pleasure to operate on me. I was fifty at the
time and felt quite flattered, though I hoped never to give him
the pleasure again. Sister, standing by him, gave me a look as
lethal as a laser beam; I was now properly in her bad books,
especially as earlier she had observed a young doctor tweaking
my foot as he passed.

Twelve days was the normal stay in hospital for the removal of a gall bladder. On my eighth day, two days before Christmas, Sister told me acidly that there was no hope of my being sent home for Christmas. Some others were to be discharged early to clear the ward for the expected holiday casualties. I was not dismayed; it had never crossed my mind that I might be sent home so early. 'I don't mind at all,' I told her. 'I'm quite happy to stay, thank you.' I was, too. I had of course endured quite a lot of post-operational pain, and I still had eleven painful constraining clips in my flesh, but the last few days of comparative comfort in the hospital bed was something I could appreciate.

Besides, Syd and I had got it all worked out. On Christmas Day all patients well enough could have a visitor to high tea. Syd was quite looking forward to it, although there would be no buses. 'Might get a lift in or out,' he said cheerfully. 'Anyway, I'd enjoy the walk. Give me an appetite.'

Christmas Eve, the surgeon and doctor came round with Sister to decide which patients could be allowed home early.

'Mrs Foley could go. She's making an excellent recovery,' said that turncoat.

'But she still has her clips in.'

'Yes, but it's all healing nicely. I could arrange for her district nurse to take them out. We're very pushed for beds.'

Obviously the surgeon felt the force of her character, and anyway I smiled cheerfully up at him about the idea just to show her. I fibbed that I could have a lazy convalescent three weeks when I got home.

At lunch time, Sister briskly informed me that my husband had been contacted at work and would be fetching me home that day. Then she hurried on and gave me no chance to ask her anything. I ate my spartan diet lunch of boiled fish, dry potato, and an apple; then I stripped my locker and sat down to wait in a visitor's chair. At heart I was grateful it was all over, and happy and excited to be going home.

We simply could not afford to buy all the nurses a present; I could only say thank you. But I had one for Sister. Syd had got me some expensive soap, which I had hidden unused, and I asked one of the patients to give it to Sister when I had gone. That cantankerous but conscientious healer; she was the one who had the most need of appreciation.

I knew Syd was working that morning, perhaps he would be let off early. Mentally I timed his actions. He could be at the hospital by three o'clock. The other two patients, a young girl appendix and a middle-aged varicose vein, had been fetched within an hour. At three o'clock there was no Syd. Oh well, he must surely catch the next bus. Confidently, I kept looking through the glass door and along the mosaic-floored corridor. Four o'clock came and went. I began to feel like a sore thumb, and imposing on their 'hospitality' when I had to be given my tea. I was still there, feeling utterly mortified, when the supper trolley was wheeled in. The other patients did not have to say, 'Your husband isn't in much of a hurry to fetch you.' I could feel them thinking it.

I had no idea how I was to get home. Sister had made no mention of ambulance transport, and it was too late to request it now even if I had had the nerve. Perhaps she assumed we had a car, and she was not to know we lived a mile from a bus-stop.

Then I spotted him, that tardy rotten husband of mine, hurrying up the corridor to the ward door. 'Took your time, didn't you?' I said tartly. 'And where's the case?' He handed me one of our old well-worn shopping bags, with my down-at-heel winter boots and on top the smart little red felt hat that

Meg had retrieved for me from a West End dustbin. Over his arm he had my topcoat. He looked a bit harassed.

'What case?' he said absently.

'The one under the bed, with the clothes I wore in here.'

'Haven't looked under the bed. I just put in what I could find of yours in the chest of drawers.' Camouflaging the old shopping bag with my topcoat I hurried through the ward to the bathroom.

By the time I had unpacked the shopping bag my cheeks were burning red with embarrassment, but my feelings towards Syd were more bitterly cold than the frigid weather outside. He had packed me a tatty vest, a petticoat with a broken strap (that was my fault), a tatty blouse, two tatty cardigans, and a pair of odd stockings. There were no knickers, no skirt, and no suspender belt to keep my odd stockings up! Draped along the side of the bed the lot might have fetched twopence in a rag-and-bone shop. I put them all on, twisted the top of each stocking and tucked in the resulting knot in the hope that they would not fall down on the way to the bus-stop. Thanks to good old Meg for that long button-up topcoat! But I knew my nether end was going to feel the cold outside. That would be nothing to the cold venom gathering on the end of my tongue to spit at Syd.

I got out of that ward as quickly as I could, giving a general wave of good wishes to the remaining occupants. I shook Syd's arm off and turned my cheek away from his kiss. The draught hit my bum as soon as we went down the hospital steps and across the car park, and then luck stepped in in the shape of my eldest brother-in-law. He had come with some Christmas goodies for me on his rounds with the presents for their friends and the family. He was delighted to hear of my early discharge, and I was more than delighted to accept his lift home.

He would not come in, not even for a cup of tea as he still had quite a few calls to make. My teeth were gritted as Syd opened our door, but when he did my mouth fell open and my temper evaporated. I was walking into surely the most cosy and delightful room in the world! A banked-up fire was just breaking into glorious flame, the brick fireplace and tiled hearth glowed with polish, the big hearthrug had been given the beating of its life, the red tiles surrounding it gleamed in the firelight, and so did the bits of furniture that could be seen between the bowls of flowers and dozens of Christmas cards. Glorious chrysanthemums, a jug of hot-house jonquils, pots of primulas on the windowsill, all sent by family or well-wishing friends. In the immaculately tidy kitchen there was not so much as a dirty cup. I understood why Syd had been late. I flung my arms round his neck.

'Oh, it's beautiful, it's just beautiful here! It's just like heaven to be home!'

'I had to do it all in a bit of a rush,' Syd admitted. 'Well, I hadn't done a stroke indoors since you went. I just couldn't; there wasn't time. The grate was piled up with ashes, dust everywhere, not a clean crock in the house, the bed just pulled up every night. I was going to do it all tomorrow morning and Boxing Day. Sorry about the case. Richard must have forgotten to tell me.'

I stood in front of the fire, lifted up my coat, and showed him my bare-cheeked effrontery. 'They say red hat, no drawers,' I said, then I had to sit down and hold the clips as the laughter shook me in the stomach.

'Sorry, darling,' said Syd. 'I'll make you a lovely hot cup of tea. That's another thing, I had to get a bit of shopping today. I've not had the chance to get much in the way of food in, but there's a big parcel come. It's in the pantry. I'll bring it out to you and open it.' It *was* a big parcel, delivered by rail, a box containing a chicken, tinned ham, Christmas pudding, cake, mince pies, dates and biscuits. It had come from Syd's sister. I was so happy I began to cry.

'I don't care now if it snows,' said Syd, and it did. Next morning we awoke to a world under several inches of it. It was still there on Boxing Day when the kindly district nurse called. She had to leave her car at the bottom, and trudge up to us through the snow, to take my clips out. Well, that was her intention, but it appeared that the surgeon had used some new-fangled clips that left a minimal scar, and the pincers she had with her could not deal with them. By the time she had got hold of the right sort, and the weather enabled her to get up, the clips were becoming embedded. She removed them with great skill and gentleness to ease the discomfort. Once again I could stand up straight.

The snow thawed, the sun came out, the children came home, and I proudly showed off my two jars of gallstones.

Mother's health had been failing for some time. To relieve the burden on my younger sister who lived near her, I sometimes took a 'day off' to help out. This meant I had a seven-mile bus ride and a mile walk each end.

As soon as I started up the woodland path that led to Mother's gate, in that familiar habitat of childhood my middle-aged identity slipped away. The child me took over, and the path became peopled with characters from the past. Here, in imagination, was elderly Mrs Box, stepping out briskly for such a short little dumpling of a woman. A fresh white apron was tied over her ankle-length black skirt, and on her head was balanced a large square basket. This, I knew, contained a choice selection of home-grown vegetables and eggs fresh from her hens. She had her shopkeeping customers, and would come back with tea, sugar, flour and rice in return for her wares. My mind ran ahead to her garden path, walled at the bottom to accommodate the slope of the garden.

There her equally plump dumpling of a husband would be tending his neat rows of vegetables, fruit, and flowers. To save her treasured garden space he grew his flowers in long wooden boxes atop the path walls. Oh! The nose-level beauty and perfumes in their season; old-fashioned pinks, sweet williams, narcissi, ranunculus, tulips, leading to the bushes of lavender, peonies, and roses round the cottage door. What pleasure to peep inside and ask please for a penny egg for Father's home-from-pit tea. The tiny interior was always spotless and tidy. By day the scrubbed-top table was bare; at dusk the red plush cloth went on, and the shiny brass paraffin lamp in the middle vied with the firelight to sparkle on the steel fender and on the pretty china on the shelves. She never asked us in lest we soil her scrubbed flagstones or her well-shaken rag mats, but just to look on such cosy domesticity was a privilege.

'Mind you fasten the latch on the gate properly, or them dattlin' sheep'll get in the garden.' In its tiny sty and run at the bottom of the garden a fat pig snorted friendly greetings. They always had a pig, and there was perpetually a flitch hanging on the white-washed wall of the back-kitchen, and everlasting manure for their garden.

These two lived comfortably enough on their joint old-age pension of ten shillings a week. Their daughter had married well from her domestic job in London. Twice a year she came down from somewhere called Wimbledon, and always left them enough gold sovereigns to keep any wolf from their door.

Growing near the house they had a laurel known locally as a box-laurel. One day Mr Box was standing on a box to trim this laurel. Overcome by ego and puerile childish wit, I piped up at him, 'Mr Box stood on a box to cut his box.'

'An' you mind I don't get down an' box your ears, you cheeky little wench,' he answered. He was grinning, though. He was just as pleased with his wit as I was with mine.

Perhaps the excitement of the biggest marrow even he had grown on his manure-rich mound killed Mr Box. He was found dead with his head close to this prize-winner. Despite his age, eighty-four, the sudden break-up of this seemingly imperishable old pair shocked the village. Mrs Box still appeared hale and hearty. With loving intentions her daughter persuaded her to sell up the cottage and go to live with them in Wimbledon. In a matter of weeks the old lady was dead. ''Twould 'a' bin better to 'a' let 'er bide at wum,' was the villagers' verdict.

Primitive tribes are often credited with better manners than their superiors. In our backwater little village we children were brought up strictly to be polite and to respect our elders.

All the same, I did not have to say 'hello' to Ferretty as he came into view with his lurcher dog and his pocket bulging with a ferret. He was not walking on the path. True to his character, he was taking a devious route between the tall thick ferns. If he got near enough I would practise my monkey-face on him, and serve him right! I took my attitude from the grown-ups. Ferretty was a thief; we all knew that.

Since his major crime, stealing Mrs P.'s Christmas puddings, he had been mentally hung, drawn and quartered and sent to Coventry by his neighbours. Now he became the guilty peg on which to hang the blame for stolen cabbages, missing hens, and sometimes even their eggs. Had he not trained his lean lurcher dog to sneak into hen-runs and bring the eggs out unbroken in his mouth? He was as sly as mustard, and too fly to be caught in the act, but two and two could be put together. He would not work, but his wife and two children could eat meat most days, and it was not always rabbit that a curious nose might sniff roasting in their oven. He grew no onions himself, but plenty went into their stewpots. Suspicion became confirmation when from his own wife's mouth he was shown to be the pudding pincher.

Mrs P. was perhaps the most respected woman in the village; a hard-working widow of impeccable character, who by her hard-earned shillings and frugal ways had brought up her family and never asked a crust from anyone. A few weeks before Christmas she made her puddings from ingredients scraped from savings throughout the year. Top-notch puddings they were; six of them, to last as special treats until the next Christmas. So rich were they in fruit and spices, they went almost black in the boiling. For their cooking she used the wash-copper in the back-kitchen built on the end of her cottage. She boiled them for eight or ten hours, gathering and chopping the fuel from the surrounding forest.

Late in the evening she flour-sprinkled six snow-fresh pudding cloths to re-cover the basins for their long storing. Then, lantern in hand, be-shawled against the cold, she went out to the copper to fish out her gourmet treasures. The long copper-stick poked nothing solider than the sides of the copper. Shocked, dismayed, and shaking with disappointment, she realised her puddings had been stolen. There was no police-man in our village; short of murder it would not have occurred to anyone to call on the services of one so high in rank. No-one had a touch of the Conan Doyle talents, either. The news brought suspicion, fury and disgust, and the vexed question of who could bring such disgrace to our village. Few other women made this festive luxury; now none would, in case when put on the table it would arouse suspicion. Even the guiltless could not rest easy in their minds, for all knew the power of gossiping tongues.

Suddenly, months later, the mystery was solved. It came out during one of the heated rows that Ferretty and his wife indulged in. He must have driven her beyond the realms of caution, for she was heard to scream at him, 'I'll go an' tell Mrs P. who stole 'er Christmas puddens!'

'An' doosn't thee ferget to tell 'er thou 'st 'elp to yut 'em.'

From then on the pair of them were ostracised, and the pity hitherto felt for the wife was dissipated. ''Adn't thic good Mrs P. brought up 'er own tin o' linseed meal an' clean rags to make poultices when Ferretty's little boy got the pneumonia? And 'adn't 'er sat up day an' night 'elpin' wi' the nursin' of 'im? Saved thic boy's life, that's what 'er done, an' that was the thanks 'er got for it!'

There was not much I could say to poor old Liza Baa. I could hear her cackling moans before I saw her, holding up her sack apron to gather kindling wood. Why ever did God let people be born deaf and dumb? It was so difficult to know what they were trying to say. All one could do was to try to put on the right expression and pretend to understand. Sometimes she seemed angry about something; then I could shake my head and mutter 'tut-tut', as the grown-ups did when talking about things that we children were not supposed to listen to. It was lovely when Liza Baa smiled; she was not really like a witch at all, although her grey hair hung in straggles down her face, and she was so thin, and her hands looked like claws.

It was an advantage having her living at the top of the village. When some of the school bullies from the Hill chased us home threatening us with sticks, they all stopped in their tracks if we beat them to Liza's gate. It was handy to tell them she was a witch, and would put spells on them if she saw them. I knew she was quite kind, really. When Mam sent me up with some coal in a bucket for her she cut me off a thick piece of bread and dripping, although I kept shaking my head to say 'no thank you'. She showed me what she had in her chest of drawers by the fire; nice clean ironed pillowcases, and a proper tablecloth with a green border round it. I could tell by the noises she was making, like a cat purring, that she was very proud of these nice things. Mam and all the other women were just the same when they'd got something to show off, but because Liza couldn't talk none of the women ever went into her house.

Now, I had to stand and listen to her; she put the wood down out of her apron so she could 'talk' with her hands. What a job it was trying to make head or tail of it. She seemed to be pointing at our house. Now she held her arms together and rocked them as if it was a baby. How could *she* know if the nurse was coming to bring somebody a new baby? We didn't want any more; the nurses ought to have had more sense. Instead of taking some to Mrs Harper who'd got none, they kept bringing 'em to people who'd already got a lot! Wonder why Liza hadn't got any babies? Perhaps it was because she'd married old George who was a bit simple and didn't know how to write a letter to order one!

It was no good, I couldn't stop; I could see our Dad coming down the dip in the path on his way to work. There, I've put your sticks back into your apron and somehow I've told you that I'm in a hurry. She'd spotted him, too; I thought she loved him nearly as much as I did. How different she looked when she saw our Dad; her face lit up. It was because he knew how to 'talk' to her with a lot of funny signs he learned from a book on deaf-and-dumb language. Fancy, when she was young, Liza was sent to a home a long way off to learn it. But there were no other deaf-and-dumb people in our village for her to talk to.

How odd it always seemed to see Dad's clean face and hands when he started off for the pit in his clothes all stiff with dried pit dust. He'd got the nicest most handsome face in the world; if he had had a beard he'd have looked just like the sailor on the Navy Cut packets. I ran to meet him before he got up the other side of the dip.

Now everything has gone misty. Dad is not here; no-one is here; just the path, the ferns, the birds, the sky and the trees. The little girl that took me over is gone too. She has probably run down under the one huge chestnut tree to play with Gladys, Lill, and Dolly, those other creatures of memory. Wipe your eyes, woman, for goodness' sake. There, I can see Mam's gate already. Don't forget you have come to give her a surprise and cheer her up; don't let her see you have been crying.

It was hard not to cry as I approached the gate. The roof of the little stone pigsty beside it had fallen in, and the door had rotted off, forlorn reminders of our 'Sukey', 'Squealer', 'Tig-tag', and 'Rush-at-the-bucket', grunting great softies that Mam had miraculously reared from the runt piglets given her by other villagers. The flat piece of trod-down earth by the gate was no longer marked with hopscotch scratchings. A growth of tall nettles filled the ash-mix hole now the village had been upgraded for the services of a dustman. Fecundity was out of fashion; there were no children scrambling among the ashes and the rusty tins for the wares for their 'shops' and 'houses'.

No little girls were playing five-stones on the grassy bank we called the tump, or pulling each other down it on old sacks for helter-skelters. It was all so quiet.

As I passed her window I was glad to see Mam busy with some sewing. With her physical strength so weakened by age and ill-health, she was hard put to find ways of making herself useful to her family. Sewing had never been one of her skills, but now despite her bad sight which had got much worse, and holding the material almost to her nose, she would turn every bit of fabric old or new that she could lay her hands on into pinafores for us daughters, pillow-cases for the children's beds, or teacloths from the best pieces of worn-out tablecloths. On the table by her side she had her treasure-tin open. In this once gaily-painted toffee tin were kept the garnered baubles of her life-time. Stripped of association, their worth could be measured in shillings, but among the pretty buttons, and the cross and chain given her by her first mistress in service, and the bracelet with a broken safety chain, and the cameo brooch with no fastenings, among all these were two things of price-less value to Mam.

One was a brooch of pretty coloured stones with the word Mother in imitation mother-of-pearl across it. This was a present from my brother, all the way from a day's outing in Blackpool when he was a young man. The other was the first Mother's Day card she had ever received, bought for her by my younger sister, Gwen. It was quite small and dainty, with roses and violets surrounding a verse of tribute to a beloved mother. We had been brought up in a childhood devoid of greeting cards of any sort, too poor for such mementoes to be indulged in. This graceful gesture of Gwen's from her first few shillings earned in a factory had thrilled and pleased Mam beyond words.

Our mother was not a demonstrative one. Once we were able to get off her lap, I cannot remember her kissing any of us, yet she would work her fingers to the bone on our behalf. That brooch and that card must have seemed to Mam like the words 'I love you', words her heart ached for. I am sure that none of the gifts any of us brought her in later years, or the large fancy Mother's Day cards we sent when the custom had become commonplace, ever competed with those two little pledges of love.

It took her a second or two to blink me into recognition through her thick-lensed glasses. 'Hello, my wench. Oh, I *be* pleased to see you. I'll get the kettle on.' With belated wisdom I kissed her, told her not to get up, and bustled about with the teacups, preparing the meal I had brought to cook for her.

'Them broad beans I planted be showin' up!' and as she said this a rare look of pleasure lit her face.

'Never!'

'They be! I scrawled up the garden somehow wi' me walkin' stick, an' they be all up through the ground.'

Mam had inherited a passionate love of gardening from her humble Welsh forebears. When even her tough spirit could no longer conjure up enough strength in her frail body to dig the ground, she had given almost all the garden to my sister to cultivate. Almost all. Unwilling to accept complete defeat she had kept a tiny portion for herself, and to humour her my brother dug it over. A couple of months previously, Mam had filled her apron pockets with broad bean seeds, hobbled up to her garden on her walking stick, and then used the tip of it to make the holes and drop the beans in, and then worrit the earth over them with it. Had she lived till those beans had podded, her ulcer-ruined digestion would not have tolerated her eating them, but they enabled her to give and to keep a contact with the earth.

What a bustler-about Mam had once been, banging the daylights out of her rag mats, dolly-tubbing the washing, polishing the grate till you could see your face in it, scrubbing a grain into everything! Now unable to indulge in energetic domesticity herself, how she enjoyed watching me play out my role as her surrogate. 'What job would you like me to do to-day?' I asked her.

'Well, I expect the bedrooms could do with a bit of a turnout by now.'

Mam had long since given up sleeping upstairs. A very cold winter had made it expedient to have a little bed downstairs beside the fireplace. To the old, the ill, and the lonely a fire is like a friend and companion. Mam kept hers going summer and winter, although her cottage now had an electric cooker and kettle. Her life was narrowing to the confines of the two downstairs rooms of her tiny cottage, but just the same it worried her to think of the dust settling upstairs. No doubt as well, the empty half of the double bed up there discouraged her from climbing the stairs at night.

That small domain, the bed. That six feet by four feet private island, where love, travail, illness, and death had waited their turn between the sheets. Now it stood shrouded in its old-fashioned best white coverlet, and mourned top and bottom by the black iron of the bedstead. A layer of dust filmed the washstand, the chest of drawers, and the bedside stool. A few dead leaves blown in by a capricious breeze through the narrowly opened window added to the melancholy unused atmosphere. Hanging on the wall above the bed was a framed text. Gold letters on plywood spelled out the words, 'Put thy trust in God for I am with thee.' But there was no-one there.

From the wall over the tiny fireplace a large photograph of Mam as a young woman looked down at me. Not a conventionally pretty woman, but the smooth, plump, youthful contours of her face, topped with a mass of dark hair dressed in the fat rolls fashionable at the time, the shapely bust set off by a white lace blouse, and the sweet round neck, made a charming picture. I remembered Mam telling me, 'It wasn't all my hair, see, we used to put pads of paper inside to puff it up more.'

And Dad often mused, 'A reg'lar pockut Venus your mother was when I met her first,' and he had first met her through the good offices of one of her four brothers. It came about through Dad going down to Wales to work. With six younger stepsisters and a baby stepbrother crowding his mother's cottage, and with a slump in the Forest coalmines, Dad had taken himself off looking for work in a Welsh coalfield, near Abertillery. He walked most of the forty miles, found a job in the Six Bells colliery, and obtained a mean, cheap lodging in the town.

Dad's pit butty was a young Welshman, the son of a farm labourer. He came down daily from the mountain to earn a bit more than the pittance he could get on the farm. He was quick to notice the inadequate rations that Father's landlady gave him for bait, and every day he supplemented it with a lump of his mother's home-made cake. Eventually he suggested that Father might be better off lodging at his home. The young man's mother was willing to look Father over. He passed her scrutiny, and went there to lodge. Now he had his own bit of home-made cake in his bait bag.

Dad used to tell us of our Welsh grandmother, 'A fine-lookin' 'oman, your granny was. Must 'a' bin a 'andsome wench when 'er was young. 'Er was good wi' the vittles too; 'twas plain but plenty on't. And 'er give us plenty o' sharp

tongue to goo wi' it. 'Er 'ad a temper like the weather, never
two days alike, 'specially if 'er runned out o' baccy for the little
clay pipe 'er smoked. I s'pose that's why your grancher left 'er
when the young 'uns was growed up an' able to stand on their
own vit. 'Im didn't goo far, just a bit further along the mountain, to the littlest house you ever saw. But 'twas big enough
for'n, cos 'im only reached about 'alf-way up your granny. Like
a ugly gnome, 'im was, but I never met a man I liked better.
I reckon 'im could 'a' charmed a rabbit out o' 'is bolt-hole. And
talk about an artist! Give thic mon a bit o' paper an' pencil
an' 'im could draw a bunch o' flowers lookin' real enough to
pick off the page. 'Im an' your granny was still sort o' friends;
'er done 'is washin' every week an' baked 'im bread an' cakes
an' such. It was just they couldn't stand each other's company
any more. 'Twas a civilised arrangement when you come to
think on't.'

At the time Mam was working as a servant on a farm nearly
four miles away. Every Sunday on her afternoon off she walked
home. Her first impression of my father, confided to her
brother, was 'Indeed, he's nothing but a white-faced
Gloucester tup.' Father thought her a bit of a 'hoity-toity'. It
took a long time for him to pluck up the courage to offer to
replace her brother as escort for her long lonely walk back to
her job.

Summer came, and sometimes they sat down for rests on
the way. Mother was twenty-three years old and all woman,
for time was to show that babies, housework, cooking and gardening was all she needed to fulfil her life. Father was just
twenty-one and into full manhood. One balmy evening they
sat too long in a mountain dell with only the sun, the birds
and the wild flowers for company; and as the old song says,
'they found the way'. Two months later they were married,

and seven months afterwards Mother gave birth to a beautiful baby girl. By then they had come back to our village to live with Father's old great-aunt who had always loved him like a son.

It was a relief to roll up the mats, take them downstairs, and make sure Mam could hear me beating them against the garden wall. I made plenty of noise sweeping into the corners and down the stairs, before asking her for the duster, cloths, and polish. By the time I had put the upstairs to rights, my efforts had inspired Mam to action. She cooked the lamb chop I had taken over, laid the table, and made a real effort to eat her dinner. I changed her bed, and gathered her washing together ready for my sister to collect. I knew well enough what to do next. In the narrow back-kitchen behind her living-room Mam liked to keep a handy indoor supply of fuel. I re-filled a row of baskets from the coal-shed, and carried down a good portion of the sticks my brother-in-law had chopped for her. Then it was time for me to go. As usual, I had cut it fine, and would have to run the mile to catch the bus to take me home; and run I did. I was running from the problems of the unhappy, frail, lonely, old and ill woman that was my mother now, running back home for the relief that the life-force of my vital and demanding young family would bring.

Mam did not live to see the broad beans come to pod. One summer morning she collapsed in a coma in her tiny courtyard; she had been potting a geranium cutting someone had given her, and the broken pot with the cutting and the little bit of soil lay scattered beside her. My brother fetched me to her, and with my sister I kept a thirty-six-hour vigil at her bedside. She slept like an unconscious child while we wiped the sweat from her face. Just in case she could hear us we whispered words of love to her; it was as though she were our child now. At last her laboured breathing ended in a sigh, and the downstairs of her cottage became empty too.

Meanwhile the stealthy years had taken our children and turned them into adults. The parent–teenager battles were over, with honours even.

'Aw, Mum, all our mates stay out till two in the morning sometimes, and their mothers don't nag them.'

'If I save up enough, I *shall* buy that motor-bike off Jimmy. It's *not* a load of old junk, and of *course* I shan't break my neck speeding.'

And oh, the lecture I gave those three boys, often enough for them to know it off by heart. 'Now mind what you get up to; I've heard about those parties you lot have in your friends' houses when the parents are away. Just remember the consequences if you do anything silly. Look what happened to young Rowena, had to leave school in the fifth form because she was having a baby. That was the result of a party and letting the lads loose on her parents' drinks cabinet. Just think how Daddy and I would feel if it was Jenny. And as for these one-night stands I've heard about, it won't be a bus you'll catch hanging around for them. I hope none of you will ever make me an illegitimate granny, but if ever you are daft enough to, I'd want to know. I don't want any grandchild of mine growing up not knowing who its father was, whoever the mother is. It's the greatest insult to a human being to beget it and forget it, and it means a chap has a very low opinion of himself, no higher than a tomcat.'

Then seeing their crestfallen faces, 'Yes, of course I trust you. It's old Mother Nature I can't rely on. Don't forget I had to struggle with her when I was young.'

With so many lectures preceding her, and with her own innate morality, we never had a minute's worry over Jenny in these matters.

How often in those turbulent years, when I became convinced of our young offspring's thoughtlessness and chauvinism, did I long for them to be married and off our hands. But there were also times when I was puffed up with pride at their achievements. To see our Chris's name on his featured articles and sports reports in the local paper; the joy and excitement of his wedding to his lovely Carole; the news of Richard obtaining a second-class honours degree at Sussex University.

Joyful though these events were, they presented me with a problem. Over the years I had developed a fairly severe type of agoraphobia. I expect the isolated position of the cottage, the fact that we had no car, and that I had been kept too busy for social life, had contributed to the aberration. Going to Gloucester for shopping had become such a terrible trauma for me that Syd had almost given up his kindly persuasions and mostly went on his own. I was quite willing to go down to the milk-box and help him carry the bags up. But beyond the milk-box was a no-man's land for me, except the familiar tracks to work, and, contemplating unknown territory, sweat would ooze from my palms and I would get palpitations. How I was going to face the journey to Dorset for the wedding was a constant dread, and I did not even contemplate going to see Richard receive his degree.

At least not until Jenny took the matter in hand. She was now a seventeen-year-old sixth former, and she had developed a live-and-let-live attitude to my eccentricities, but this was stretching her tolerance too far.

'Mummy, now listen, of course you're going, as well as

Daddy. You *must* see Richard get his degree. He's worked so hard for it. What kind of mother are you?'

'Agoraphobic.' 'Nothing to wear.' 'No transport.'

She admitted these were impediments, but not impossibilities. It began to look as though I was going. The idea of spending money on new clothes for myself had not occurred to me for years. Meg, and Syd's sister, and jumble sales, had kept me adequately covered for next to nothing. Besides, I just was not worth the effort. I have my vanities, but they do not include dress sense; I am just naturally untidy. For once at least, Jenny was determined to defeat this failing. With every penny we could muster she took me, palpitations and all, to Gloucester. Luckily the sales were on, and she 'allowed' me to choose a cream crimplene suit reduced to eight pounds. I was not permitted to point out that, for me, cream was the maddest and most impractical colour. Cutting me out of it altogether she then decided on a black straw hat, sale price a mere ten shillings, and cheap black nylon gloves. There followed a ruthless round of the shoe shops for a pair of black court shoes going cheap. The nylon stockings she treated me to herself, from the pocket-money she earned by working in Woolworth's on Saturdays. She would cut, shampoo, and set my hair for the great day, but she insisted that I bought some setting lotion to keep it tidy.

Transport was now the problem. How was Cinderella in her crimplene and nylon to be got to the ball? Richard had learned to drive, but we had no vehicle, and hiring one would stretch our pockets badly. My brother came to the rescue. He had a Lanchester of ancient vintage, a grand old upright dowager of a car, but full of the coughs and wheezes of old age and liable to stop altogether if too much mileage were demanded of her. A self-taught mechanic of considerable talent, he gave her a Harley Street examination. He oiled and greased her, put in false joints to boost her rheumaticky ones, covered her cracked old visage with a cosmetic coating of black enamel, polished her to Rolls-Royce standards, and drove her over. She looked a real old aristocrat.

'She's a bit heavy on her drinking, and only likes stuff from the best pumps, but she'll get you there and back all right, don't worry.'

If my eyes popped out at her grandeur, Syd's nearly popped out at the sight of me when I was ready to step into her. Jenny had transformed the old scruff into someone approaching an elegant woman. I was still slim, five-foot-five tall, and had retained quite a good figure. Jenny's choices, the plain cream suit and black accessories, my work-swollen hands hidden in gloves, made up in taste what they lacked in quality. I hardly knew myself!

Richard had been given two guest tickets for lunch at the university. Jenny was quite willing to stay at home, so we left her in charge, and set off. On the way back we were going to have a night at Syd's sister's in Pinner. Once I was settled in the car the long drive that I had feared became an exciting novelty. I was all ready to be impressed by the architecture of the university, for I knew it had been designed by Sir Basil Spence of Coventry Cathedral fame.

Well, we got there, and I did not think much of it. It seemed to me more austere than many a factory on the Great West Road approaching London, but I did approve of the oblong pool of water just inside the entrance, its tranquil depths encouraging the philosophies of the studious mind. We sat in one of the study rooms; to me it had a hard distracting influence, with its plain brick walls and its modernistic, brightly-covered but comfortable chairs. The cold lunch, served in the students' dining-hall, was excellent and we were ready for it. We caught a glimpse of some of the selected guests going into a more luxuriously appointed dining-room. Among them were a Cabinet Minister, Douglas Jay, and his wife, and she was wearing a cream suit with black accessories. I began to feel that stuck-up I remembered the old rhyme, 'The Colonel's Lady and Judy O'Grady are sisters under their skins.'

The degree ceremony was held in the Brighton Pavilion; a confection of overstated architectural curves and trimmings, enough to give Sir Basil a nightmare, but I could not stop gawping at it. We squeezed into a great crowded room, and the stage itself was crowded with dignitaries, among them Harold Wilson and Yehudi Menuhin. We found seats right at the back, and in front of us was a gangway along which the students filed their way to the steps to mount the stage as their names were called. Among them were the pretty twin daughters of Mr Jay. When Richard's moment of glory came I had to bite my lip and swallow hard to choke back the tears of love and of pride in him. I noted that he had got a better degree than the Jay twins.

Syd's sister and one of her sons had driven down from London; movie-camera in hand, they filmed us proudly walking on the campus with our capped and gowned BA son.

It was a wonderful day. The old Lanchester felt quite proud of us, and purred her way back to Pinner. We did not let her hear us say she would not look out of place on the London-to-Brighton vintage car rally. Nor did we tell her straight to her old-fashioned black bonnet that she looked impoverished and outdated among the expensive streamlined models peppering the drives of that select area of Pinner.

Before my agoraphobia had the chance to settle on me again I was taken on another long drive. Richard took us in a smart modern hire-car – the old Lanchester had gracefully retired. We went to Bridport for our Chris's wedding. The Brighton journey had helped me break the ice on the social scene, and I had gained enough courage to play my part at the reception and carry it off smoothly. We all chalked up another wonderful day. After the long journey home through the cold evening, we sat round a lovely fire and talked, and much of the talk was of Chris and his bride. It was a happy time, but when the chatting stopped there was a little chill somewhere in the back of my mind. The first fledgling had flown the nest for good.

Soon enough our Richard followed. He had got his degree, and he took it up to Birmingham and obtained a teaching post. At a vacation party he looked into the eyes of one of the prettiest guests. They both liked what they saw so much that they were soon holding hands for the romantic trip to the altar and domestic bliss in Perry Barr.

While Richard was studying sociology and economics from the tomes of learned professors, our Nicky was not so definite about his going, and chose to take several short dangerous flights rather than one clean break. Unable to tolerate the disciplines of the sixth form he sought the harsher regimes of the outside world. Farm labouring, dustman, bottle washer, battery-hen cleaner, lorry driver, gate-maker, he learned a lot about life. He was an astute observer of character and incident, and enlivened our evenings with his amusing mimicry and stories. It is true to say that we often laughed till we cried, and so did he in the telling.

Eventually he settled down to train properly, as a carpenter, getting his qualifications at the technical college, and embracing a useful career that stretched his brains as well as his muscles.

Home from his day as farm labourer we greeted Nicky with the stock question, 'Did she?' This referred to the peculiar habit of an enormous sow. Every morning when Nicky filled her drinking trough with fresh water, she would rush to foul it. It had become a battle of wits and strength between them to get her snout in before her bum.

'Talk about pig-headed!' Nicky would laugh ruefully, looking down at his mucky trousers. 'You should see the mischief in those old piggy-eyes as soon as she spots me with the water bucket. No matter how I heave and push and grunt trying to turn her round, she *will* put her arse in that trough of clean water and do her business.'

'You did not ask me what happened today, Mum,' he said one evening as I put his food in front of him. There was an expression on his face I had never seen before.

'Well, what did happen, then?'

'I helped the farmer to born a calf. It was so wonderful, Mum, seeing that dear little calf, all legs and head but all there, and in no time at all struggling to his feet to find his Mum's udder. And the way she nuzzled him, and the look in her eyes. That poor old cow, what she went through to have him, and how pleased she was with herself. I could shoot those farmers that take the calves off 'em for veal.'

However, Nicky soon discovered that being sentimental about animals was not part of a farmer's life, or a farm labourer's. So he left.

Meanwhile Richard was at university, and to manage on his grant, had digs in a run-down boarding-house in Brighton. Nicky joined him there, and looked for employment open to the non-skilled. He started off in a beer-bottling works, washing the bottles, noisy, dangerous and monotonous work. Most of the employees were coloured, and accepted the conditions and the poor pay with a remarkable lack of complaint. Everyone had to wear goggles to protect their eyes from splintering glass. One Monday a flying piece cut Nicky's top lip open. Only the day before, in the business supplement of Richard's quality Sunday paper, he had read the profit figures of the company. 'Bloody brewers,' thought Nicky, and collected his cards.

The landlady gave no credit, so he had no choice but to start work the next day cleaning out the cages in a battery-hen establishment. The smell was abominable, but even worse was the plight of the incarcerated hens, egg-laying machines without room to turn or even stretch their legs properly. It was an economic way of producing eggs, and fertile manure, and tasteless packaged chickens for the super-markets. It was also a foul, inhumane commercial practice. After a few weeks Nicky could not look those poor hens in the eye.

He came back home and got a job as a council dustman. Now, I doubt that if a hostess needed to make up a number for a dinner-party, she would plump for a dustman. Not even a sedate, church-going hostess; though, if cleanliness is next to godliness, dustmen should be well-seated in the celestial dining-halls. It was Nick's best job to date as regards wages and shortish hours, but it was early start and hard dirty work. The older hands did much better. They sent the newcomers home and then sorted out their perks from the rubbish. One dustman was on the way to becoming a minor property tycoon. He rented empty houses in the less salubrious areas of town, furnished them with cleaned up discards from the rubbish, and let the rooms out to immigrants at a handsome profit.

Eventually he was able to buy up some of the properties. He ran a pricey Rover car and lived in his own lavishly-furnished house.

One might think that Nicky's succession of dead-end jobs was due to his being less intellectually bright than his siblings. This indeed was not the case. Soon enough the novelty wore off, and he decided to train as a carpenter. One day a well-meaning ecclesiastic, undeterred by the stony ground of our acquaintance, made one of his calls to persuade us back into the fold. Knowing that Nicky had been a bright pupil at the grammar school, he was commiserating with us, in Nicky's hearing, about the way this son had thrown away his chances, and was now ambitious enough only to become a carpenter.

'I dunno,' Nicky said to him. 'It was a good enough job for your Master's Son to follow when He was on earth.'

When our Jenny was eighteen she had seven O-levels and three good A-levels, and was awarded a County Major. To our surprise and chagrin she was determined not to go to university. Some of her friends had done so the previous year, and their acquired accents, flashy college scarves, and new conceits, quite put her off. 'If that's what it does to you, I'm *not* going.'

Parents are often a poor match for a sensible strong-willed eighteen-year-old. We said our piece, and left her to make up her own mind. She had already done so, and went on to get a good secretarial job, and a fiancé. When she was twenty she became enamoured of a handsome young engineering student, and now wedding number three was looming ahead. This time, as the bride's parents, we would be the most involved.

Knowing how I would probably get the jitters, Meg, and Syd's sister, and our Yorkshire friend from London, came to stay and to help. Often in the past I had regarded white weddings and their paraphernalia and pomp as an absurd ritual and expensive nuisance. Now I could see something in it. It was an absolutely beautiful day; the little village church, cleaned and decked with flowers, was filled with the two families and beloved friends. The organ, already murmuring something sweet, burst suddenly into triumphant song, and every head was turned. Our Jenny, lightly resting on her proud father's arm, walked stately down the aisle.

Such a blissful compound of profound emotions hit me that like all mothers I could not hold back my tears.

The reception was held at a nearby hotel, and after the wedding repast and the speeches, the stars of the show, the reason for the gathering, swiftly disappeared and left the assembly rudderless. Many of the sixty guests came to us for the evening, and my three wonderful helpers roasted chickens, boiled hams, made trifles and dainties, and lent their best cutlery and glassware. I was not allowed to wash even a glass. Chris, Richard, and Nicky co-hosted with Syd, and an entertaining well-fed evening was enjoyed by all. Little thanks to me, but my own heart was full of gratitude.

Our children were spreading their wings. In a few short years all four of them had gone and now we were only two; just Syd and me. For the first week or so, with only undemanding Syd to cater for, I felt as if I was on holiday. Then the loneliness began to trouble me. My back had got worse, so there were now very few jobs on the land that I could manage, and I missed the company. I kept as busy as I could at home, weeding and hoeing the garden, gathering kindling wood, and making pickles and jams, augmented by anything I could gather from the hedgerows. One lovely sunny September morning I went blackberry picking; plenty were growing near at hand in the hedges of the adjoining fields. Hating to see this free bounty going to waste I took a large basket for my gatherings. It was almost full before I had gone half-way round the field and the thought hit me, what did I want all these daily pickings for? To give them away locally was carrying coals to Newcastle. There was no need now to rush home to get the pastry bowl out, and make a pile of pies and tarts. Who was going to eat them?

I looked down the hill, and oh! the emptiness of the landscape! No school children hurrying up with their satchels swinging, their faces rosy, their caps on the back of their heads.

'Hiya, Mum. How long to tea? We're famished.' No longer would I hear it; nor 'Ooh, that was scrumptious. Can I have some more?' No praises to give, no reprimands to administer, no schoolday chatter to listen to. The child days were over; they had gone like Peter Pan to Never-Never land. The blow hit me full force right below the belt. Like many a newly-retired man, the relief of being free from the daily grind brought with it a feeling of uselessness. The loss of old mates and of the stimulus of discipline; no wonder so many men just dropped dead when their working days were over. A tear of self-pity dropped on the blackberries. Oh, well, Syd liked blackberries and I could make pots and pots of jam to give the children when they visited us. And Syd's sister, and Meg, when they came. There was still plenty to pick and plenty to do. Comforted, I sniffed my way home.

Going to grammar school had made the children late earners, but from their very first wage packets they all contributed to their keep. By this I mean they paid for their food; services and accommodation were thrown in with our love. We had managed tolerably well.

Despite the fact that I was no longer fit enough to go out to work on the land, with only the frugal pair of us left I was surprised to find I had some housekeeping money left at the end of the week. Our life had not been complicated by bank accounts, so I started to put my savings in a jam jar, and postponed the decision on which of the multiplicity of uses I might put it to later. All my life I had lived on my daydreams from time to time, but they had never been ambitious enough to imagine that we would ever own a car. I was a bit taken aback when practical phlegmatic Syd broached this possibility as we sat cosily each side of the winter's fire.

'And pigs might fly,' I thought, especially as he based the idea on the hope of one of our premium bonds coming up with a big prize. He knew nothing of my jam jar savings. Nearly a year had passed and I had amassed almost eighty pounds, and was toying with the idea of wall-to-wall carpet in our living-room.

One winter evening when he came in from work, Syd sat wearily down by the fire. 'Gosh, it's good to be home. That bloody hill gets steeper every day. Wish Ernie would come up for us. Peter, the carpenter at work, is selling his car. It's an A35, and an old 'un, but it's in smashing nick. Pete looks after it like a baby.'

'What's he asking for it?'

'Eighty pound. A bit above the average for a car that small and old, but it's a real bargain because he's looked after it. No rust, good tyres, sound little engine. He's a genuine chap; wouldn't sell anyone a pup.'

I fetched out my jam jar of hidden treasure, gave it a magic rub with the corner of my pinny, and began to count out the notes and silver on to Syd's knee. Talk about Aladdin and the Genie's magic lamp! Syd's mouth fell open, and his eyes lit up like a pair of lamps.

'There you are. Seventy-nine pounds four and eightpence; tell Peter we'll have it!'

After all, a magic carpet to get about in was better than a static one on the floor.

Syd was in his fifties. Apart from the small tractor in the sawmill yard, he had never driven anything. Driving lessons were a pound an hour. Our euphoric anticipation of becoming car-owners was tempered by this snag. We had reckoned without our children. They contacted the young, ex-police, driving instructor, and between them paid for a number of Syd's lessons. At last, during a bitterly cold February, the great day of the test came.

Through the kitchen window I watched Syd coming across the yard (as he knew I would). His face blue with the cold, and his expression impassive (as I knew it would be).

'Kettle's just coming to the boil.'

'Good. I could do with a nice hot cup of tea.'

The blighter! Why didn't he put me out of my misery? Had he or hadn't he? I handed him his cup of tea.

'Well?' I said.

He drank half the tea, put the cup and saucer carefully on the mantelpiece, and said casually, 'Yes, I passed.'

How could he be so calm? Such an achievement, at his age, a first-time pass. I made up for it; I literally danced around the kitchen, and heaped unstinted praise on him all the evening. We had a car, and I had a driver.

But I still had my agoraphobia, and even now I invented excuses to avoid going into Gloucester for a few more weeks.

Eventually shame gave me the courage, and I found that getting in at home and getting out at home made all the difference. Years later I still get a feeling of relief when we get back past the milk-box, but the agoraphobia is as good as cured.

There was an exciting unreality about getting into our own car with Syd at the wheel. I could not help it, it made me feel like the Queen Mother; I had a job not to wave graciously at the people we passed.

By the time Syd's holiday came round in August, Chris and Carole had persuaded me to let Syd drive us up to Staffordshire to stay for a few days with them. All the way from Gloucester to Staffordshire, and on the motorway at that! Proudly snug in our little A35, I was indifferent to the sleek modern cars streaking past us. However, when a tiny dumpy little car went by with a middle-aged couple in it, I could not help observing how comical they looked, like some Enid Blyton characters in a Noddy car.

'Look at them, Syd.'

Syd almost smiled. 'Have a good look, then,' he said dryly, ''cos that's just how we look from the back. That car is exactly the same as ours.'

We took rather more than twice the time that Chris did for the same journey, but we got there, and tried hard to look nonchalant about the achievement. Nevertheless I could see an extra shine in Chris and Carole's eyes as they welcomed us in.

The car was also a blessing to one of our most favourite visitors, Meg, who over the years had become one of the family. Her childhood in Swansea's dockland, and the rest of her life in London, had made Meg a townswoman by choice. She regarded us as amiable lunatics for making a move to such primitive isolation, and this opinion was strengthened every time she walked the mile from the bus-stop on her occasional visits. When an unforeseen tragedy struck her, the visits became much more frequent.

Meg's handsome Canadian husband was seventeen years her junior, and she had sometimes pondered what would happen to him when she died. It never occurred to any of us that the boot might be on the other foot. His fine frame gave no clue then of the ravages going on inside it. When the symptoms of his trouble appeared, Meg hustled him to the doctor. A few weeks later he underwent heart surgery and the discovery of other troubles. The remarkable skill of the surgeons gave him a few more years' lease of life. Then he was hospitalised again. Meg, bewildered and heartbroken by the turn of events, but never able to believe that he would die, watched him do just that. Over the years she had made their rooms in the tenement house luxuriously cosy, but now they held too many memories for her to endure living there.

So she was glad to accept an offer to make her home with an elderly sister and brother-in-law on the outskirts of Swansea. The area might be drab and run down, and her sister's house one of a small terrace on a main road. But its front door opened on to an interior that could be fairly described as a little palace; carpeted, polished, perpetually painted and papered, it was a superb example of the best that working-class women can achieve. Meg was now an old-age pensioner, a fact that she ignored, and indeed she was soon at work again, this time in a bake-house, despite the fact that it meant long hours on aching feet, plenty of minor burns, and arms almost too tired to carry home bread and cakes for her sister's family.

Meg loved cooking and had become quite an expert. Throughout the years on her visits to us she always gave me marching orders out of my own kitchen. This arrangement met with high approval from the boys. Meg took infinite time and trouble with her superb cooking, and the boys gave her a chorus of praise. Like a surrogate mother she would stand, arms folded across her pretty frilled pinafore, shining-eyed, lapping up the compliments.

'Wish Mumy could cook like you, Aunt Meg.'

'Don't you go running down your mother, or I'll box your ears.'

Utterly tactless, but without a scrap of spite, she would sort us all out.

'For goodnesss' sake, Win, go and get yourself changed and smartened up a bit before Syd comes in from work.' And from her capacious handbag would come yet another lipstick and partly-used compact for me.

'Nicky, I saw you put that other spoonful of sugar in your tea. You'll end up with diabetes if you don't look out.'

'Now, Jenny, you eat up those Brussels sprouts. Never mind not liking them, eat 'em and you'll have skin like me, not a blemish, even at my age.'

And God help me if I had not a stock of saucepan scourers, Vim, and soda and polish in the house. My pots and pans got a birthday inside and out till they shone like new, in a kitchen that she kept as tidy and clean as a hospital. Her scoldings ran off us like gentle rain off a duck's back. In between her visits we lapsed into our old ways, but we loved to have her bustling, cheerful, organising presence around us as often as she cared to come.

Meg was always in the forefront at the weddings and the subsequent christenings; dressed up to the nines in honour of the occasion, and looking far more like the groom's mother or the proud granny than I did. Her presents to mark these occasions were always too generous. We got truly cross with her but all our protests were as ineffective as catching Niagara Falls in a bucket. My home is full of mementoes of her visits: a really sharp carving knife; a sensible unbreakable cruet set; a wall tin-opener; a kitchen clock; and all sorts of gleanings from her various jobs. I could never catch up with her generosity, so I bided my time. She was a good deal older than I, and the time would come when she would be unable to work. Then our door would be wide open for her to spend long periods with us 'on the house'.

Alas, she only did this once.

Chris had grown dissatisfied with his situation in Staffordshire, and felt that he was not realising his potential. Seeking more job-satisfaction, though with less money, he obtained a post on the outskirts of Swansea. By a pleasing coincidence this job was within walking distance of where Meg lived with her sister and brother-in-law. Chris and Carole and their little daughter Lorna were soon settled down in a nice bungalow on the Gower coast side of Swansea, but still only a few miles from Meg.

'Auntie' Meg was soon a welcome and frequent visitor of theirs; she adored Lorna as if she were her own grandchild. Whenever they drove up for a Sunday, or a week-end visit, Meg came with them.

Meg had at least one thing in common with me; she suffered from a chronic indigestion. She was a sucker for every tablet, powder, or medicine that came on the market, giving me her unused stocks as she tried a fresh cure. At last it drove her to the doctor, who diagnosed a hiatus hernia but advised against an operation at her age. After that, Meg stopped worrying about it. She enjoyed eating food as much as cooking it, and put up cheerfully with the burps and discomfort that followed.

She would not allow advancing years to interfere with her vitality. She would not tolerate a grey hair, the tiniest flaw in her nylons, or any difference in standards or colours for her appearance. In spite of evidence to the contrary she believed that Endocil cream kept the wrinkles away. It was a pricey cream, but it solved for us the problem of Christmas and birthday presents for her. The rest of us grew older, but, as our boys would say, 'Auntie Meg doesn't alter at all.'

And so it seemed for a long time, until one pre-Christmas visit from her. During the couple of months since we had seen her, Meg had suddenly aged. Though Chris and Carole saw her about twice a week, they too had noticed how tired she looked. Despite my pleas she insisted on doing the cooking for all of us.

The following Easter she spent with one of her nieces near London, and did not come to us again until a week-end in June. This was most unusual, and how glad we were to see her, but her appearance alarmed me. It seemed that the shadow of death was already smudging her sunken eyes. Nevertheless, she would cook us all a perfect roast chicken dinner with all the trimmings, and then for herself only a piece of bread and butter.

Now it was my turn to sort her out. 'Meg, you aren't well. Don't you dare come up to us again until you've seen the doctor. If you don't go, I'll come down to Wales and take you myself!'

'It's all right, Win,' she said, with calm resignation. 'My sister has been nagging me to go. I've been feeling bad in the night; terrible sickness and stomach pains. I sneak downstairs quiet as a mouse not to disturb her, but she's caught me twice, and she's made an appointment with the doctor for me next week. It's that old hernia playing up, I expect.'

I could not help thinking it was something worse than that. Apart from my gall-bladder operation, I had been in hospital twice for minor operations. After each one, Meg had wangled time off from her job to make sure I enjoyed a week's rest. After the children were married, Syd had been suddenly rushed to hospital for a week. Again Meg had come up at once to keep me company. Meg, our true friend. I wanted desperately to help her now.

'Meg, you must give up going to work; remember you're seventy-two now, not seventeen.'

'Well, I like to earn a bit. I don't want to be a burden on my sister. She and Dai are only on the old-age pension themselves.'

'Well, you can come and stay with us a lot. Our kids are off our hands now, and there's plenty in our pantry for one more mouth, and you'll be doing me a big favour, giving me your company.'

The doctor made her an appointment at the hospital for an X-ray; almost immediately after that she was admitted for an urgent operation. Two days later, Richard, who had moved from Birmingham back to Gloucestershire, had a day off and took me down to see her. Chris was already at her bedside.

Morriston Hospital had a drab, run-down look, but the atmosphere inside was permeated with the aura of kind friendliness so evident in Wales. Meg looked very weak, and was obviously in great discomfort. Round her bed was a miniature Covent Garden of flowers. Apart from her many relatives and friends, her local Jones the Meat, Evans the Shop, Lewis the

Fish, and Owen the Coal, had all sent a summer memento to gladden her eye.

'I keep telling the nurses to share them around. Now look, you've brought me some more.'

'And you deserve them. How are you, love?'

'Mustn't grumble,' she said, wincing. 'Some of the poor women in here are in a bad state; it's pitiful to see them suffering. I'm not too comfortable myself; whatever they've done, it's knocked the stuffing out of me just now. I can't even raise myself on to my pillows. I don't like to keep worrying the nurses: they're lovely girls, they are, but they're run off their feet.'

'Shall we try and sit you up?'

'Yes, please.'

I watched my two six-foot, rugby-playing sons gently ease her up in the bed. I saw the stricken look they exchanged over her head.

'Ta, that's better.'

'Have they given you any idea how long you'll be kept here?'

'No indeed, they haven't told me anything much. I know they've cut me right across my stomach but they didn't say what they'd found wrong. I asked the doctor that came round this morning, but he just said he wasn't the one who did it. Still, it's over now, thank God; now it's just to get my strength back.'

Richard and I stayed as long as we could, and as we left we found Meg's sister and Carole in the corridor waiting to go in. Their sad faces prepared me for the answer I now dreaded from her sister's lips.

'It's hopeless, Win. They found a malignant growth, and it's spread too far for them to do anything. They say she could last up to six months. She doesn't know, God help her. They think it's best to keep it from her.'

Six months! When the truth is unpalatable, a belief in miracles can creep in. Had I not read more than once of sudden inexplicable cures happening to people stricken like Meg? Of course it's possible, said my heart. On the evidence of your eyes, it's not, argued my mind. By the time Richard and I got home we were both feeling years older.

As soon as her stitches could be removed Meg was discharged from hospital. Syd and I went down to stay overnight with Chris and Carole so that we could visit Meg at her sister's. She looked so frail it hurt me to ask the conventional inadequate question.

'How are you feeling now, love?'

'Oh, I mustn't grumble. I think I'm improving. I wish I could get my strength back a bit quicker. Our Jean here grumbles at me if I try to help her with the housework, but some days I do get up to the shops for her.'

For a moment or two, Meg dredged up a little of her old brightness, and I felt a bitter helpless anger with the fates, so indiscriminately dealing out their suffering.

Although Carole was a lavish hostess, we had no option but to sit down again to a laden table. Meg proudly brought in Syd's favourite fancy sponge she had made specially for him.

'I have to go to the doctor's Tuesday for a check-up. I'd like to ask him if I could come and stay with you for a couple of weeks, if you'll have me Win?'

Would I have her! 'Have you, dear? I'd love to.' My heart was aching to do something for her. 'Tell you what,' I enthused, 'Syd and I will bring your bed downstairs into the sitting-room.'

I had made the room downstairs, which had been the boys'

bedroom, into a cosy sitting-room with armchairs and a television for viewers to watch in peace, away from the chatter of the living-room.

'Indeed,' said Meg, 'you'll do nothing of the sort; a bed in there would spoil it. I can sleep upstairs. You're not to get spoiling me or treating me like an invalid.'

Why, oh why, had I not kept my big mouth shut, and given her no option?

The following Sunday Chris drove her up with Carole and Lorna. I had a dinner up to Meg's standards all ready to put before them. I could see that it was only to please me that Meg struggled through some of hers. Her rouge, lipstick and powder mocked the wasted pallor of her face, but she made no complaint and her talk was full of lively concern for all of us. Nothing would stop her helping with the washing-up.

Meg was obviously still grateful for her life, such as it was, and had no knowledge of her illness. All we could do was to hide the truth from her. To forward this ploy, Carole, who was an excellent sewer, had bought some very nice material and measured Meg up for a new dress. 'I'll take you out to dinner somewhere posh at Christmas, and show you off,' Chris promised her. And so began the bitter charade, in which our children were willing accomplices, paying back a little of the debt of love they owed her. They brought her fruit and flowers, make-up and her special Endocil cream, and plenty of her favourite reading, romantic paperbacks by Denise Robins and Barbara Cartland.

For years Meg and I had had a sisterly relationship, and I took a well-meaning advantage of it. When I took up her early morning tea, I told her to stay put with a book until I had got all spruce and tidy downstairs and the fire lit. And what could I bring up for her breakfast? Poor dear, her appetite and pleasure in food had gone. For her, I stopped my slap-happy, plonk-it-on-the-table habits, and put a dainty cloth on her tray and a posy of flowers; grapefruit carefully segmented; egg boiled just right; or a crisp rasher of bacon and fried bread as she used to love it. I took the crusts off her toast, put home-made marmalade on a pretty china dish, tried to be a credit to her past example, and she tried to eat some of it.

It was late summer, but I knew she loved the comfort of a fire. When I had one blazing well, I called up that she could now get up when she liked, and I would help her have a strip-wash in the comforting warmth. About eleven o'clock she would totter down. Despite her pain-killing tablets, I had heard the pages of her book rustling in the small hours, but she rarely complained. Just sometimes the pain would wring from her a little apologetic grumble.

'Ooh-ooh! Sorry, Win. This old pain in my side is playing me up a bit; I wonder what it is? It can't be anything *very* bad, can it, Winnie, or I'd be having some sort of treatment?'

I knew what she meant, though she never uttered the dread word, cancer. If a Harley Street consultant could have eaves-dropped on me, he would have given me the Baron Munchausen badge for medical fibbing. From my small glean-ings of medical knowledge I had a comforting diagnosis ready for any pain or discomfort that might, or might not, follow a major stomach operation. Sometimes I was right, and that made it all the more convincing. 'The only thing, Meg, is that it may cause you to get anaemic but they'll give you injections for that if it gets bad.' I knew the time was coming when mor-phine would be inevitable.

She became too weak even to help with the lightest house-work, but still I had to discourage her. 'Now look here, Meg, it's a fat lot of good me having you up here if you don't rest. Besides, you're doing me a favour keeping me a bit busier. I *need* more exercise; just look at my behind, half-an-acre round, I reckon.' Sometimes I could sense she was too weak for my mouthy chatter; then I would take myself out to do some gardening or gather kindling wood. She still enjoyed watching television. I would light a fire in the other room, and after tea she would watch *Crossroads* and *Coronation Street*. When the sun came out and it was warm she would totter out into the courtyard, and feel very pleased with herself for walking up and down the length of it, but each day she grew weaker. At the end of a month Chris came and took her back to Wales for her check-up. With some difficulty, we got her fairly comfortable in the car, and she turned and said, 'If he says it's OK, Win, can I come back for a while?'

'Yes, oh yes, of course, love.' I am not an over-tolerant or kindly-disposed woman. My patience was often stretched to its limits when I looked after my elderly mother and my mother-in-law, but somehow I felt it a privilege to be in the company of my brave dying friend. Her lack of self-pity, her genuine interest in other people's burdens, and her ability still to extract some pleasure from her restricted miserable existence, still finding touches of humour, filled me with admiration, and love for her. I had little hope of her coming to us again, but a week later there she was, holding on to Chris's arm and struggling back across our courtyard to our welcome.

This time we had brought her bed downstairs, and we bought a very comfortable high-backed armchair for her to watch the television. Jenny had got her a bed-ring for she was now little more than bones, except for her swollen stomach. Still her spirit was unbroken. 'Oh, I don't know,' she would say, 'there's plenty worse than me.' We played a little game. When I took her morning tea in, I told her I was the night nurse just going off duty, but first I would help her to the toilet and tidy her bed. Then I assumed the role of wardmaid, cleaning the grate, lighting the fire, dusting and carpet-sweeping. Next I would be the day nurse, giving her a wash and taking in her breakfast. Her appetite was pitiful. I put a supply of her novelettes, fruit, and a drink just in case, and let her rest, popping in frequently and racking my brains for any ploy that could bring her any pleasure.

At first she would struggle out for an hour or two by the living-room fire, and we would talk of our days in the tenement house, the amusing things that happened there, her West End jobs, the children's antics. At first, once up, she would want to get dressed and made up. 'I must look respectable, Win, in case you get any visitors.' At last she took to her bed and only got up to go across to the toilet. It distressed her when I told her I could borrow a commode to put by her bed.

'Your consultant will be in to watch the telly with you this evening.' She could still grin at this. After tea Syd would wash and shave, and change into his Sunday suit especially to keep her company. Meg, all woman to the end, would insist I hold a mirror for her to make up, and change into her prettiest bed-jacket.

After another month she was too weak to stand up on her own. Syd went to the phone box and called Chris to tell Meg's sister that we had to bring her home. We would come on Saturday, stay with him and Carole, and return the next day.

'We're taking you home this week-end, dear,' I told her. 'It's high time your doctor started giving you some injections to build you up a bit. Then we'll fetch you up to us again.'

This time she looked at me with eyes full of undisguised sadness. 'I'm beginning to wonder if I shall ever be able to come again, Win.' I wanted to go down on my knees, put my arms around her, and tell her whilst she could still hear me how much we admired and loved her. But in so doing I would have destroyed the flicker of hope that her expression showed she still wanted to cling to.

'Of course you will,' I lied.

'I don't want to go home in my nightie and dressing-gown; it will upset my sister. Help me to dress, Win, and to put my make-up on.'

During the eighty-mile drive there were times when I wondered if she would survive the journey, but with our arms each side of her she made it from the car to her sister's door and into the cosy loving atmosphere inside.

On our way home we called in to see her. She was in bed, propped up on pretty pillows in a comfortable bedroom. She was dressed in a dainty lacy bedjacket and was waiting patiently for the doctor. I kissed the ghastly remnants of her wasted face, and she gave me a long steady look. 'Goodbye, Win,' she said with dignity, and I knew she knew.

She got her injections. Tears of relief as well as sorrow welled up in us when, two weeks later, we heard that Meg had died.

Meg was gone, never to return. Syd's sister and her family, now well off, had moved into deepest Sussex among the millionaires, too far for a day trip either way. Our old friends from the tenement house had all dispersed. Of our children, Richard had come closer to us, but Jenny and Nick were in the Cotswolds and Chris in Swansea. People say that routine is good for you; sometimes I wondered if that were true. With my life now almost totally governed by Syd's going and coming and by petty household duties, any little distraction from my loneliness assumed heroic proportions.

One morning, hearing a lot of early clatter round the back of the cottage, I rightly assumed that the workmen had arrived to repair the roof. When I went up the back garden I could see a young man throwing down the perished tiles. Young man? These days it was difficult to distinguish the sexes; the fashion for masculine long hair had spread even to this rustic back-water. He turned his head and gave me the cursory glance which is all a plain, middle-aged frumpy woman could expect. I took a good eyeful of him; scruffy shoulder-length hair, lurid stencilled T-shirt, skin-tight drainpipe jeans on skinny bean-pole legs. What was modern manhood coming to? No wonder, all youth thought of today was cheap popular music, cheap sex, discotheques, and even drugs. They seemed cynical and world-weary before they had cut their wisdom teeth. Still, I had to admit he was tackling our roof with gusto.

By mid-morning the day was turning into a scorcher, and I was more than ready to brew myself a cup of tea. Better give that lad some, I supposed, and a wedge of cake for the skinny ribs. I put it with a jug of tea on a tray. 'Drink here,' I called to him, putting it down.

'Ta!' He climbed down, took the tray, and disappeared, no doubt, I assumed, to eat it in the battered old van he had parked on the piece of waste ground.

At one o'clock I put him out a jug of lemonade and a sand-wich; I had heard him working well all the morning.

This went on for several days until he had worked his way round to the front of the cottage. I was busy doing my weekly baking and suggested he should knock for his one o'clock tray. Promptly at one o'clock he did so, and said, 'Would you mind if I brought my friend in to see you, missus?'

Friend? My mind uncharitably conjured up a girl; no doubt one of the tousle-headed, dirty-footed, long-skirted, hippy types that were much in evidence then, battening on to any male rather than going to work. I am often a coward at speaking my mind, so I gave a very reluctant consent, and put another cup on his tray.

Presently he came back across the yard, but I could see no-one with him. Then I noticed a tiny fledgling bird of unidentifiable species perched on his shoulder. It was a wild variety and I was amazed that it did not fly away.

"Ere 'e is, then. This is my friend Joey.'

You could have knocked me down with one of its immature feathers. 'Where'd you get him?'

'Found 'im in some grass under a tree. Must 'ave fell out o' the nest, or been pushed out by 'is mother. The poor little bugger was bald when I found 'im.'

In the larder I had a bit of liver cooked for the cat. I scraped a bit off finely, and put it in my palm under the bird's beak.

"E ain't ready to take it like that yet, missus.'

He held a finger out for the bird to perch on, then, taking a morsel of the liver, gently held its head back and put it down the open beak. As a mother of four grown-up children, I felt rather mortified at my lack of maternal instinct.

He said, 'I've got 'is lunch box, anyroads,' and from his pocket he took a matchbox filled with tiny worms and bird seed.

'What does your mother think of you bringing up a bird?' I asked.

'She ain't in a position to think anything about it, missus. My Mam died when I was a little 'un, probably to get away from the old man.'

I looked at his gangly thinness, his ill-washed T-shirt, the cobbled-up stitching that nearly held together a large tear in the knee of his jeans.

'D'you live with your Dad, and what does he think of your bird?'

'The only thing 'e thinks of, missus, is what goes into a glass, wi' a froth on the top. 'E's all right when 'e's just got a skinful, but me an' Joey keeps out o' 'is way other times. We go up in my bedroom. He threatened to smash Joey's cage and wring 'is neck. I told 'im, 'urt that bird an' I'll smash your face in. I ain't scared of 'im any more since I got Joey. I do think o' goin' into lodgin's but a landlady mightn't take to me 'avin' a bird in my room.' He laughed at his pun. 'Besides, there'd likely be a cat around. Can I bring his cage round in your yard this afternoon, missus?'

'Of course you can.'

'Usually I leave 'im in 'is cage while I'm workin', and I've made a nice little nest in the dashboard for 'im to sit in when I'm drivin'. But I'd like to give 'im a bit more exercise.'

He came back with Joey in a large home-made cage, and he was also carrying a piece of cloth. 'I put this on one side of the cage so he can 'ave some shade.'

He put the cage down in our yard, and got back up his ladder to the roof. Some time later I went into the front garden to pick some flowers, and the lad called down asking me to open the door of the cage.

'Oh, I'd better not; he'll fly away and you'll lose him.'

'Don't worry, missus. He'll be all right, you'll see.'

Reluctantly I opened the cage door and waited to see. The lad made a few whistling sounds, and Joey hopped out and flew straight up to perch on his shoulder.

'Now off you go, and have a bit of a fly around.'

Off went Joey, up into the leafy branches of the rowan tree behind the cottage and out of sight. Nearby there were other trees and hedges and meadows to tempt him. 'Oh dear,' I wailed. 'You'll never get him back now.'

'You stop frettin', missus.'

It seemed a long ten minutes before the lad made his special whistling call again. Almost at once back flew the little bird to his shoulder. They gave each other a couple of kissing pecks, and then the finger of authority was extended, and pointed towards the yard. Joey hopped on to it.

'Now be a good boy, and go back in your cage.' Fascinated, I watched the bird do just that.

'Shut the cage door, please, missus, in case your cat comes round.'

For the next week or so until the repairs were finished, Joey took up his residence in the yard, making his social calls at his master's break times, taking his afternoon airings in the branches of the rowan tree.

I was sorry to see them go, Joey perching proudly on his saviour's shoulder. I never saw them again. I hope that young man has found a wife to be as tender to, and one who will mother him a bit. If he is now a dad himself, I am sure he is a good one, long hair and all.

Every decade of our lives brings its sorrows and its joys: the bewilderment of babyhood, the struggles of schooldays, the trauma of the teens, the problems of parenthood, the miseries of middle-age, and then the lingering sadness of senility. Shakespeare summed it all up in the seven ages of man, and then sought his own oblivion from the trials of advancing years in the bottle. When young we look on time as something to be spent without thought, but old age makes us look back on what we have purchased with it and realise how little we have left of the precious hoard. By then our appetites for living have changed, most of our emotional needs have been spent, and physical deterioration too often limits activities. Looking forward into a rapidly shrinking future daunts the boldest spirit; far better to indulge in the comfort of re-living the past. Now I was approaching sixty, and with long hours of my own company, I fell easy victim to this temptation.

Faces from the past loomed up with an importance magnified by time. Granny, for instance. Granny, next door, had been one of the soft cushions that protected me from the harder knocks of childhood. I recalled with guilty pangs how little I had shown my appreciation while she lived. In a fit of contrition I took pen and paper and wrote down my thoughts about her. I wanted to share my admiration of Granny with others. With only a stamp to lose, I sent it to a quarterly country magazine. It seemed quite an achievement when it was accepted and published, with the added bonus of a six-pound cheque!

A little encouragement of that sort goes a long way with me! Now I had an incentive for something to do in those lonely hours. I began to write down some of my early memories. A request in a Sunday paper by a professor of Social History for pieces by working people about their lives soon got one of mine on the way to him. Again I had an encouraging response, and eventually a piece in his book, *Useful Toil*.

Most days, by means of the radio, I enjoyed an hour's vicarious company with some charming people in *Woman's Hour*. The pleasant style of the presenters and producers made them feel like friends. One in particular who appealed to me was named Pamela Howe; I sent her a pile of my writings. Excitement mounted when she wrote that she was interested, and even more when eventually she said she would bring them to the notice of *Woman's Hour*. They decided to have them read out in serial form on the programme. So far, so good.

So far, so *incredibly* good, it seemed, and then came the bombshell; a letter from Miss Howe to say she would like to come and visit me, and bring with her her secretary, and the actress June Barrie who was to do the reading. June wanted to hear and study my accent in order to imitate it on the radio. They were coming at midday, and would take me to lunch at the Speech House.

My life as domestic servant, waitress, charwoman, and land-worker, had convinced me that I was a second-class citizen in the eyes of those who were blessed with the social graces. I was ashamed of my rough, swollen and work-toughened hands, and of my inferior clothes. How wrong I was on this matter; a fool with a fool's sense of values. Yet there was some justification for unease. I knew these ladies to be clever talented people who had earned their fame. Had I been meeting the Queen, I do not think my apprehension would have been greater: after all, I knew nothing about her except the inherited trappings of her birthright.

The Speech House is a famous old inn at the heart of the Forest of Dean. Queen Elizabeth the First really had slept there! As a young woman I had once called at the back door to apply for a job as maid, and had been too intimidated by its antique grandeur to accept the post. Now I simply had not the nerve to go there for lunch. So I wrote suggesting that I would like to cook a lunch for my three guests if that would suit, and I got a charming letter of acceptance.

I cleaned our cottage from corner to corner. I told Syd he must have a day off; his ability to take events in his stride would be a help. I planned the meal. I sorted out our mixed bag of crocks and cutlery to see if I could match up four settings without chips or cracks. I actually bought some serviettes, and some new serving-dishes, and even a bottle of sherry. Knowing that my stomach would have too many knots in it for me to sit at table, I intended to be a waitress hostess.

They arranged to come at one o'clock, and promptly at one we heard the car draw up. I had timed my cooking exactly right for once, but my heart seemed to be thumping in my throat. Within a couple of minutes of opening the door to our guests my nervousness had almost evaporated. They were not just charming; they were downright friendly. By the time they had eaten their lunch, with obvious enjoyment, and got down to discussing the scripts, it was not like being in the company of strangers at all. After a drive into the Forest to show them the village where I was born, they came back and had tea with us.

We waved goodbye to them about half-past six. It had been a wonderful afternoon, but there was a feeling of relief that it was over and had gone well. I made another pot of tea, and just sat gloating about how well we had managed, and how easy they had made it for us. Then I remembered with considerable embarrassment that the celebratory bottle of champagne that Pamela had brought with her for our lunch was still keeping cool in the pantry. We had no refrigerator at the time. We treasured the three warm thank-you letters we received.

From a standing start, I felt I had taken quite a plunge into the social whirlpool. I was more than satisfied with this one exhilarating dip, to last me the rest of my life, but I was in for a few surprises. Sweeping the chimney, for instance.

In the good old days our living-room, the one with the peculiar ceiling and so full of character and inconveniences, had been part of a series of one-storey buildings. It had had a copper in it, and as a result the flue was short, narrow and contorted. The chimney was regularly swept by a local man, a friend of ours, who was familiar with its peculiarities. He was in poor health, and sometimes unable to work. At such times it hurt his feelings if anyone else was employed to do the job, and messages were sent that we were not to worry, he would soon be up and about with his brushes. Now he was incapacitated again and our chimney was belching terribly. Syd would not blackleg on his mate, so I decided to do it myself. I poked about in the woodshed and found some long pieces of thin, pliable but strong wood. I tied them tightly together and fastened a bunch of holly on to the end.

I covered myself up in an old dirt-ingrained, land-working coat fastened at the neck with a safety-pin, a tatty head-scarf, and wellington boots. I got the holly right up through the chimney pot, wangling it somehow round the convoluted corners, and then down came the soot. Buckets-full of it, and a good percentage on my person, especially my face and hands. I had just started to shovel it up out of the hearth when an elegant young man knocked at the open door. In an accent to match his appearance he said he had called to take some photographs of 'Winifred Foley, the writer', to illustrate a feature to be published in one of the quality newspapers! He only batted his eyelids a couple of times when I told him it was me. I suggested hopefully that the idea could be scratched. That did not suit; he needed to take the photographs that morning.

I had to think quickly; I had to stall. What was I going to do next? Get the milk – that was it. I got a shopping bag, held it out to him, and suggested he might like to fetch our milk and paper from the box down the hill. If he took his time admiring the view, I would try to make myself presentable while he was gone. It was a case of noblesse oblige, and he obliged, tactfully finding the view much to his taste.

I made a rush job of the hearth, and dusted and polished a chair for him. I washed my face – never mind my neck, I had a clean high-necked blouse. A quick comb through my grey-ing, soot-dyed hair and my toilet was complete. Two cups and saucers quickly rinsed of the soot that had wafted through the archway all over the kitchen dresser, and I was ready to make him a cup of coffee and have my photograph taken. He was awfully polite and took quite a number of shots. I realised why, when he kindly sent me some copies! He has quite a name in his profession, his equipment is high-grade stuff, and it did not hide the soot still embedded in my wrinkles!

By now I should have begun to realise what to expect, but I was quite unprepared for my next caller, a few days later. It was mid-morning, and I was in my muddy gardening gear. Anyone who knows me will testify to my flair for spreading mud about me, or soot, or paint. My hair was still in curlers, pipe-cleaners pinched off Syd, and I was smelling like a gypsy from the garden fire I had been making up.

This time it was a gentleman who obviously recognised me from a photo in the local newspaper. To his credit he did not flinch, nor make some excuse to conceal his intentions in call-ing. He asked me if I would open the annual summer Fete of Dean. What a ludicrous idea, I thought, and I could not help laughing outright. I gave what I thought were good reasons for refusing, but he would not agree. 'You're famous in the local-ity now, you know.' Famous! I did not feel very famous. Fame must be, like beauty, in the eye of the beholder, then. He con-tinued to be persuasive, so I half-heartedly gave him a semi-promise to consider it by the time he called a week hence.

I had never even attended the opening of a fete, but I had seen photographs in newspapers. If it were a lady, it was always one of repute, smartly dressed and wearing a posh hat. I had not even got a hat. My ten-bob bargain buy had done duty for four weddings and now had our scarecrow's head pushing through it after two years in the garden. Anyway I felt sure that Syd and the children would back me up on the absurdity of the idea.

'Don't see why you shouldn't,' said Syd, the traitor.

Jenny backed him up. 'Good idea, Mum. It might make you start to smarten yourself up a bit.'

I gave in, and promised to go with Jenny to buy a hat, some gloves, shoes, and a blouse to suit my crimplene costume. This was still almost as good as new.

Gilding the lily is a superfluous exercise, and spending a lot of money trying to tart up an old dandelion was equally silly, I thought. So I mentally compromised. I could augment the funds of the 'Help the Aged' shop in Gloucester by getting my things there cheaply. I dodged into the shop before Jenny realised the ploy. Patiently she followed me in. Taking care not to catch her eye I spent about a pound and got it all except the shoes, which I would have new. Jenny waited until we left the shop well behind us, then she exploded.

'You're *not* wearing that lot, Mummy.'

'Why not? It's all in good condition, and the hat's OK.'

'It's ghastly! I reckon every other old-age pensioner was wearing one like it about ten years ago. If you're too stingy to buy things yourself, I'll buy them for you.'

I could not let her get away with that. 'Oh well. All right. I'll give these things to Nanna.' (Syd's mother.)

'Don't you dare! Nanna would be offended. She *does* care how she looks. She probably gave them that hat in the first place!'

I got home with a smart new hat, matching gloves, a new

blouse, a pair of smart shoes, and the awakening of some dormant feminine instinct that made me feel that a new hat is a tonic!

On the day of the Fete I felt that I looked the part at least, although the high heels on the new shoes made me feel a bit tottery after my habitual slippers and wellingtons. The weather was dry and sunny so I had no worry about my posh hat; the big worry was getting the few words out to open the Fete. For this I had to climb on to a decorated farm wagon, its body camouflaged with a sheet of plastic grass. On it sat the pretty Beauty Queen, whom I had to crown, and her six small attendants.

Feeling every inch the lady, I graciously accepted the helping hands guiding me on to a box that was strategically placed for me to get on the wagon. The curious upturned faces were all friendly and reassuring. I said my piece, crowned the Queen, introduced her and her attendants to her subjects, posed with 'her majesty' for photographs, and then, very relieved and distinctly swollen-headed, I made to get off the wagon. Someone had removed the box; no matter; in my euphoria I felt light-footed and agile enough to jump down.

I took off, but the heel of one of my shoes did not. It caught in the edge of the tailboard concealed by the cover. I landed on my posh hat with my feet in the air, and it was not just the rush of blood that the angle brought to my face that made it rosy-scarlet. There were a good many displays and exhibitions put on for that Fete. Oh well, I thought, they have had an extra one now for their money!

My little interlude in the limelight would soon have died a natural death, for I am sure the amount of demand on a person is nicely geared to publicity. However, the radio scripts were published as a book, and it sold surprisingly well from such modest beginnings. Now more invitations began to arrive, some of a perplexing nature. As a child, the fact that I had nothing to show off about had never stopped me doing so when the chance occurred. Over the years this trait had taken enough diminishing knocks to make me now refuse politely the grander invitations.

I did not even want to accept those from Women's Institutes. I had meanly subscribed to the notion that their members were a toffee-nosed lot, and I had never had the courage to join them or any other women's group. On the whole, I was not fond of my own sex. How wrong I was! How friendly, tolerant, and sympathetic were those rows of faces to the nervous old chatterbox on the platform! The aims of these groups are all based on kindness, help for others, and friendly competitions among each other. There is an atmosphere of sisterhood that I found uplifting. I have a new respect and affection now for my own sex; their claws are shown only on occasions.

I did once accept a request to speak at a WI that accidentally gave me a peep into grandeur. We were now on the phone, and one day a very worried female voice rang through to ask could I possibly act as a stand-in for their booked speaker who had been rushed to hospital. The call came from a place some thirty miles away with which I was totally unfamiliar. The lady sounded distressfully urgent, so after warning her that I was not a 'proper' speaker I accepted. She gave me the address, which I wrote down, and rang off.

'Underberry' Court,
Underberry.

A funny address. 'Underberry' Court? Still the name was nothing to go by; it could turn out to be a little wooden meeting hut, or more likely an old house turned into a community centre. Our own local Westbury Court had become an old people's home taking over from the old workhouse. Anyway I had no time to dwell on it as I had to be there the following evening. Also I had not much time to consider what to talk about. My habit was to think about a subject and then just get up and open my mouth. I never knew myself what might come out. Once I had tried making notes, but my glasses kept falling off. I lost my thread and had to ask the audience what I had been on about! Some of them knew! I made a mental note to have the National Health frames changed one of these days.

This time I decided to talk about my days in domestic service, its amusing side, with a few digs about the humiliations of being a servant thrown in.

With his meal still undigested Syd had to have a quick wash and change to drive me there by quarter-past seven. En route, after we had left familiar ground, we had to ask directions more often than once, because the place was definitely not sign-posted. Other villages, even hamlets, in the area were sign-posted, but not our mysterious destination. Syd began to get rather annoyed; I could see his jaw working. Assured again and again that he was on the right road he drove on, puzzled and angry.

We were now in the middle of a very rural area indeed. The tiny settlements, each a handful of cottages, became smaller and smaller and even farther apart. The road dwindled into a lane neatly ditched and hedged. Here and there where the roadside was a little sloping embankment some loving souls had cut out patches and literally filled them with flowers, and trimmed the weedy grasses all around. I do not remember ever seeing that before. While we were almost lost in admiration of these and the far-flung pastoral beauty that surrounded us on every side, we passed a little church, old and almost hidden in yew. A narrow gravel road, unmarked, led towards it. 'That's it,' I cried. 'Stop, Syd, that must be it.'

He stopped, reversed to the gravel road and looked gloomily down it. 'S'pose it must be, but why isn't it marked? We could drive round here for hours!' Advancing stealthily up that road as if we were trespassers, we passed the church, and stopped by a really imposing wrought-iron gateway of what must be one of the most stately homes in England. Old, sound, and beautiful, with a large square courtyard and strips of close-cut lawns, not a weed to be seen. Everything about it seemed to be so well looked after, as if the owners wanted it to last for ever. The gateway bore a coat of arms, but no name, and there was absolutely nobody about. Not daring to enter we drove up a pathway that we thought might lead round the back, but it led into a woodland with grass paths running here and there and even these were mown and edged. We retreated again, back to the front of the house.

Nearby was a row of four old-world cottages, absolutely immaculate and with neat clean gardens laid out in the same patterns and flowers. The weedless paved road beside them ended in a field. There was no sound, and not a soul about. Desperate, I knocked at the door of the first cottage. Almost immediately, a pleasant old lady came to the door and confirmed that this was indeed the place written down on my piece of paper. Apparently we were in the middle of an estate covering several thousands of acres, she was one of the retired tenants, and the big house was the residence of the lord of the manor.

It was obviously not the meeting place of the WI! Then an idea struck me. Perhaps the lady of the manor let the estate WI members hold their meetings in one of the outbuildings around the house. In a lesser courtyard we could see a few cars parked, and they were not all Rolls-Royces! So we entered the majestic gateway to inspect the fine stone outbuildings; an estate office, stables, sundry others, all in the grand manner, but not a sign of life, apart from the horses. Everything so immaculate; more wide sweeping paths unsullied by a migrant blade of grass; more great lawns, well-mown, brushed and combed and edged, not a blade missing or even out of place. Then a view of a beautiful landscaped garden with a huge ornamental lake. We were definitely in the wrong place!

We were creeping back out through the courtyard and trying not to crunch the gravel, when a gentleman appeared, a very natty specimen in a dark suit, white shirt, and bow tie. Gosh, we had bumped into the lord of the manor himself. Syd politely raised his hat, apologised if we were trespassing and explained our errand.

'Oh yes, yes. You are expected, Mrs Foley. Please come this way.'

'See you later,' said Syd with relief, and disappeared.

I was ushered into a palatial hall with arched ceilings, hung with the sort of paintings one sees in the National Gallery. My gentleman escort excused himself and knocked and entered some grand double doors. 'Could you tell me where Madam is?' I heard him ask.

Good lord, I thought, this must be the butler. Wherever had I landed myself? Just then a lady entered the hall from another door. I had seen her type before, in the pages of the *Tatler*; elegant, charming, with an aristocratic accent. I knew this must be the mistress of the place, and she introduced herself as such.

'I do hope we haven't kept you waiting, Mrs Foley.'

I was Winnie in Wonderland as I followed her through the

doorway from which she had emerged. I was in another nobly-proportioned room, wood-panelled, with an enormous window overlooking the garden. Here at last was my audience, sitting on rows of chairs, some of them looking more like house guests. I took my seat behind a priceless desk with a bowl of flowers and a carafe of water on it. How I wished I had hopped it with Syd!

All the way on the journey my talk had been churning over and over in my mind. It now seemed terribly tactless, in view of my hostess and her friends. They had obviously been used to ordering servants about for generations, taking them for granted, a part of life. I would have difficulty in changing the subject. What was I to do? A picture flashed into my mind; my father's drawn and undernourished face covered in pit dirt. 'This above all: to thine own self be true', and I was.

I had been ushered in in style through the front door by the butler. Maybe I would be ignominiously chucked out through the back one by the same major-domo. Nevertheless I rattled on, editing a little, as I went, some of the past hurts and indignities. In fairness, I did not entirely overlook the problems of the mistress class.

My hostess was the president of the estate WI, and graciously invited them to have their meeting in her home once a year. Their choice of speaker must have surprised her. There was no sign of it in the charming vote of thanks she gave me. She warmly invited me to bring Syd in and stay for coffee and refreshments. I politely declined. On the way out she introduced me to her husband and her daughter, which I thought was lovely of her. Then she handed me a long wrapped box and an envelope.

I had explained on the phone that I did not charge a fee, but would accept the petrol expenses. Our little car could

have done the journey three times on the generous amount in
the envelope. Inside the box were some punnets of the biggest
juiciest raspberries I had ever seen, and some cartons of clot-
ted cream, doubtless produce of the estate farms and garden.
We shared some of these out, but kept plenty for our dinner
the following day, and what a dinner Syd came home from
work to! For once, I had mixed with the aristocracy, and for
once we were going to eat like lords. I did soup for starters,
rump steak with all the trimmings, and raspberries and cream
for pudding. All we were short of was the butler!

Indecent exposure is a crime in law, and self-exposure can feel
like a crime committed on one's own spirit. The transition
from agoraphobic home-body to extrovert public chatterbox
stretched me to a vulnerable thinness in the middle. It was
disturbing trying to maintain the two identities, each impov-
erishing the other, and I had brought it entirely on myself.
Having had the sauce to write an autobiography for public
scrutiny, I could hardly grumble if the public were interested
in me. Not fair now to want to hide away in a corner. I could
not have my cake and eat it, and we were certainly getting
some cake.

So long as it covers the bare essentials and a little over to
save for replacements, living hand to mouth does have its
advantages. There are no problems wondering how to spend
the money, no income-tax forms to fill in, and no feelings of
guilt about robbing the rest of society. No conscience about
not giving to charity, for charity must begin at home. In fact,
one is in the honourable position of owing the world nothing.

Getting used to having more money is as easy as falling off
a log, and the assertive voice of self-indulgence can overcome
the still small voice of conscience with little effort. When the

cheques began to roll in I gave vent to some of my generous impulses, but the habits of a life-time of thrift soon intervened. Generous impulses became curtailed or postponed, or were very strictly examined. We were none too generous to ourselves either, but we bought a few things. A new, good-quality, firm mattress for my back – the price made us reel. A new, electric, very easy mower for our lawns. A new suit for Syd, and his first dressing-gown! Persuading him to buy these brought me out in more of a sweat than the old lawn-mower did.

For some time we had been fighting our children's notion that they should pay for us to have the phone. 'You've no excuse, now, Mummy. Look how awful it was for you when Daddy was taken ill at two in the morning and you a mile away from the nearest phone! Just think what it would mean to us if we could phone you any time. Think how you could check up every time you heard one of the grandchildren had sneezed twice!'

There was sense in it; we had the phone installed. After that I had to recuperate from such a glut of spending.

The book went into paperback, and an edited version for schools. An excerpt from it was made into a film for television. For the first time in our lives we opened a bank account. By the time our old car was ready for the scrapyard we were affluent enough to buy a modest brand-new one (to last us out). Surely now our lucky streak would go away and find another home? It did not. I wrote a little sequel which went well, too.

If I wished, I could now replace much of our shabby home, but the novelty of spending lump sums on things that were not strictly necessary was wearing thin. Or was it that I was daring to harbour a germ of a dream, and this was reinforcing my frugality? I honestly do not know.

We tried to share our savings with our children. All such suggestions were met with adamant refusals. 'For God's sake, haven't you two done enough for us? D'you realise you've never been away on a proper holiday in your lives?'

'That bit of money that's worrying you so, why you could blow the lot on a cruise in Daddy's holidays!' And so on. We kept on saving.

After four years my little dream had grown enough to come out into the open, and to challenge a problem that grew more menacing for us all the time. What was going to happen to us when Syd retired and our tenancy of the cottage came to an end? That would not be long now. We would have loved to end our days where we were, but there were several factors against it. The huge garden we had cultivated with blood, sweat and tears, with joy and temper, was now too much for us. We had empty rooms that could be better used by a young family. Also there was no doubt that the estate would be under no obligation to let us stay on, and if their legal rights were waived, or if we were offered something smaller and humbler, it would be an act of charity. We did not want that. We might get a council old people's bungalow, but waiting for death in one of these I would feel a fish out of water. No fire to poke, almost no garden to potter on, the convenience-packaged soullessness of their architecture! Why, it would be like putting a free-roaming mongrel into a pampered Peke's silk-lined basket!

If only we could save up enough money to buy a tiny cottage of our own. A very humble sort would do, with enough garden to keep us busy. Something a bit old, not an ancient monument, but not a box either. Something with a fireplace and just a little character. It was not impossible; one such might turn up!

Syd was willing to share this dream, but he shared little of my hope of ever realising it, the old pessimist. The children, however, encouraged me and thoroughly approved the idea.

Many years ago when I was girl, our Dad was doing a patched-up repair to our cottage. He had no means to get the proper materials. Ruefully scratching his head, he observed, 'Well, my wench, I do reckon that if a mon do want to get 'is own back on a enemy, 'im could do wuss than leave'n a old cottage in 'is will.'

Father was no fool, but there must be plenty of fools about now, for any old cottage that comes on the market attracts a queue of customers in no time. We joined the ranks when Chris took us to see one for sale a few miles away. The price was so low that we did not expect much, and we certainly did not expect to get a feeling of affection for it as soon as we saw it. Yet we did. Like a little sister standing for protection by an older one, this cottage leaned against a larger one of identical design. It was a typical home-built shelter of the humble labourer some two hundred years ago. Like the smattering of cottages nearby, it was built of stone from an abandoned quarry some fifty yards away.

It had two small windows up, and two down, and a good door surmounted by a porch. Though this cottage was very small, it was set in a sizeable L-shaped garden which swept right round the back. Even for early April the garden looked outstandingly clean and well-cultivated. Looking down from the garden gate the walls and the roof seemed sound. Feeling like trespassers, we tripped down the garden path to have a peep through the windows. Though the place was empty, it was still fully-furnished, and you needed no degree in psychology to conclude that the occupant had been elderly, and that death had come unwanted and unexpected. But it had not caught the unwary napping; the crowded interior was in neat order and spotlessly clean. There was even a bundle of kindling wood beside the hearth ready to light the sitting-room fire.

This room was about twelve feet square. It had a low undulating ceiling propped up by an extra beam, tidily boxed-in. This must have raised a few bumps on the unwary heads of tallish visitors. All the same, I mused, with a nice fire glowing, this would make a cosy room for Syd to come in to from work. The other window revealed a six-foot sliver of space contorted into a kitchen. There was a sink-unit, a cupboard, some shelves, and a string line across, with a precisely-hung towel, tea-cloth, and dish-cloth. Everything looked scoured and monastically tidy.

All this tidiness left us unprepared for the jumble of decrepit out-buildings round the back. There was a pervasive inescapable odour that revealed the identity of the smallest one before I unlatched the door. It was a primitive flushless privy with a wooden seat in which were carved a big hole and a little one covered with lids. All was scrubbed to whiteness. There was a carton of powdered disinfectant, a toilet roll, and an aerosol can of air-freshener to prove that the occupant had not turned his nose up at modern inventions.

We had a proper Twenty Questions session about object number two! A nine-foot high, six-foot square, extension abutting on to the back wall and the side of the chimney-piece. It was as sturdily stone-built as the cottage itself, and about the same age. There was no way of getting into it from outside, and a quick glance through the window showed it was not accessible from inside. What was it? Our imaginations ran riot. An underground passage to buried treasure? A secret grave for murdered bodies? A buttress to help hold the cottage up? Perhaps an obsolete bake-oven? A bake-oven, that size? This was my inspired guess, and that is what it turned out to be.

Tucked in against the other side of the chimney-piece was a tiny back-kitchen with a rusting corrugated-iron roof. The rotting wood was held together by layers of paint, and inside was a wash-copper with a tall chimney, one brick wide, held together merely by its own weight. There were two rickety rotting sheds, for fuel, tools, oddments, and a worm-eaten ladder. We were glad to look the other way, over the thick hedge that bordered the garden, across a panorama of farmlands, and into the misty distance of the Malvern Hills. Never mind the old sheds; this view was priceless, and the garden too was worth looking at. Just the right size for us, and its clean black soil looked invitingly fertile. A few yards down the sloping garden was a valuable acquisition, a fine upstanding plum tree in its prime of age and health, and around it the pink tips of a clump of rhubarb were forcing themselves up for a share of spring sunshine through a bottomless old bucket.

Next to it two gooseberry bushes carried a bumper crop of green flowerets hanging between their new leaves, and a huge blackcurrant showed plenty of healthy tips. Like cupped green hands the outer leaves of three rows of May broccoli protected the forming curds from the late frosts. There would not be much summer shade under the gnarled old apple tree; most of its branches were dead, and the hollow trunk had a hole big enough for birds to nest in, and enjoy a perpetual larder of insects in the soft rotting interior. The path from the front gate to the cottage door was bordered with the most prolific show of giant-headed daffodils and narcissi I had ever seen.

I looked all round once more. Now I had seen enough to make up my mind.

'If we can get it, I'm willing. How about you?' I asked Syd.

As a rule, Syd does not exactly chew the cud before he answers; he just chomps on his old pipe stem and thinks of all the cons to dash the pros of most of my ideas. With his eyes still roaming the garden, he answered without hesitation, 'Do me.' From him, this was the seal of approval.

'Could be a smashing little place. Just right for you two,' said Chris.

Twenty-three years previously we had turned the clock back by leaving our modern flat and returning to cottage life. Back to emptying the privy bucket, back to no bathroom, back to pumping the water, back to mysterious bulgy ceilings and inexplicably bulgy walls. Well, we could do it again, and maybe have the mod cons installed later. Syd could leave the sawmill; that would please the children. The snag was that we had not saved up enough for the price of the cottage.

'Leave it to me,' said Chris. 'We might be able to knock the price down. Estate agents always try their luck. Anyway, I'll see my bank manager and persuade him to give you a loan; I'll be the guarantor; and don't bloody argue, Mum, because I've made up my mind. You and Dad must think it over well, and I'll come up later for your decision. That place will have to be snapped up quickly, it's a real knock-down bargain!' Knock-down was a prophetic description.

As we left, the next door neighbour 'happened' to be by her garden gate. A pleasant 'good afternoon' from her was enough excuse for my probing tongue to winkle out all the information about the cottage. She was charming and informative. An old widower of eighty had recently died there. An independent sort who had never taken to his bed, he had been digging his garden that very day. He complained of not feeling well, and a few hours later the neighbour from the cottage below called and found him dead in the chair. A merciful end? Who can tell, but if it was he deserved it. His only child, a son, lived up north with his family. He had put the cottage up for sale, and was supposed to be coming down soon to clear it out. This nice homely woman was obviously of a similar background to myself, and if we did get the cottage, she would help me feel at home.

Soon we were looking over the property with an agent, and there were other customers waiting for him, too. With everything still as the old gentleman had left it, it seemed an intrusion to enter. This had been *his* private little world, the photographs on the sideboard were of *his* grandchildren and relations, the diplomas proudly hung on the wall had been obtained by *his* son. The clean-sheeted bed had been waiting for *him* to get into. The very furniture and walls seemed embarrassed by the curious eyes of a bunch of interlopers. Traitor to my agnostic beliefs, under my breath I said 'sorry' to the spirit of the old man, and I told him he could teach me a thing or two about the housework. However, I was diplomatic about the state of his ceilings; there were some enormous bulges showing signs of cracking, and over the landing, plaster was actually falling off. In the bedrooms, the furniture and the layers of mats and nailed-down lino made it impossible to inspect the floor. All the same, we made our offer; it was all we had and not enough. Chris saw his bank manager, who came out, looked at the cottage from the garden wall, and granted the loan. That fine solid heavy stone garden wall was worth the money by itself. There was a little money over, to pay the solicitor, and to do, as we thought, some ceiling repairs. Six weeks later the cottage was ours. We owned a fruitful little piece of England, we owned that panoramic prospect of Malvern's miniature mountains, and that plum tree, and that rhubarb.

We also owned that smelly cesspit and those ugly derelict sheds, and God alone knew what else in those ancient partitions and crumbling ceilings.

Syd was all for moving in at once. We had not had the money for a survey, and I was surprised at my cautious husband's reaction.

'Look,' he said, 'if that old fellow could live in it, we can live in it. Let's get in there and bodge it about later.'

I could not agree. I felt I had done my share of bodging, and what about that lavatory, and did he expect me to walk all round the house to get into my back-kitchen every time? He took some persuading, but eventually agreed to some repairs.

We already knew of an obliging jobbing builder, and we asked him for a quote to see to the ceiling bulges, and lent him a key. A couple of days later, he called on us, and his pallor was not entirely due to plaster dust. He was gingerly carrying some pieces of ancient wood. He let them drop on the yard and they practically disintegrated.

'These were so-called helping to hold up your so-called bedroom ceilings. I know, because I've just fell through it. You've got dry rot over there, missus.' He sounded slightly aggrieved. We had got dry rot, and woodworm, and rising damp, and floor joists rotting at the ends that had been reinforced by the boxed-in beam, actually a steel girder in disguise. It became clear, and we reluctantly accepted it, that the interior would have to be gutted. Chris had remarked that we had bought a knock-down bargain; well, the three of us now began to knock it down.

We started with the bake-oven. The summer, what we had of it that year, had come at last. We heaved and hammered, we pulled and prised. The veins came up in knots on Syd's forehead, and the purple flush spread behind his ears. I was wearing my surgical corset, but even so my back felt it had been jumped on in a rugby scrum. We carried the stones to the bottom of the garden. Exhausted, we looked at our work; we had made practically no impression. We knocked off for a cup of tea. 'Well,' I kept on saying for comfort, 'it *is* a lovely view, and it *is* our very own ground we're standing on.' If the way to Hell is paved with expletives and bad tempers, by the time we had got that ancient monument of a bake-oven down, and destroyed the old sheds, and ripped that old back-kitchen off the wall, we had widened that way a fair bit.

I doubt if we shall last long enough to cough up the dust we inhaled knocking down the ceilings and partitions. A couple of hundred years of accumulated debris sent us running and gasping for air while it settled down enough for us to see what we were doing. The mouldering nests of long dead rats and mice and birds came down with it, and we got an occasional bonk on the head from rotted timber, broken bricks, and stones. When all the rotten stuff had come away, there was enough left of the internal structure, like a noble skeleton, to gladden an artist's eye. Luckily the roof beams were of oak; the defeated worms had given up after their initial penetration, and all they needed was a good spray of Rentokil. Of cleft natural limbs roughly adzed, they were put together with haphazard beauty and formed a beautiful arch to support the roof. Had we been affluent enough, I would have left them exposed. Many of the limbs that had formed the partitions were sound inside, though as bent and twisted as an arthritic old man. We marvelled how they had stood the test of time. Their contours were so much better than the sawn timber that would replace them. Of the shell that we had left, thankfully the tiled roof was sound, and the thick stone walls would only need a damp course to cure their gout. It is a fact that a quart cannot be put into a pint pot. We began to doubt this as the piles of stone and rubbish mounted up in the garden. And that was only the start!

Well, there we were then. Four walls and a roof, nothing else of any use, piles of rubbish and almost no money. We had some top-level conferences about the next step. At this point Lady Luck stepped in. Sorry, I mean Person Luck. I had co-written a play which got accepted by the BBC, and I had an advance fee from the publishers. That was still nothing like enough for our new plans. We wanted a kitchen extension built on the back, and the inside of the cottage renewed and a flush toilet and shower included. We saw an architect who did us some drawings which were very good but pricey and knocked a sizeable hole in our diminishing nest-egg. We applied for a council grant; after all, this would really be a loan, for the rateable value would go up and gradually pay it all back. The council promised us a grant, and we went on through the bureaucratic maze of permissions. The all-clear came and we could make a start, but now it was winter and we were short of light and time as well as money.

Summing up all our resources, and some of these were merely hopes, we thought we might manage if we did all the labouring and digging ourselves. Chris and Syd studied the puzzling drawings and the metric measurements.

'Let's start with the hole for the plastic septic tank,' said Chris.

'Right,' said Syd. 'Let's go out and measure up.'

After a few minutes I heard a cry of anguish from Syd. 'Oh, no, it can't be!'

'Yes, it is,' said Chris, 'right under the plum tree!'

'No, no! We can't! We just can't lose that tree!'

'Well,' said Chris, 'you will. Think about it; the architect's right. That's the best place. In fact, you look, it's the only place!'

And it was. Soon afterwards the sacrilege was committed, with a borrowed chain saw, and the root was heaved out. Where that beautiful fruitful tree had stood soon became a miniature wasteland. We had had just one crop off our tree, a good crop of large clean tasty plums.

There was no means of getting a digger into there; the job had to be done with pick and shovel. Eighteen inches below the surface, the soft black top soil ended and the picks hit the stone. It was stone all the way then, and it was a gargantuan task to cut out a hole eight feet deep and seven feet square.

'It's too big,' moaned Syd, 'it's too bloody big.'

Chris was so patient. 'No, Dad, they must know what they're talking about.'

Sometimes I would leave what I was doing to see how they were getting on. As they leaned back sweating against the stone, their muddied faces grey with fatigue, Syd looked up at me. 'Dunno about one foot in the grave, Win, I've got two. Reckon I'm digging my own here. Do the sexton a favour, old butty, chuck the bloody stuff back over me.'

I promised him that when the system was finished he should have the very first flush! Reinforced by this honour, and some tea and cake and a smoke, he soon changed his tune. They became quite fond and proud of their hole. The helpful young builder whom we had contracted to do the skilled work came and looked at it and tended rather to pick holes in it. It did not quite suit.

'And when you've done that,' he said cheerfully, 'I'll show you where to dig your soakaway!'

During the week I cadged lifts over to the cottage and began to wield a pick-axe for the base of the extension and to wheel away barrow-loads of spoil to make a new path under the hedge. Surprisingly, my dodgy, sixty-four-year-old back, which could come out so often with a simple movement, stood up to this for weeks; and I stood up to the nagging I got from Chris for doing it.

We were reaping some of the rewards of parenthood. Our elegant dainty daughter came when she could, and showed a surprising ability to shift large stones, and push heavy-laden wheelbarrows, and even drive the pick-axe well into the stony subsoil. Our carpenter son Nick left his wife and family thirty miles away for several week-ends to do the woodwork inside the cottage, charging nothing for his labour, time and trouble, and losing what he could have earned at home. Eventually, he reluctantly agreed to accept something later, if and when we could afford it. Our daughters-in-law never complained. Even Richard, so far away, came to do what he could and fretted when he could not. Rome was not built in a day, and now we know why. Even in a tiny humble place like ours there was a great deal of dirty, hard and painful labour. Love will not hold stones together as well as mortar, but if old houses can be said to have a spirit, then ours will have a good one.

As soon as a plastered wall dried out enough, I got cracking on the decor. It was a crack-crack here and a crack-crack there from my arthritic joints as I knelt for the skirting boards, stretched for the ceilings, and contorted into the corners. I am sure that Picasso did not get any more happily absorbed with his brushwork. Unlike him, I stifled any original ideas, mostly from fear of possible reactions from the family, and simply laid on many coats of conventional pastels on the walls, and glossy white on all the woodwork. When the weather was dry and sunny, which was not very often, I tackled the piece of garden that was not covered in rubble. Barring the ravages of slugs, birds and blights we shall have peas and beans, and raspberries, gooseberries, and strawberries to pick.

Now our cottage is nearly ready. I should be, and am, grateful, yet each remaining day in our old home becomes in part a requiem. Rooted deeper than us are the clematis scrambling up its trellis for the sun, the climbing roses splashing the grey stone with their scarlet miracles, the honeysuckle by the staddle-stone caressing the old oak pillar, the lilac trees, and the flowering shrubs, vivid reminders of Father's Day and Mother's Day gifts from Jenny. The flower beds abound with shrubs presented by friends. I stand outside where every prospect pleases. I tread the familiar and beloved paths. To leave the old stone barns, our protectors from the icy east winds, seems like leaving old friends. I shall not see the seasons changing the leaves of the rowan tree. My own spring, summer and autumn behind me, now comes perhaps the winter of my discontent. After its icy finger has spent its grip we shall not come into fresh bud again. We must warm ourselves selecting and rekindling memories.

Start at the beginning; turn the pages; but one page will not turn. I see a seventeen-year-old girl running up the basement steps of a house. Upstairs in an attic room a servant's cap, apron, and print dress are folded over the end of an iron bedstead. For the next eight hours she can enjoy her own identity, free from the incarceration of servitude. Her legs are lithe and long; London spreads out before her. She too can now walk miles of the pavements hallowed by its history – she knows some from her schooldays – down the cobbled streets of the old city, where the carts once trundled to collect the plague-stricken dead, where ragged urchins once played in sewered gutters, muffin men rang their bells, and lavender, 'three bunches a penny', was proffered to the passers-by.

Standing on Westminster Bridge she can share her most daring thoughts with Old Father Thames. Oh yes! The Houses of Parliament are noble buildings, but what devious schemes are hatched under their roofs by the politicians inside them. Serve them right if Guy Fawkes came back and put a squib under some of them.

A cat may look at a king, and princes have been known to marry beggar-maids; so she can stand at the gates of Buckingham Palace and imagine she were Queen. And if she were, what knuckles she would rap, what bonfires she would order of servants' caps and aprons. God gave ten commandments; if she were Queen she could think of many more to whisper insistently in the King's ear! She turns up her snub nose at such wasted opportunities. Not that she feels poor herself; the wind has whispered hints of magic feasts in store for her. She has only pennies in her pocket, but her head is full of dreams.

BOOK 2

No Pipe Dreams for Father

A Washing Day

It was the worst day of the week. It was washing day and the signs were ominous. True the weather was dry, but it was worried by a spiteful icy wind. Mother was already in a lather carrying buckets of water through our little living-room to fill the copper in the dark back-kitchen. Old Auntie was irritated at the small amount of rainwater in the brick-lined covered well, outside the front door, that housed the precious water from our cottage's guttering.

Old Auntie was a washer of the old school, a believer in starching, blueing, and plenty of rinsing. Mother, who would work like a Trojan at the dollying and scrubbing, had no time for such laundering refinements. She was glad to get it washed at any price. Intolerant of each other's methods, they were as likely to come to the boil as the whites in the copper. They would have a row before the day was out, and treat each other to a list of their respective shortcomings in all directions.

The fire in the big black-leaded grate had the miseries, too, suffocated as it was by a huge black iron saucepan full of swede and potato peel and coarse cabbage, boiling to add to the bran in the bucket for the pigs' dinner. My sister had been packed off to school in a bad humour because the pair of drawers old Auntie had made her from some striped flannelette 'is showin' all down below me frock'.

My toddler brother was crying to be picked up. Mother, heavy with child, could hardly find room to squeeze with her loaded buckets between the table and chairs. The last thing she wanted was an uncooperative three-year-old who had soaked up the atmosphere of tension and irritability.

'Now get from under my feet,' Mam warned me as I stood by the copper while she tried to poke the fire beneath it to a blaze. Determined to help, I threw a pair of my sister's black woollen school stockings into the copper among the whites when Mam had to rush to the kitchen. The saucepan of pigs' food had tipped into the fire, and poor Auntie had not the strength in her rheumaticky old hands to straighten it.

'I'll get the little varmint outside,' said old Auntie, and wrapping me up in a parcel of old scarves, she shoved me outside with a couple of currants in a piece of paper. With a mutinous scowl I sat on top of the stone steps leading up to the garden. My nose was level with a group of early narcissi and their perfume drew it to their white-petalled beauty and the thin scarlet edgings of their trumpet centres. At three years old I felt 'drunk' for the first time, intoxicated by a little piece of nature's living artistry. The coldness of the stone step on my bum soon sobered me up and I crept indoors again.

Old Auntie had poured the saucepan of pigs' scraps into the bucket with the bran, where it waited to cool enough for Mam to take it to the pigs, and now she had got my little brother on her lap, soothing him to sleep. To sit over that steaming bucket would be just the job to warm my bum, I thought, and

I knew that her arthritics and having my brother on her lap would prevent her stopping me for a bit. I ignored her warnings and edged myself over the bucket. Just a little too far: my behind, and a whole lot more of me, got a warm-up as down I went into the mushy smelly contents. Wedged a prisoner, there I sat till Mam rushed out from the back-kitchen and truly hotted up my nether end with her soapy hands.

'That's all I be short of, a yup more washin',' Mam wailed as she peeled my clothes off. 'I know what we'll do,' said old Auntie, 'we'll shut the little toe-rag up in the front room.'

The front room was a narrow slip of a room which contained old Auntie's single bed, a mahogany chest of drawers with glass knobs – her finest piece of furniture – a small wooden table under the window, and a couple of chairs. There was also a hanging basket over the window, from which grew a trailing plant much cosseted and watered, and old Auntie's family Bible.

Re-dressed in what Mam could find me, I was pushed inside and the door locked. Kicking and banging brought no response. Presently, from the back-kitchen, I could hear the two women's voices raised in argument. All the washing in the copper had boiled to a dingy greyish-blue. Mam had fished out a pair of ruined, once-black, woollen stockings, and now each was blaming the other for putting them in with the whites. Suddenly Mam exclaimed, 'I'll warrant it was that little tartar in the front room what done it. I'll give 'er the good 'idin' of 'er life, that I will.' Mam's mood made Auntie act as defence counsel on my behalf till she had cooled off. 'Leave 'er be till we 'ave finished the weshin'! Anyroads, none on't'll need the blue bag for a bit.'

Unrepentant, my martyrdom increased. 'I'll rip your bloody plant down if you don't let me out,' I yelled as they came within earshot. 'Doosn't take any notice on 'er,' advised old Auntie; "er can't reach up to touch'n.'

I couldn't, but there was the chair to climb on, and the little table. Not quite tall enough, so I took the chair, and from it reached the Bible off the chest of drawers. It was a huge illustrated volume with metal clasps to shut it. I struggled and heaved it on to the table, then tip-toed to reach some of the trailing foliage and ripped at it with all my energy.

I knew I was in for a good hiding, and I meant to have my hide's worth! When they opened the door, I intended to get under the far corner of the bed. They would have to drag me out! My apprehension soon changed to hope when I heard the sound of Father's heavy pit boots across the yard. I put back my head, opened my mouth, and began to howl piteously.

'What's all this then? What's goin' on?' asked Father as he unlocked the door and picked me up in his dirty pit clothes. 'That's right,' said Mam sharply. 'Make me a bit more weshin', as though the little 'ussy ain't made me enough already.'

I sniffed and sobbed as tragically as an Ophelia, whilst Mam listed my misdemeanours of the day, interrupted by a little scream of horror from old Auntie. 'Me plant, me plant! 'Er 'ave ruined me plant!' I clung tightly to the refuge of Dad's neck whilst he inspected my horticultural rape.

'Now, doosn't thee fret, Aunt. I 'a' bin meanin' to prune thic plant f'r a long time. Thee see, 'im'll shoot out better'n ever now.' Father put me down and followed Mam into the back-kitchen. There was some whispering, and sounds of kissing going on, and Mam came out looking all soppy with her mouth twitching at the corners as it did when she had a nice secret all to herself.

Dad sat down at the table, took my little brother in the crook of one arm and me on the other knee, and began to eat his boiled-egg tea. Times were hard, but never in my life did I ever hear Dad complain about whatever Mam could muster up for him to eat. Enthroned on his lap I ate the bits of crust he broke from his own bread and butter and dipped in the yolk of his egg, a bit for my brother and a bit for me.

Naughty, undeserving, I drank the tea he poured into his saucer, but I remember . . . I remember . . .

Early One Morning

The feather bed, made from plucked chicken feathers by ancestral grannies, was warm and soft. My sister, little brother and I slept in its dents as cosy as beans in their fur-lined pods. Winter and summer, Mam had quite a job prising us out of it.

From our little back bedroom it was hard to see what season it was. The bottom of the tiny window rested on the garden level of the cottage above ours, and weeds often obstructed our minute view.

On school mornings our Mam kept calling up the stairs threatening us with the stick on our behinds to start out with, and very likely the same from the headmaster at the other end, if we were late for school. We became quite expert at measuring the irritation in Mam's voice, and we mostly timed our jumps out of bed just as she started up the stairs. We thought of a good ploy to fool her by banging our boots on the wooden floor without actually leaving the bed, but it did not always work!

On summer mornings, once up, it seemed just as good as being in bed. My sister and I washed first, in the little dark back-kitchen. Our little brother could take his time; he was still too young for a stint of water carrying before breakfast.

My sister had a proper yoke with a bucket at each end, and I had two wire-handled tins. Mam would be getting our breakfast, toast done in front of the fire bars and kept warm on the hob, while we went down the garden path, then through the gently sloping woodland, and down to the well at the side of the main road. Converging from other paths, we could hear the voices of other children on the same errand.

The pure, exhilarating morning air, the sunshine benediction, and the thought of the warm toast to come, plus our sleep-renewed energies, often drove us mad with joy. In those days, wild sweet days, we had the privilege of behaving like lunatics. We could yell our heads off, take running jumps into the lush green fern between the trees, make drums out of our buckets with banging sticks, and pause to look at all the wonders along the way.

'Look at this bloody yup under 'ere!' The flat upturned stone revealed a mass of sluggish wood-lice. Poor stupid things, hiding from the summer's day! Whatever did they do all day! Unlucky creatures. Lower the stone again, very carefully, not to squash them. Oh, how lucky I was, born me instead of a wood-louse!

'Eh, thee come 'n' zee wot I 'ave found. The cu'st 'a' some, there's plenty a growin' just 'ere.' We picked and relished the pale green juicy sharp-tanged leaves of something we knew as wood-sorrel. It often sharpened our imaginations as well as our taste buds.

'Coo, I just zeen a girt great fox over there, wi' blood round 'is chops. 'Im 'ave 'id behind thic tree over there.'

We knew it was not true, but in an ecstasy of terror we would run screaming down to the well. Fear-tightened throats

were soon eased with cupped handfuls of sparkling spring
water. In the mossy stream from the well overflow we observed
the progress of the black spot in the frog spawn, via the tad-
pole, to the endearing ugly croaking frog; a fairy prince, of
course, under a witch's spell.

Water slopped out of our containers as we raced to pluck
the rare white foxglove amid the myriad pinky-purple ones
growing among the ferns. These special ones were for Teacher.

By the time I heaved my tins on to the back-kitchen table,
the water content was well down.

Toast in hand, and off up the hill to school. Spring brought
the leggy lambs running up to their mothers for short and
urgent sucking sessions. We saw the afterbirths, we knew that
hens laid eggs and that baby pigs came out of the mother sow,
but we never doubted that we were young, God-like creatures,
mysteriously deposited under the gooseberry bush to be
brought to our mothers in the midwife's bag. How I scolded
Mam on one occasion for just lying in bed all day with our
new-born baby when she should have been getting our tea.
That she must be there to keep him warm seemed a poor
excuse.

Autumn brought the fluttering leaves, piled by the winds
into banks of confetti to jump and roll in and scatter back to
the winds.

Winter seeped through our boots, aggravating our itching
chilblains, but they were soon forgotten in the snowball pelt-
ing with our 'enemies'. Icicles made lovely lolly-ices to suck,
but summer mornings were the best of all, mornings to recap-
ture when I listen now to the evocative genius of Beethoven's
'Pastoral' Symphony, taking me back to the well-springs of my
childhood, to fetching water from the well.

No Pipe Dreams for Father

I stood with uncharacteristic patience whilst Mam tied up my
pinny into a sort of pocket, put old Auntie's pension book in
it, then made it extra safe with two large safety-pins. I was
going on a very important errand and well aware of it!

'Now mind,' old Auntie warned me, 'if thee dost get playin''
about and lose me pension book I'll never let thee 'elp to
scrape out me Nestlé's milk tin agyun.'

It was an unnecessary caution; I had every intention of
making a sedate bee-line down the rutted track to the post-
office-cum-shop at the bottom of our village. I intended to
keep well to the forest side of the path to resist the distracting
temptations of other children engaged in the ordinary pastime
of playing. I was six years old and for the first time trusted
alone for this very important mission.

I had old Auntie's livelihood in my pinny; her old age
pension book from which she could draw five whole shillings
a week. It was a fortune – even old Auntie thought so and was
apt to give as much praise to Lloyd George as she did to the

Almighty for His munificence. She sang God's praises every Sunday and dratted the Devil for the rest of the week.

It was fair shares really, considering that a life of hard work, absolute honesty, and much kindness to others, had left her at seventy-six years old a housebound arthritic with only enough savings put by to 'putt I under the ground dacent'. Rigidly independent of spirit, God knows how she would have managed had Lloyd George not come just in time with the five shillings a week old age allowance.

Fairly speaking, she could have accepted the little sustenance she required from us, for she had shared her home with Father from the day he had got married. We children had broken many of her treasured ornaments, kicked the legs off her best table, piddled on her feather beds and trodden on her rheumaticky toes.

Mother had kept her lap filled with a succession of babies to be hushed and comforted to sleep. Father revered her and we children adored her; this squared our books, for never by the slightest imputation did she make *us* feel indebted to her.

Too crippled to walk down to the post office to draw her pension herself, she entrusted this task to Father, and on this particular Friday afternoon I was going to meet him at the post office on his way home from his early shift at the pit.

Friday was a very special day for us children. It was pay day! However short work was at the pit, Mam always insisted Dad must have his shilling a week pocket-money. Ninepence of this went on two packets of his beloved Stanfield tobacco, twopence on a slab of marzipan toffee for us children, and a penny on liquorice all-sorts for Mam and old Auntie.

Waiting outside the post office provided me with a lovely extra treat. In its little shop window was a shelf with a beautiful baby doll priced at half-a-crown. It had been there a very long time. Flanking the doll on each side was a doll's tea-set in a cardboard box and a set of doll's furniture in another cardboard box, each priced at sevenpence. I was pleased no-one could afford to buy them, for it meant that I could 'pretend' play with them. Magic worked in those days. I 'got' them out of the window and sat down on the grassy bank outside to 'nurse' the doll and 'arrange' the furniture using little stones as substitutes – then I pretend-drank my tea from the tiny cups, holding my little finger crooked in the manner my aunties in service told me their mistresses did.

It was a wonderful treat, too, when I had Father's company all to myself. Father was a bottomless source of fascinating information, and all us children loved him to distraction. However, I got so engrossed playing with my pretend toys it was only when I noticed Father's mud-caked pit boots near me that I sprang up for my pit-grimed hugs.

I marched into the post office with him, my snub nose stuck even farther into the air; after all we were cash customers with a whole shilling to spend!

When we got home Mam shared out the marzipan toffee, and magnanimously letting her have Dad's company I ran out to play – out into the beautiful green forest when school holidays and summer days lasted for ever. Yet winter came with its ills and chills, thinning us out with its icy brittle fingers, etching for ever on the memory a trail of black figures bent against the cruel snow-flecked east winds carrying a coffin in front of them, and the matching mourning of leaden skies, the creaking moans of dark leafless trees, and the black tread marks in the snow. That winter I came close to the edge of 'the pitty hole' myself.

*

Though by no means a particularly sunny-natured child, my persistent grizzling one evening attracted Father's notice before he went off to the night shift. He picked me up on his lap, felt my burning forehead, and noticed my heavy eyes and quickened breathing with some concern.

'Mark my words, thic young 'un be a-sickening fir zummat. The best place for 'er is bed an' a bit o' quiet.'

He put a brick to warm in the oven, helped Mam to make a bed for me in their room and lit a fire in its tiny grate. When the fire had warmed the bedroom and the hot brick my bed, Mam gave me a washdown mustard bath and covered me with extra blankets borrowed from a kindly neighbour; my worried father went out in the darkness to walk to the pit.

When he came home in the early hours of the morning I was worse.

Father's only culinary achievement was invalid's sop and he proceeded to make me some. He poured some boiling water on a piece of bread in a basin, beat it to a cream, adding sugar, a little knob of butter and a drop of milk. When my normally greedy little stomach refused to touch the delicacy, alarm set in.

Mam made some invalid drink – boiling water poured on a piece of toast and allowed to get cold. My siblings went to bed with hushed voices and tip-toe manner.

'I be goin' for the doctor,' said Father.

For the doctor's and pride's sake two shillings off the arrears we owed him had to be multiple-borrowed from our impoverished neighbours, and Father ran through the woods to the doctor's house before going on his night shift.

Old Auntie, who had given up the struggle of getting upstairs to sleep, made a tortured ascent to sit with me whilst Mam did her evening chores and attended to the baby.

The doctor came, shook his head on my account, advised that the crisis would come shortly and my chance of surviving it was nil. His visit did not register on me; a black coma kept sucking me down. When I opened my eyes it was to unrecognisable surroundings. I could hear far-away voices and someone crying softly – 'I be afeared we be gwine to lose the little wench, Maggie, fir I never knowed anybody as bad as 'er is to get over it – and to think that only a couple o' days ago 'er was threadin' me needle for me as right as rain.' I could see no-one, only weird terrible shadows on the wall and a pair of fiery tiger's eyes gleaming in the corner ready to pounce on me and eat me up. I must have screamed. Old Auntie pounded the floor with her walking stick. Mam rushed upstairs carrying the oil-lamp. Some of the shadows disappeared, the tiger's eyes became the fire's reflection on the toe caps of a pair of treasured boy's boots someone had given Mam for my little brother to grow into. Mam had kept them shined and polished on the bamboo what-not in the corner of the bedroom.

'Dad, Dad, I want our Dad,' I begged from this little oasis of lucidity. Dad would make the witches' shadows go, and the tigers, and save me from the black pit that kept sucking me down. Several times I struggled to consciousness to see Dad's face – but he was still down in his own black pit hacking on his knees for the coal that nearly kept our bodies and souls together.

'Dad, Dad, oh I want our Dad' – and he was there – allowed straight up to the invalid's bedroom in his pit dirt. That dear kind face with the crinkles at the corner of his eyes as he held my hands in his pit-calloused ones. I was safe now. Dad was home.

'There there, my little wench, Fayther's wum, an' I'll stop 'ere till thee bist better – now mind thee'st got to make up

thee mind to get better – for who's goin' to putt the taters in
the dib 'oles for 'er old Dad, an' who's goin' to play wi' the
babby whilst Mam do get on wi' the washin'? – now thee take
a sip o' thee Mam's drink and goo to a nice nap and I'll stop
'ere by thee bed.'

I took some spoonfuls from him whilst Mam fetched him
up a cup of tea.

In the morning the doctor was amazed to find me still in
the land of the living.

I had survived, but only just. I could make no headway
with appetite or strength despite all the love and attention
lavished upon me. My ten-year-old sister filled jars of flowers
to put by my bed, Mam got little luxuries she couldn't afford
to tempt my palate, but best of all I loved it when Dad came
up to sit with me, to tell me stories or just to sit and read
himself from one of the books a pit butty of his used to lend
him.

One Friday, Dad came up with a cup and spoon in his hand
and an expression of great pleading in his eyes. Beastly little
daughter I must have been, for this was an ominous sign. Dad
was a great believer in herbal medicines and often brewed
his own from the herbs he gathered. I thought they tasted
terrible and my pig-headed nature made me the most uncooperative of swallowers, but I noticed what I thought was a
book wrapped in brown paper in Dad's pocket. Perhaps Dad
was going to sit with me for a long time.

With the patience of Job, and his own incredible gifts of
love and encouragement, he got me to take eight spoonfuls of
his little brew; then to bolster the undeserved praise he lavished upon me, he drank the dregs from the cup himself.

Then from his pocket he took the brown paper parcel, but
it wasn't a book! He unwrapped it and put it on my bed. I

could hardly believe my eyes. It was the box of doll's furniture out of the post office window!

'There then, that's fir bein' a good little wench. Now thee try and start yuttin' a bit better and then thee'lt be able to get up and goo out on the tump to play to thee 'eart's content wi' all the t'other young 'uns. Now afore I do go out to do a bit o' gyardening I'll 'a' me a little nap.' It was a little nap. As soon as he woke up it was always Father's habit to feel round for his beloved old pipe. He did so now, put it in his mouth, then took his baccy tin out of his pocket. There was nothing in it. He put it and his pipe back in his pocket, then sat sadly staring through the window.

I remembered – today was Friday, pocket-money day! Sevenpence for doll's furniture, twopence for marzipan toffee, a penny for liquorice all-sorts – there was only twopence left!

I looked at my Dad, and I looked at my present, and I wished that doll's furniture was where old Auntie sent the 'tarmenting Devil', all the way to Halifax.

The Rivals

They had been rivals in love. If 'Hell hath no fury like a woman scorned' it has no greater rivalry than when two females set their caps at the same man! In the case of Vernie and Lydie, whilst enjoying the flattery of their attentions, the young man in question had been smart enough to escape his dilemma by marrying someone else altogether.

This mutual loss did not bring them together. Each blamed the other, and though they eventually acquired a husband each, they remained bitter enemies, ever trying to outdo each other, especially in the matter of dress.

Both were talented needlewomen. Chapel Anniversary was the highlight of their year and to outshine each other on that day was the summit of their ambitions.

Paris has its yearly bonanza of Haute Couture, and fifty-odd years ago our chapel had its fashion parade, too, on that important Sunday. Any girls lucky enough to be home from service on their annual holiday paraded the finery their hard-earned shillings had bought them for the delectation of the village boys, but the 'stars' of the show were always Vernie and Lydie. Much to Lydie's chagrin, Vernie was always voted the winner. 'Wonder wot they two show-offs'll turn up in this time?' was a frequent conjecture of the village women who could not afford such indulgences.

At seven years old, ribbons and laces, frills and bows met with my undiluted approval and a determination to indulge in them when I grew up and could earn some money. I was always happy when chance permitted me to sit on the corner of Vernie's fender and watch her sewing. Even her rag-mats had a glamour. She didn't just poke the bits of rag through the sack at random; she patterned the colours and once earned a spate of childish praise from me when she fashioned a black cat in the middle of one from scraps cut from a dead old woman's skirt. But it was her drawers and chemises I especially envied; on the legs of the former she threaded pink ribbon through slotted borders and added frills of lace. Her washing day was 'a sight f'r sore eyes', as one man remarked – the women were not so charitable. 'I bet they never even go on 'er arse; 'er do just dip 'em in the wayter an' 'ang 'em on the line to show off.' No doubt the shape that Vernie possessed to fill them, which went with a very flirtatious pair of eyes in a pretty face, didn't endear her to them either!

Lydie also was no mean looker and she had the advantage of a crowning glory of naturally curly auburn hair. Her luck, however, didn't last as far as her legs. They were fat and shape-less, with ankles that hung over the high-heeled shoes she wore on Suudays.

Having little sensitivity about how my 'social calls' were regarded, on occasions I took up my perch on Lydie's fender too, thus one summer becoming the innocent decoy in Vernie's underhand machinations.

'D'you know wot!' Vernie said to me one day a few weeks before Anniversary Sunday.

'D'you know wot!' she repeated, her eyes shining, hands clasped together in apparent ecstatic anticipation – 'I be going to make meself a real classy dress f'r the anniversary, summat different. I be sick o' bright colours, I be goin' to wear black: a black velvut frock trimmed wi' black braid – I shall 'ave long sleeves to look different, an' a nice little close-fittin' black 'at an' I shall wear me pearls, an' very 'igh-'eeled black patunt shoes.'

I was rather less than enthusiastic at this description. I thought black was the awfulest colour to wear and only fit for funerals.

Vernie enthused on – 'Wot made I think on't was a picture of a actress – on a postcard; 'er 'ad lovely ginger 'air and thic black frock 'er was wearin' set it off summat lovely. I read somewhere as well that all the smart 'igh up women be goin' into black – they do reckon bright colours be too common. Oh I do wish I 'ad ginger wavy 'air, but I shall wear black just the same an' I'll bet I shall look smarter than all the t'others put together!'

My hitherto unqualified admiration for Vernie's taste, plus her persuasive enthusiasm, nearly brainwashed me into thinking it a good idea; she went on so much about it I knew the details off by heart before my belly told me it was time to go home.

I had to go by Lydie's cottage farther up the hill, near the chapel. I was passing her gate and got quite a surprise when she beckoned me inside from her doorstep.

'I've got a bit o' custard left in a basin if you'd like to yut it up?' Though my belly at that time was my god, and I took every opportunity to send it down an offering, it was ingrained in us village children not to accept from neighbours, who in general had pantries as bare as our own; but the temptation of custard, a rare treat for Sunday tea only in our house, and the fact that Lydie had no children to feed, made my scruples on this score give in without a murmur. 'Come on, set down,' Lydie said in a most kindly manner. She showed me a butterfly she was embroidering on a corner of a pillow case – the subject got round to sewing, then to the Anniversary Sunday – then to the problem of what to wear for that grand occasion?

Without much prompting, and automatically imitating Vernie's fervent manner, I told her all about Vernie's plan to wear black. 'Vernie said – ooh 'er wish 'er'd got ginger 'air 'cos then 'er'd look like that beautiful actress in the photo 'er got the idea from. Ginger 'air like you got,' I added artlessly.

I had finished the custard, and was further astounded with a piece of bread and jam. Meantime Lydie skilfully got all the details of Vernie's forthcoming outfit from my mouthy chatter.

To augment the pittance they could get from their husbands' meagre earnings both Vernie and Lydie tramped the surrounding country in the autumn to earn their pin and needle money. They gathered acorns at 2d a bucket under the forest oaks for a local pig-keeper, and had their own blackberry territories. The 'Jam Man' came in the evenings to the main road at the bottom of the village with his horse and cart to buy this wild fruit. He was a proper Shylock; having no competition, he paid very stingily for his wares – he may not have got his pound of flesh but I reckon he got pints of blood from the scratches these two gathered in their pickings.

*

It was a perfect, very warm sunny Sunday on Anniversary day. Pretty outfits for me were still a figment of my imagination; meanwhile I must put up with whatever Mother could muster for me to wear, being one of five children. No matter, I had my bit of glory to come; ever ready to show off, and blessed with a good memory, I was always given a 'spot' in the proceedings reciting a poem. We children who sang or recited sat on raised seats facing the congregation.

The chapel was soon packed, but the preacher, a local man, well knew that two of his flock had not yet arrived, so he hung about in the pulpit. Vernie was hanging about, too, crouched down behind her gate waiting to see Lydie emerge from hers. Lydie had been impatiently waiting for Vernie to go past. She looked at her clock – it was no good, she would have to start out.

Funereally garbed, hobbling painfully up the rain-rutted path ('Like a pig on stilts,' as Vernie gloated afterwards) – Lydie was hot, bothered and perspiring in her black velvet before she was half-way to the chapel. When she was sure Lydie had got as far as the chapel door and the point of no return, Vernie started out.

What eyebrows I had shot up under my fringe when I saw Lydie hobble in and sink into the only vacant space at the back of the chapel. I thought she looked a miserable sight, and serve her right for copying Vernie's idea; for now the penny had dropped as well as the custard.

It was the turn of my big mouth next. It opened wide enough for all the trapped flies beating their wings against the chapel panes to come in for a flight, when Vernie made her entrance.

She was a vision in a cream silk sleeveless dress, a wide-brimmed cream straw hat trimmed with a peachy-pink rose and ribbons, cream dainty shoes and, crowning touch, a cream silk parasol, sprayed with roses to match the one on her hat! No black for her! The male organist had kept his seat right in the front row warm for her; he kept other things warm for her, if local gossip was anything to go by.

Lydie's face went a quite dreadful red that clashed with her ginger hair. The look she gave Vernie's back view ought to have set fire to her rival, and the one she gave me wasn't suitable at all for the chapel either!

Aches and Pains

When I was a child, as they aged, the old people in our village drew up their chairs nearer the fire, accepting their physical deterioration with a fatalistic stoicism, waiting for the Almighty to take them in His own good time. The doctor's pills and potions had not then superseded the powers of the Almighty. God and His angels were still up in the sky watching over them.

Sophisticated technology had not yet sent men soaring to the moon, destroying their comfortable illusions.

They still fought sickness with all the means at their disposal. Pneumonia might be cured with linseed-meal poultices on the chest – raw sheep's kidneys tied round the feet till the kidneys went putrid, drawing the poison out – and boiled onion liquor to ease the throat. Often these 'cures', bolstered by love and encouragement, worked!

When the doctor diagnosed consumption, heads were shaken and the slow heartbreak began. When it was 'galloping consumption' the heartbreak came quicker.

*

Sonny Banes was only eighteen years old when the horrified whispers began to circulate that "im 'ad got it'.

The scourge could not have hit a less likely victim. Sonny had always been regarded as 'a regular caution', a cheerful extrovert ready for any mischievous fun afoot. He brought rosy blushes to the girls' cheeks with his welcome ribaldry, and he was a very good-looking boy, too.

At fourteen years old he cheerfully plodded to the pit in his heavy boots with the village men and other boys. A bit of 'chestiness' was so common he wasn't especially noticed. When opportunity gave Sonny the chance for a bit of idling underground the older men laughingly observed he was the exception to that old saying, 'One bwoy'll do one bwoy's work – two bwoys together'll do 'alf a bwoy's work – and dree bwoys together be nothin' but a 'indrance.'

His bouts of coughing and obvious exhaustion were put down to 'the bwoy's outgrowin' 'is strength findin' 'is road to monhood'. When, however, the ebullient Sonny kept lagging behind them on the walk home ('Me bloody boot laces be undone agyun') sympathy turned to alarm. 'Better take thic bwoy to the doctor f'r a tonic and 'ave a check-up, missus,' they advised his widowed mother.

'I zid 'em comin' back dru the 'ood on their way wum from the doctor's, and thic 'oman was carryin' twenty more years on 'er shoulders than wot 'er started out wi'.'

The doctor had broken the news to Sonny's mother that he had the symptoms of advanced consumption.

She made him up his bed downstairs by the fire and fed him with the best at her disposal augmented by 'a bit o' this and a drap o' that' from sympathetic neighbours.

Poor Sonny's youthful contours dropped to skeletal proportions, but between his blood-flecked coughing bouts he was as cheerful as ever, flirting outrageously with any female from nine to ninety who popped in to see him.

He was fond of my father, who visited Sonny for a chat and a game of snakes and ladders whenever he could spare the time. One fine mild day Sonny made up his mind that he would come down to our house to visit Father for a change, and he was determined to make it on his own; it was all of three hundred yards. When Father heard this he got out our wooden chairs and asked some of the neighbours to place one every few yards for Sonny to have a rest. Then Father resisted the impulse to give the boy his arm – 'Let 'un come on 'is own if 'im can make it,' he begged us.

Eventually Sonny got to the chair in our little courtyard. Mam poked the fire to a blaze under the kettle to give Sonny 'a nice 'ot cup o' tay' – and cut him a cheese sandwich from Dad's pit rations.

When he could get the strength, Sonny accepted the cup of tea placed on another chair near him. He was too weak to hold the cup for long, and he shook his head refusing the sandwich – 'It's a waste o' your victuals, missus,' he grinned, 'for 'tis no sooner in one end than 'tis out o' the t'other. There's a pretty wench thee bist gettin'.' (I wasn't, I was as plain as a pikestaff.) 'Thee 'urry up an' get old enuff f'r me to take thee to the pictures.'

Sonny couldn't stay long; Father walked behind him between his chair-rests and let him totter up unaided to his own cottage door.

Sonny never took me to the pictures. We never saw Sonny again. A week later his neighbour called asking if we could spare a couple of coppers towards a collection to help his mother with the funeral expenses.

Jarge

Normally, simple old Jarge was as placid and untemperamental as the sheep lying under the trees in the surrounding forest chewing their cud. After a few days of uncharacteristic grumpiness from the old man, one of his butties asked, 'Wot's the matter, old 'un? 'Ast thee bin gettin' out o' the wrong side o' the bed lately?'

One worthy who could have been a born medico in more affluent conditions hit the nail on the head with his diagnosis of Jarge's trouble.

''Ow long is it since thee'st went to the mon 'ole, old butty?'

The 'mon 'ole' was a natural hole in the forest, well hidden by surrounding undergrowth, where the men went for nature's calls and left the bucket privies in the gardens for the use of women and children.

Jarge rubbed the stubble on his chin and shook a negative head until enquiries had gone back a week.

'That's the trouble with thee, old 'un; thee bist bunged up – I reckon a lump o' thy old 'oman's bread pudding 'a' got stuck an' caun't goo up or down – thee'lt vill up wi' gas like the cows do. Thee goo to the doctor's tonight an' tell 'im thee bist constipated.'

Like most simple souls, Jarge was apt to do what he was told. That evening he turned his muffler cleanest side out and walked the two miles to the doctor's surgery.

'And what is it that's troubling you, Mr Dobbins?'

'I be constipated, zir.'

'I see, when did you last pass anything?'

'On the road 'ere, zir.'

'And what was it like?'

'A 'oss an' cyart, zir.'

A bottle of senna mixture and a few sprints to the 'mon 'ole' and old Jarge was chewing his twist of baccy again as contented as the sheep. He outlived the doctor, and when he was in his nineties the doctor's successor, by now an elderly man himself, humorously suggested to the old man that the only way he could send him on his way was to shoot him!

A Bargain

When old Jarge had a couple of coppers to spare he toddled down to the pub at the bottom of the village, there to reflect on the vocabular glory of his peers. He loved to pick up what he considered smart sayings to pepper his own limited conversation. When the two Wills cousins were arguing about the selling and buying price of a young pig, Jarge was all ears.

'Dree pound I do want for thic pig, and 'im's wuth every penny on't.'

'Two pound ten I'll gi' thee, an 'im byunt wuth a grunt more.'

'Dree pounds.'

'Two pound ten.'

'Dree pounds!'

'Two pound ten!'

And on and on.

'Tell thee what then, I'll split the difference. Give I two pound fifteen.'

'Done.'

'Two 'alf pints o' zider, missus, and charge 'em to thic Shylock,' demanded the seller.

Split the difference! Split the difference! The saying sounded very grand in old Jarge's ears. One evening some time later, he went into the pub with a dead cockerel he had fattened up in the coop. It was a fine fat bird.

'I'll gi' thee one-and-six for thic 'un,' offered one of the men.

'I'll gi' thee one-and-nine fer'n,' said another.

'I'll make it two bob,' and the offers went on mounting up until the grand sum of half-a-crown waited for the hammer of Jarge's fist.

Blue eyes a-twinkle with his own importance, chewing hard on his cud of tobacco, rubbing the grey stubble on his chin with the effort of getting his punch-line in the right order round his tongue, old Jarge kept the last bidder waiting. Looking round his eager audience and savouring his moments of drama, he brought his fist down hard enough to spill drops of cider from the glasses of the more parsimonious drinkers. Then Jarge got it out. 'Split the difference,' he boomed. 'Give I one-and-drippence.'

'Avin' a Goo

'Thee 'ave a goo, old butty' is the Forester's way of expressing encouragement. Fifty-odd years ago, when I was a child, the lack of necessary skill did not deter a Forester from trying to help another in distress, even a bit of dentistry on one occasion!

One day when there was no work in the pit, Joe, Tim and Albert were squatting on the grassy slope outside Joe's house, when Dan lurched up, moaning and groaning and shaking his head from side to side.

'Wot's the matter, old 'un?'

'The bloody jawache, that's wot's the matter; it be got that bad I'd be willin' for ern o' you to chop me yud off wi' a 'atchut.'

'That's a bugger that is, I've 'ad some on't in my time,' sympathised Joe. 'But I'll tell thee wot: if thee bist willin' I'll take thic tooth out for thee.'

"Ow?"

'Wi' me pinchers as I do castrate the animals wi'. Tim and

Albert can 'old thee down, an' I'll pull on the bugger till 'im do come out. We wun't take no notice o' thee 'ollerin'; it'll be wuth the agony for to putt thee out o' such misery.'

Desperate, Dan agreed. With four hard knees on the chest, and two pairs of pit-toughened arms holding him down, and a mouthful of castrating pinchers, Dan had little chance to get a holler out, but a cry of triumph came from Joe as he fell over backwards on to the grass.

'Thee'lt be all right now, old butty; I 'a' got the bugger!'

His enthusiasm was not shared by the patient. Dan continued to roll his stricken head, and after poking about in his bloodied mouth, though grateful for the well-meant intentions, he said sadly, 'My jaw do veel wurs than ever; I be afeared thee'st took the wrong bugger out, Joe.'

Big Ambitions

I could see my auntie was nearly crying when she kissed us all goodbye before going back to her job in domestic service. All my five aunts who lived next door in Granny's cottage cried when their holidays came to an end. From what I heard them saying it was horrible being a servant. True, they came home smelling all scenty and powdered my nose with little pages from a paper powder booklet, and they got three-and-sixpence a week wages to buy pink silk stockings and pretty blouses, but I knew they would much rather be at home.

I was nearly five years old and was well aware that when I left school I, too, would have to go into service.

I hated the thought of leaving my Mam and Dad, and the family and our village, so I began to lay my own future plans.

I decided I would *not* go into service. I would go to work daily at the village pub, where I knew the landlady paid two shillings a week for doing the scrubbing and cleaning, with a bread-and-cheese dinner thrown in. I would live in Miss Phillips's cottage at the end of our garden. Miss Phillips was already old; she would have to be dead or go in the work-house by the time I left school.

I loved babies, so I planned to have a dozen – six boys and six girls – all bastards, as I had heard the grown-ups say. Bastards were very easy to come by, and I knew you didn't have to bother with a husband for that sort. I was puzzled why the women bothered with husbands, they were often so grumpy about them afterwards. I wouldn't mind one like my Dad, but of course he was a very special sort of man: there wasn't another like him in the whole world.

I hated cheese, so I would bring home my cheese for the twelve babies and I could feed them on the forty-eight half-penny ice-creams my two shillings would buy. I kept my plans all to myself – until the day Miss Gabb called.

Mam was emptying the slops between the cabbages when she spotted Miss Gabb approaching our gate. Mam rushed in all in a tiz, taking off her sack apron, removing the nappies from the fireguard and the newspaper cloth from the table. 'Quick,' she urged me. 'Goo up to Mrs Brown's and ask 'er if 'er can lend me a bit o' sugar – 'tis no good askin' Granny. 'Er've let me 'ave 'alf o' wot 'er's got in 'er sugar basin. Tell Mrs Brown 'er shall 'ave it wi'out fail when our grocery do come tomorrow.'

Dear Mam, she loved to put the rare visitor a cup of tea, especially such a grand caller as Miss Gabb.

I put on my pig-headed, uncooperative, bribe-demanding expression.

'If you can borrow me a bit o' sugar you can 'ave a suck o' the babby's sugar teat when 'er's gone.'

It was bribe enough – Mam sometimes kept the baby quiet with a spoonful of dampened sugar tied in a piece of clean rag.

I got the sugar from kind Mrs Brown and I had the gump-tion to take it into the back-kitchen behind my back. I had long sensed that Mam did not like to advertise her poverty in these circumstances.

Miss Gabb was sitting by the fire, and I took up my perch on the corner of the big steel fender to give her one of my thorough optic going-overs.

How prim and neat she was: snow-white blouse collar over her navy-blue costume, hair drawn back into a tight little bun, and black shoes as shiny as brand-new ones – all very suitable for a prudish middle-aged spinster who taught at Sunday School, had a preacher for her father and who was of independent means. She began to wilt a bit under my intense scrutiny and tried to break my concentration by asking me when would I be starting school and what I intended to do when I grew up. So I told her all about my twelve bastard babbies, my job at the pub and my intention not to be bothered with a husband.

She went very red in the face and slopped her tea into the saucer. Mam went red, too; they didn't share my enthusiasm at all. Granny seemed quite pleased – I could see her trying to keep her mouth straight, and her soft child-rearing belly shaking under her pinny.

She cut off a lump of the bread pudding she had brought in as an excuse to be in on the *tête-à-tête* and 'cup o' tay'. Holding it in front of my nose like a carrot to a donkey, she got me outside.

''Ere you be, my wench, thee'st better goo off to play with the t'others afore thee'st put some o' thy ideas in Miss Gabb's yud, and I shouldn't hurry back if I was thee – I don't think thee mam's in a very good 'umour.'

I went down the path well pleased with my bread pudding, but very puzzled about the frequent oddness of grown-ups' reactions to my bright ideas.

The Meeting

Only those too old, too ill or too young did not come to the Meeting. People came from the outlying villages and hamlets to converge at the Hall, a plain oblong building used for the social activities of the community.

This particular evening it was not for pleasure – we wouldn't be laughing at Mr Stott's comic recitations, or, come to that, the rather unappreciated singing of the grand local lady contralto.

We were going for a scolding – at least our dads, brothers, uncles and granddads were, so it amounted to the same thing.

The menfolk were miners – miners who had dared to come out on strike rather than take a cut in their already pitifully inadequate wages.

Now the bosses and their managers were holding this meeting to remind these common, two-a-penny sparrows how grateful they should be for the crumbs thrown to them from the rich man's table. They were not a lot in number. As benefited their superior social and economic status, they sat on the stage looking down at their crowded, standing audience.

How marked was the contrast! Proper suits, starched white shirts, gold watch-chains across well-filled bellies. Their ladies, grand in Sunday-type hats, fur-trimmed coats, well-shod feet and plump pink faces.

In the audience it was mufflers and caps, down-trodden boots, the gaunt, grey, underground faces of the men, and mostly pale, under-nourished faces of the women and children. Chesty coughs punctuated the waiting silence.

One of the men on the stage stood up, cleared his throat in an important sort of manner, and advised the men to go back to work – *or else*. Time has dimmed his speech but not his pompous, condescending, down-his-nose attitude; but time has not dimmed the expression on my father's face as he listened to this rhetoric. Though Father was a great man in my eyes, physically he was a slight, pale-faced man, who had of late made extra holes in his leather belt to hold up his shabby trousers where his stomach should have been.

He looked at the speaker – then his eyes travelled round the audience, and the compassion in them came from what, for want of another word, we call the soul.

Father was gifted with the sort of exceptional intelligence that made him a good man – a widely-read man, a thinker, slow in his judgements and willing to see both sides of an argument – and Father had made up his mind now which side he stood on.

The cruel economic systems geared to profit instead of human needs, man's foolish inhumanity to man culminating in wars and poverty, man's capacity for self-destruction, was a burden he carried in his mind that often found him staring sadly into space. He had his blessings, too – a great sense of wonder and appreciation for all the beauty that came his way, from the flora and fauna in the forest around us to the genius of artists, composers and scientists, to the very Earth itself.

He waited until the speeches from the stage had finished. The down-trodden audience had sighed and coughed on, seeming visibly to shrink in their hopelessness. Then Father raised his hand to ask questions. Again the words are dimmed by time, but never their effect.

At first this upstart miner got some sarcastic comments – but, quietly, Father continued to demand answer for question.

Soon their pomposity and bluster were pierced by his shafts of truth – it was they who began to look small, to squirm, to fidget, to get angry.

A change came over the audience. They had got a voice – an advocate the bosses had not the means to put down. Dull eyes shone, heads were lifted, shoulders squared to the world – they were men again, and as one man they called 'no' to their oppressors' demands. Belts would be pulled even tighter, for their future's sake women and children must suffer further, their backs were against the wall but now they had a pillow to support it.

During Father's seven-year victimisation from the pits these men did not forget us.

Father was killed in the pit in 1945, aged 57 years. He did not live to see the affluent miner, or the garage, car and bathroom a common-place in workers' homes, but I wonder, if he were still alive, would he smile wryly to read as I did the other day that one per cent of the population still have control of eighty per cent of the nation's wealth!

Entrance and Departure

In our village, life was simple and 'near the knuckle', food for an extra mouth was hard to come by, yet it could not diminish the glory of each new birth.

The stairs to the bedroom might only be of scrubbed wood, but the new father, perhaps too many times over, would tiptoe up them reverently to marvel at the tiny fingers he could curl around one of his pit-calloused ones.

'Well done, my wench, that's a little beauty thee'st got there!' would be thanks enough for the tired face on the pillow.

However long the black angel hovered, the deaths of even the oldest inhabitants got their share of sighs and tears.

'I be afeared 'er time be come,' the bed-watchers whispered out of hearing of old Ginny, when the indomitable old woman could no longer infuse the strength of her spirit into her worn-out body and took to her bed.

Resigned at last, she saved her gasping breath to talk over

old times with the old faces still around her. There was no need to dip into the carefully hoarded pittance, saved 'to putt I down dacent', for a doctor's diagnosis.

'We'd better get Edie Paine to come and 'ave a look at 'er; thic 'oman can see death in anybody's eyes as soon as it be knockin' on the door.'

'Ay, an' 'er can see by a 'oman's eyes when a babby is on the way, sometimes afore the 'oman be sure of it 'erself.'

Edie Paine, widow, washerwoman, midwife and layer-out of the dead, dispenser of goose-grease for the chest, herb-teas for the colic, and a trusted friendly ear for private troubles. When called she went to old Ginny's bedside.

Honest kindly eyes looked into honest eyes.

'I do know wot thee bist come for, Edie, but I ben't quite ready for thee yet.'

The soap-and-water-wrinkled hands took the emaciated geriatric ones in hers for a warm goodbye.

'Some time between midnight and six o'clock,' Edie advised the neighbours who accompanied her to the door.

Old Ginny didn't let her down. Just after 4 a.m. she gave up watching the flickering candle on the wash-stand and let the darkness come.

Conscience Stricken

Big-eared, chopsy and tactless, with a penchant for letting cats out of bags and for exposing the skeletons in the family cupboard, I was the sort of child mothers like out of the way when visitors are around. However, this was a special occasion and Mother was determined to show her brood off.

By our terms this visitor was a proper somebody. I had learned that he was elderly, a lay preacher who had settled many years ago in Yorkshire after leaving our impoverished mining village to look for work. He had made himself 'a tidy bit o' money' keeping a grocery shop up there, and, most important to a mercenary little six-year-old, 'There might be summat in it for you if you be a good little wench.'

'Summat' might mean a toffee, two toffees! a halfpenny!! or even a penny!!! My optimism travelled like a kangaroo by leaps and bounds. I decided it was worth cooperating with Mam. It was quite a trial; it meant giving in without a struggle to having my knees washed as well as face and hands, the tangles combed out of my hair, the responsibility of a clean

pinny, and, worst of all, sitting still and keeping my mouth
shut. Strictly speaking he wasn't really our visitor at all; he was
coming to see our aged great-aunt with whom we lived.

Old Auntie who was chair-ridden with arthritis didn't have
to have her knees washed – no one could see them under her
long black skirts – but we brought her a wet flannel and towel
for her face. Mam tied a clean pinny on her and brushed her
sparse strands of white hair into a tidier little bun, assuring her
that she looked 'quite respectable'.

The freshly-nappied baby lay on the sofa contentedly
sucking his sugar teat, Mam kept rubbing over the big, black-
leaded grate until it shone. We youngsters tried to be as still
and as wooden as the chairs we sat on. It was purgatory, but
after one of Mam's quick peeps outside, she dramatically
hissed at us that ''im was a-comin' down the garden path'.

He took his time, for he was quite old. When he came in I
thought he looked like a cross between Methuselah and one of
the Disciples. He had white hair and a long white beard,
watery blue eyes below bushy white eyebrows, puffed pinky
cheeks and a moist pink mouth I didn't take to at all. It wasn't
his physiognomy I was particularly interested in; it was in listening for the crackle of a sweet packet or the chink of coins
in his pockets. He looked affluent enough for both; in a black
suit grand enough for funerals, starched white shirt and gold
watch-chain shining across his chest. Mam pulled up the
other best chair with arms on nearer the fire opposite old
Auntie's. They took an interminable time reckoning up the
dead and gone, and recalling old times, before Mam's polite
coughs got a bit apprehensive regarding our forbearance, but
at last he turned his attention to us.

The baby got a short nursing on his lap, spent a penny in
the form of a big wet patch on the visitor's knee, and made a

profit of twopence by getting a silver threepenny-bit in his hand. The omens were good! My little brother next. He was soon off his perch having tried hard to pull the old man's beard off. I decided he was like a Disciple, for he still gave my brother a penny. I was a bit worried, though, about this sort of financial index – there was still a little sister to come before me. She was a pretty, quiet, fair little creature and sat long enough to absorb most of the damp patch and she, too, got a penny. My evaporating patience returned. At six years he considered me eligible for a sermon, advising me that if I said my prayers every night, attended Sunday School regularly, and never disobeyed my elders, I should go to Heaven when I died. I wasn't struck with this bargain –we had texts and pictures of angels hanging around the walls upstairs and I had come to the conclusion being an angel was very boring; just floating around in the sky all the time. I much preferred it on earth, where I could get broken bits of china and rusty tins off the ash-mix to play shops with, and make houses out of the lush green ferns under the trees, and only get a smack if Mam could catch me when I was naughty instead of going to Hell. However, I didn't aim to risk a possible penny by correcting him, and at last I got one, and I knew just what I was going to spend it on – lucky, lucky me! Oh! what a lovely day it was! I was up our garden path like a rocket.

As far as I was aware there was only one cherry tree in the world, and it was in Prudence the witch's garden, the cottage below ours. Many a dribble had gone down the front of my pinny longing for some of the luscious ripe cherries on it. Now I could buy a whole pennyworth and hide down in our empty pigs-cot for a feast.

We reckoned Prudence was a witch because she never wanted to mix with the rest of the village and had a nasty habit of crouching down behind her gate in the dusk, popping up like a jack-in-the-box making a weird cackling laugh if a child went by. She could perform miracles, too, because all the women said it was a miracle where Prudence's son had come from. She hadn't got a husband, was never seen ever talking to a man, and the village women seemed very annoyed wondering where she had got him. He was quite big and strong but not quite all there in his attic – but he was very good at shinning up the cherry tree to pick the wares. We forgot about her being a witch when her cherries were ripe!

I was stopped in my tracks when I reached our garden gate by a most unusual sight! A beggar-woman, *in our village*! I had heard about beggars, and how sometimes they had gold sovereigns hidden under their ragged clothes. Perhaps that was the reason no-one came out of our penny-pinched community to give her anything. Apparently it was against the law to actually knock on the doors to beg, so this old woman was supposedly singing for her supper – I thought she sounded worse than a cat on the tiles and anyway it was cherries, not charity, that occupied my mind. I ran down to Prudence's door and soon got a nice lot of cherries in a piece of newspaper. I didn't have to share with my siblings, they had all got their own money, so clutching my precious hoard I made my way back to our gate en route for the pigs-cot.

I wasn't pleased to see Dilys Pugh leaning up against it. She was a few years older than me – a 'stuck up', well-dressed only child with a caste system of her own. She regarded me as one of the head-scratching, droopy-drawered, inferior untouchables.

She had a long nose and plenty of practice looking down it. She was a born scolder, worse than a governess at school, and kept showing off by pulling her proper hemmed handkerchief out of the legs of her drawers even when her nose didn't need wiping.

If you said 'bugger' when a sharp stone went up through the hole in your boot sole she was so shocked she told your mam and probably got you a good hiding. I had no intention of offering *her* any cherries.

'I'll tell your mam if you yut any on 'em,' she warned me.

'I don't care, they be mine anyroads.'

'Pooh, don't tell lies. You've got a penn'oth there and the likes o' your mam can't give a penny fir yourself.'

'It ben't lies. We got a visitor, and 'im gid the lot on us a penny, and 'im gid the babby drippence, so there!'

Dilys pulled herself up to a bit above her normal height, pursed her lips to a thinner, narrower line, and took a deep breath through flared nostrils that swelled out her narrow chest. She looked at me with her 'God help them for they know not what they do' expression. Her eyes concentrated into accusing slits. I thought she was going to explode.

'Dost thee mean to tell I that thee'st spent a whole penny on thee own greedy guts with thic pore old varmint up there a-tryin' to sing 'er 'eart out to get some money fir summat to yut! 'Er's likely to drop down dyud afore long from starvation. The trouble with thee, thee'st got no conscience. I'll bet thee'st 'ad some dinner today, not like thic pore old creature.'

I looked at the old woman again with 'seeing' eyes. Oh, how pitiful she was, so skinny, so raggedly dressed. I remembered my dinner; Mam had made a big suety pudding and put a good sprinkling of sugar over it. Oh! what a thoughtless, wicked, greedy girl I was! If only I could get my penny back, but I didn't dare ask Prudence such a thing. Never mind, I would give the old beggar-woman my untouched cherries. I ran up to her and thrust them in her hands. To my intense

surprise and disappointment she didn't seem at all pleased.
She put them away somewhere in the folds of her ragged skirts
without even a thank you or a smile. I staggered back against
a garden wall and started to walk down to Dilys who had been
watching. Dilys, too, appeared to have lost interest; she turned
and went on her way down the village. I stood by our gate; I
had no penny, no cherries, not even a thank you.

I was square with my conscience but it brought little comfort – I decided there and then that me and my conscience
didn't get on very well together.

A Loss

There was a proper midwife who wore a navy-blue bonnet tied under her chin, a navy cape, and carried the bag 'she brought the babies in'. Most of the women managed with the village midwife, a skilled, kindly, self-taught woman who took a mere pittance for her services and was the soul of discretion regarding the lack of sheets and other necessities for the confinement. She often added the bonus of bowls of her own gruel and pieces of clean white rag for the new mother to hem napkins whilst she stayed the statutory ten days in bed.

The village midwife, the proper nurse *and* the doctor were called in on one occasion but between them all they could save neither mother nor child.

Letty was a bonny young wife who had carried her first pregnancy right up until the ninth month as easily as she carried her bundles of kindling wood home from the forest. By then her neat slim little figure had such a dimensional preponderance folk laughingly observed it would be bound to be twins there, if not triplets! There were no clinics for the measuring of pelvic bones, urine tests or the other safeguards now in practice. Only the wise village midwife felt alarm for Letty. When the girl's labour started, before it got too protracted she sent the young husband for the proper midwife. The professional midwife had no wish to diminish her own status by calling in the doctor, but after many hours she relented and the fleetest-footed teenager in the village was sent running the two miles for the doctor.

The worried, bewildered young husband was reluctantly made to go to his shift at the pit by the midwife. 'You'll do no good here – just be in the way, and with another mouth on the way to feed you can't afford to miss your work.'

He put his feet towards the pit but his head kept turning back to the cottage window where Letty suffered in the big iron bedstead. Before he reached the pit head she had bent the iron bedhead in the mad agony of her turmoil.

The good old doctor was away on an urgent case of pneumonia, but the boy left the message for him to visit. By the time his horse and trap drew up at her cottage gate, Letty's eyes were glazing over and her knuckles were bitten to the bone in her suffering. The doctor knew this child would never be born. Not for the first time he cursed Nature and its methods of reproduction. The nearest hospital then was eighteen miles away, and transport a horse and cart. He knew the girl would not survive the journey. He had not the skill, the means, or the trained help to perform the necessary caesarian operation in a primitive cottage bedroom. He had only laudanum and it was getting too late for that, but youth dies hard.

The village midwife, stricken by the turn of events, asked the weeping neighbours to send a couple of men to way-lay the young husband, now on his way home from the pit. 'Tell 'em to kip 'im away from 'ere somehow – 'tis better 'er be gone than 'im should see the wench like this.'

Sick in their hearts, two men hurried off through the woods trying to think up a ploy to keep the young man out of earshot of his cottage. He saw through their false cheer and hindrance. Sensing a conspiracy and full of foreboding, he broke from the physical constraint they were forced to use. He rushed indoors and up the stairs and watched his sweetheart wife die.

The women wept and said, 'I shall 'ear thic poor wench's screams till the day I die.' Men hung their heads in sorrow – 'Thic pore bwoy, 'im'll be like a young tater that 'a' bin nipped by a black frost – 'im'll never be the same agyun.' The young man never was the same: he never married, he relinquished his manhood. 'I'd never do anything that 'ud putt a 'oman dru that agyun.'

We children knew him as a kindly, eccentric, white-haired old man, who looked at us with tender, rheumy eyes. Perhaps we were all like living ghosts to him, ghosts of the child he never had.

A Good Clane Out

Facts are facts and have to be faced, and in truth when I was a little girl, next to my Dad, I loved my belly. It was a tyrant, always sending messages up for anything I could scrounge for it. I was a good scrounger, from old Great-Auntie's bacon-rinds and crusts, too hard for her toothless gums to chew, to the bits of corn I could peck up before Miss Phillips's fowls gobbled them when she threw a couple of handfuls to them over her garden gate. Best of all, my stomach and I mutually agreed, was suet treacle pud, and Granny was our greatest benefactor in this respect. Granny's bevy of daughters were all away in domestic service or married; only her son remained at home, but Granny never made suet pud for just the three of them. She waited until she could get enough ingredients for her household, our household and any other children within sniffing distance. Pudding cloths were her problem. Clean white rag was hard to come by and there were so many other uses for it. Babies' bums, for instance, and there were plenty of them about!

Granny's problem was solved on one occasion when one of her daughters brought home from service a couple of white cotton tennis stockings given her by her mistress. Just the job, thought Granny!

Granny mixed her puddings in her huge bread-crock, then stuffed them by the yard down the stockings. She filled her copper with water and lit the fire underneath it. When she finished her washing, it was Granny's habit to rinse the copper out with clean water and soap, and dry it. Something must have distracted her on the previous washday, for a residue gel of Hudson's Powder and soap had been left in the bottom. Now, Granny's copper was in the darkest end of her dark little kitchen, at the back of her cottage. Unaware of the soap, when the copper came to the boil and clouds of steam hid the frothy water, Granny couldn't smell it. She had lost her sense of smell from a severe sinus illness years before. The puddings bubbled about like a bunch of anaemic Loch Ness Monsters.

We children and our friends stayed near at hand playing hopscotch on the piece of hard-trodden earth outside our garden gate – waiting – waiting for Granny's calls.

At last – 'Come on in, me butties; bring summat wi' yer to putt yer puddin' on.'

We lined up with our saucers etc. by her back-kitchen door, taking our turn by her salting slab for our dollop of pudding and ration of warmed treacle. Then we perched in tiers on the stone steps leading from her garden down to her tiny court-yard, just in case a second helping might be forthcoming.

A second helping! We could hardly down the first!

Something had gone amiss; the pudding tasted bitter and soapy. We were no gourmets, and the anticipation had been so great; besides, we were well-mannered enough to hide our disappointment from our beloved Granny. We controlled our grimaces of distaste and swallowed every mouthful.

Granny always left herself till last, but there was some in the toe of one of the stockings for her.

Life hadn't made Granny a gourmet either, but she pulled a very wry face with her first spoonful; then, realising what she had done, she said, 'Laird o' merssy, this puddin' be awful. Oh my Gawd I 'ope I 'an't pizened the lot of you – oh well, if I 'ave I might as well pizen meself, too.' And she ate hers all up as well.

The stomach spasms didn't hit us all at once – but it was frequently one-in-and-one-to-go doubled up outside the garden bucket-privy.

However black the clouds gathered on Granny's horizon she always poked in them for a bit of silver lining. She found some then.

'I'll tell thee what,' she observed to Mam, 'thee ou'tn't need to give any of 'em doses o' brimstone and treacle f'r a bit – I reckon all their insides 'ave 'ad a good clane out.'

A couple of years later Granny moved to another part of the Forest. We missed her even more than her treacle puddings. Through Granny's eyes the world was an infinitely richer place. When I was a young married woman of twenty-six and visiting my parents, Granny walked through the woods the two-and-a-half miles to us for 'a squat an' a chat'.

When it was time for her to go I walked most of the way back with her. We stopped for a breather in a little valley with steep wooded sides. It was so peaceful and beautiful there: a sparkling little stream meandered through beds of watercress, birds sweetly twittered in the branches over our heads; the dappled sunshine through the trees gave a perfect mixture of warmth and shade and the moss-covered earth was soft beneath our feet.

Granny stood there for some minutes quietly gazing around, then she sighed, 'Ah, my wench, I mustn't grumble. The Almighty 'a' bin good to me, f'r 'Im 'a' let me goo past me dree score years and ten, and the time be comin' soon f'r me to goo – but oh, my wench, I shall miss all this!'

Now I am getting old, dear Granny, I know just how you felt.

Dashed Hopes

'I'll tell you what we'll do, Maggie.' Granny's voice was low, urgent and conspiratorial. 'We'll make up some pizen – we can make it out o' some deadly nightshade – then if thic Kaiser gets 'is armies over 'ere and they come anywhere near us, we'll pizen the little 'uns fust, then take zum ourzelves – I'll never let them varmints put they dear little young 'uns on the end o' their bayonets.'

I knew I was one of 'them dear little 'uns' Granny was talking about. It was 1917. I was three years old – and I knew there was something called a war on. It was all the fault of a wicked man called the Kaiser who lived in a country named Germany and was sending his armies into England to kill us all off and have it for himself. The war, the war – everyone, especially the women, kept on talking about it, but I could see no sign of it anywhere. Old Great-Auntie, sitting in the chair nearest the fire, was fast asleep, her toothless mouth agape, she didn't seem worried. It was a comfort. I had never seen a soldier – the men in our village were all miners and exempt from call-up. Coal, and more coal, was needed, all the coal that could be got to stoke the fires of this man-made hell on earth.

It was lovely when Father was home from the pit and I could take my turn with the others for a sit on his lap. Then I felt safe and secure from the Kaiser, from the war, from the shadows on the wall, even from the thunder and lightning that sent Mam cowering in the coal-hole under the stairs. Granny often came into our house from next door. Granny couldn't read herself, but she brought Grancher's paper in for Mam to read. She, old Auntie and Mam would cuddle us round the fire while Mam read all the awful news from the war front, news exacerbated by all the ghoulish rumours about the wicked Germans. Father had no patience with these sessions.

'Them Germans be no different to we lot or any other country – them soldiers over there do as they be told the same as our lot. They be no more responsible for this war than we be – and you women do want your yuds examined if you do swallow all you read in the papers, or what do get about on people's tongues. 'Twas the Boers last time – and when this lot's over, after a bit, another war'll break out somewhere else. We 'uman bein's be supposed to have brains but we be wuss than the animals. The world's a sick place – all us 'ave bin from what I've read, and all us will be till they got enough sense to share things instead o' fightin' over 'em, and they've got more gumption than you dree swallowin' everything you be told.'

Such conversations were beyond my comprehension, but even at that age Father had an aura for me that made me his ally.

The war came into our house with the grocery man. Miners

were now earning enough to keep their families' bellies well filled, but rationing kept us short. Old Auntie got a precious ounce of butter – she loved her 'bit o' best butter'. When it went missing off the table one day the house was in a turmoil. Mam and she had definitely seen it when the grocer had delivered it along with Auntie's three-cornered blue paper bag of sugar, a tin of Nestlé's milk, bit of red-rinded cheese, etc. How could it have vanished into thin air? I had been playing with a neighbour's toddler son indoors; my mouth was inspected inside and out, and my small person thoroughly frisked for evidence – despite my denial of the crime.

Only when our neighbour undressed her little boy for bed did she find the bit of greasy paper in his pocket and the oily stain on his trousers. This little tragedy was recounted for weeks.

I knew the war had ended when Granny came in and picked us up one at a time and did a dance in our tiny courtyard. Old Auntie kept thanking the Almighty for His deliverance. I almost stopped worrying about the Kaiser coming to kill me in the night. The need for coal slackened down – gradually the men were put on short time, especially when coal was imported from the Saar as reparation from the beaten enemy. Rationing finished, but our grocery deliveries didn't improve all that much.

At five I started school. On winter evenings, perched on the end of our steel fender, I often listened to Father and his pit butties talking. Their talk ranged on many subjects –war was one of them. I knew that the subject of war particularly saddened and angered Father. I sensed that he might be worried lest my little brother go to war when he grew up.

One evening, when I was about eight years old, Father came in from a meeting. He had a book in his hand, his face was white and taut. Granny, old Auntie and Mam were sitting round the fire.

'Here,' said Father to them. 'Take a look at this book, then you'll see what war is all about.'

I could see the title of the book was *War Against War*, but I was not allowed to look inside. I knew where Father put the books he thought unsuitable for childish eyes – on top of the cupboard by the fireplace. I waited my opportunity to climb up on a chair when no-one was about.

I turned over the pages and became a pacifist for life. Here was proof of man's bestiality to man – if his capacity for evil was exploited. No wonder Father worried. I could not comfort him or go to him for comfort. I had disobeyed him getting up on the cupboard. The dread of war, though often forgotten in happy playing, hung over my childish head.

A quarter of an hour before school prayers for the end of lessons one day, our teacher told us to put away our composition books because she had something to tell us. As she spoke the sky grew a more fairy blue through the windows, the flowers in the jam pots on the windowsills more exquisite, and her pleasant face with its aura of fair hair began to look like an angel's, for she was telling us about something called the League of Nations – about the treaty the leaders of these nations had signed to prevent another war.

No dawdling home from school for me that day – no joyous runs into the ferns from the woodland path. No linking arms with the other girls, whilst singing our favourite school songs. I was the bearer of magic news, weighed down not at all by my black leather-studded boots.

'Where's our Dad?' I demanded breathlessly of Mam.

'Down in his shed – wot's up?'

I couldn't stop to tell her. Father was in his little shed at the bottom of the garden. He was quite a handyman. Here he mended our boots, did a bit of amateur carpentry, and soldered his and his pit butties' carbide lamps. It was mostly an honorary pastime – there was often no money to pay for his services. He had fashioned his own brazier from a large round tin with a fire-bellows fixed in the side to heat the soldering iron white-hot. I loved to watch Father soldering. The tiny balls of liquid metal needed such a delicate touch to spread it on the cracks in the metal lamps with the soldering iron. It was not a time for distractions – but my wonderful news cast such considerations aside.

'Dad! Dad! There ben't goin' to be any more wars!'

He went on with his soldering. My words could not have sunk in. I tugged at his sleeve. 'Dad! Dad! Did you 'ear wot I said? – there ben't goin' to be any more wars!'

'And wot makes you think that, my wench?'

'Our teacher told us, Dad. A lot of countries 'ave done summat called the League o' Nations. They've signed a treaty so there won't be any more wars.'

Father lifted me up on to his work-bench. He looked through the window with sad, faraway eyes.

'I be afeared, my wench, that this treaty ben't wuth the paper 'tis wrote on.'

My spirits sank down in my heavy boots – but I had grown never to doubt the truth or wisdom of Father's words. As simply as he could, he explained to me about the moving balances of world trade – about the discoveries of natural resources and how, even by going to war, nations sought to obtain the lion's share of these things. He told me about man's ego patriotism, and ego religions, about all the things that made them enemies.

My stricken face must have disturbed him. 'There, there,

my wench, Father shouldn't 'a' worried thy young yud wi' such talk. Doosn't thee worry, there may never be a war in thy time. Eh, I'll tell thee what – I 'a' got a nice bit o' rope 'ere, and two pieces o' wood that'll do for handles. Thee goo and ex thee mother to wet I a cup o' tay and I'll make thee a skippin' rope.'

I have lived through a second world war. The powers of East and West threaten each other with atom bombs. Somewhere or other a war is always going on on this earth. Unlike Granny, Mam and old Auntie, I never believe all I read in the papers.

Kezzie

Because she was such a bright little scholar, our exasperated teachers often overlooked some of Kezzie Larkin's shortcomings, for Kezzie was a bit of a handful.

The cottage 'over on the Green' where the Larkins lived was looked down on by us villagers. It was overrun with little Larkins; 'nothin' but a bloody rabbut warren', was how one man described it

Kezzie was the eldest of six children. Despite her ragged clothes, tangled nitty hair and dirt-ingrained knees, Kezzie had enough charisma to be accepted by the rest of us. God knows we village children had absolutely no grounds to be toffee-nosed about anyone, but children, of course, form their own hierarchies just as grown-ups do. In our childish eyes, pretty girls were those lucky enough to have be-ribboned curls and tidy clothes; looks and form had nothing to do with it.

Grown-ups were more observant. I remember one man remarking to another as they watched us at play: 'I doubt thee'lt ever clap thee eyes on a purtier wench than thic young

Kezzie. I bet the kings o' England 'ould give zummat to 'ave daughters as looked like thic little wench.'

Recalling Kezzie in my mind's eye, I see a thin little face with a pair of long-lashed, expressive eyes, flecked with green and hazel, a neat, small, straight nose and a mouth that rarely turned down at the corners. My eldest sister and Kezzie were the two top scholars in their class. Kezzie was the younger by six months, but they were close chums. Kezzie knew where the rain made puddles for illicit paddling, where the best wild strawberries grew, and the right places to go scrumping apples. She organised us into 'concert parties', performed acrobatics like a monkey from tree branches, and could make up the most exciting fibs to scare us out of our wits. Her skinny, muscle-knotted arms packed a terrific punch in defence of her tribe of small brothers. Carrying no ballast, she could run like the wind, leading us to safety when pursued for our misdemeanours.

The Larkins' fecundity was a sore problem to many of the village women; they were full of sympathy when rumour had it that Kezzie's mam was 'in the cyart agyun'.

''Tis a cryin' shame, there's more mouths over there already than victuals to put in 'em.'

Mrs Larkin had her baby, a girl this time.

The words 'gone to a better place' seemed only too true when the news got round six weeks later that the baby had died. Mrs Larkin was in a bad way too, hardly able to walk, with swollen, ulcerated legs.

As it neared chapel treat time I stepped up my attendances at Sunday School to get enough marks for this special day of the year. The kindly old man who took Bible class asked Gladys, Dolly, Lil and me if we would be four little Christians and act as pallbearers to carry the baby to church. There would be no mourners and no service inside the church because the baby had not been christened. The mother was too ill to go but the vicar was willing to say a few words before she was buried in some unconsecrated ground at the back of the churchyard. We were eleven years old – too young for any depth of feeling, but we felt very sombre and important as we looked at each other for assent and nodded 'Yes'.

All our mams picked us a little bunch of flowers to go on the coffin and Lil's mam made us a black armband each to wear.

It was a lovely warm sunny day, a day to shin up trees, scamper in and out of the ferns beneath them, and jump for joy over the huge oak-roots exposed across the woodland paths, but we felt the solemnity of the occasion and walked sedately, remembering all the miserable things we could talk about. It would be cruel to the dead baby to feel cheerful.

I had never been in Kezzie's house before; I was shocked. I thought our house was a palace in comparison. Our Mam made rag-rugs to put in front of the grate; we had a pair of brass candlesticks and a vase on our mantelpiece; our Dad had made some shelves for Mam to show off the cups, saucers and plates she had got with tea coupons. Here there was only an old sack on the floor, the bits of lace curtains had more holes than lace, not an ornament anywhere, and the table and chairs looked very kicked about.

The little home-made coffin was on the table. Mrs Larkin, who looked very ill, hobbled over to it. I could see her swollen ankles all ulcerated and bleeding . . . she lifted the lid of the coffin. I had been privately of the opinion that new babies looked little different from skinned rabbits, but this one looked like a white marble doll, paler than the nightdress she was laid out in. The Larkins had to lug the water much farther than the villagers from the communal well. A little posy of wild flowers had been placed between the baby's hands. Two tears from Mrs Larkin's eyes bedewed them as she kissed the baby goodbye. There was pride as well as grief in her voice as she called on us to witness what a little angel her baby looked.

The lid was fastened down, two ropes were tied round with loops for carrying, and we started out. Mrs Larkin picked a toddler up from the floor, rocking him in her arms for comfort. A couple of her other little boys followed us as far as the well. 'Where's your Kezzie gone?' Lil asked them.

'Nowhere – 'er ben't gone nowhere – 'er's zittin' round the back o' the 'ouse wi' 'er pinny over 'er yud a cryin'.'

It was a mile to the church. We kept to the grass verge of the main road. Only one timber wagon passed us; cars were still a rare sight in those days.

The vicar stood in the church porch. He met us outside while a man stood by the open grave to let the coffin down. The vicar mumbled a few words and led us out of the church-yard.

'Don't worry,' he said, 'I'm sure the Good Shepherd will take this little lamb into His flock.'

When we were out of earshot Lil observed rather tartly, 'Of course that babby'll goo to 'Eaven. All babbies do 'cos they 'an't done nothin' wrong.' We felt quite comforted.

We didn't go back to the Larkins' house; we knew there would be no funeral meats – not even a cup of tea to spare.

By the winter all the village was in similar straits to the Larkins. Our dads – all miners – had come out on strike rather than submit to even worse conditions than they had already endured in the cruel economic climate of the twenties. It was an awful struggle for our mams to get something for us to take to school for our midday break. Our Mam had melted some mutton fat down for dripping, spreading it on the bread whilst it was still warm. It had re-congealed into hard white lumps but was going down sweet enough until our young noses sniffed the unfamiliar odour of meat. *Meat!* Who could possibly be eating meat?

We were allowed to sit in the main classroom for our lunch-break. The whispers came back up the row of desks.

'It was they Larkins lot *yuttin' meat.*' No bread, they hadn't got any bread. 'Just girt chunks o' lean *meat.*' It was astounding information. And they kept bringing meat day after day.

Then one day none of the Larkins came to school and the rumour got around that the police had taken Mr Larkin away. He had been sheep stealing. Fifty years before he would probably have been hanged for the crime. Instead he was summonsed – sent to jail – and the bailiffs called in to sell up his household goods towards recompense for the sheep-owners.

'Poor bugger, I'd 'a' done the zame livin' up there out o' sight with me young 'uns starvin'. They baillies got to leave the beds; it's the law: they mustn't sell the beds.'

We were as a rule ready gawpers at anything outside the common rut – funerals and weddings. A cat stranded up a tree, a harangue between neighbours, the odd drunk – all got our rapt attention.

But with no means to help the Larkins, no-one from the village had the heart to go and watch.

'Their veow sticks o' farniture zold over their yuds; I doubt the lot put together'll vetch a couple o' quid.'

'Poor devils. It'll be the work-house for 'em now.'

Children and mothers were segregated in the work-house; her children were all that Mrs Larkin had left.

"Ave you 'eard about the Larkins? They've gone in wi' the gypsies.'

'Never.'

"Tis right enough. Our Tom was walkin' dru the wood by the gypsies' camp and 'im zid the Larkin bwoys a-playin' wi' the gypsy young 'uns and 'im could zee a iron bedstead in one o' the tents.'

The strike was over, the beaten men went back to work, but not our Dad. There was no job for him. He was labelled a radical upstart because he had openly spoken up against the oppressors. He tramped the days away looking for work, but a day's work of any sort was almost impossible to come by. His pit coal allowance was gone, but we drew our chairs up to a good fire that winter. Buckets of coal were tipped inside our garden gate, and there was kindling wood to be gathered in the surrounding forest.

One bitterly cold night, a cruel east wind, full of icy sleet, beat against our window and blew the piece of sacking away put to stop the draught from coming under the door.

'I wonder 'ow they poor little Larkin young 'uns be standin' this out in them tents in the 'ood,' said Mam sadly. I shivered in sympathy, soon forgotten as I cuddled with my siblings under Mam's heavy home-made patchwork quilts. We survived the winter, spring came to cheer us up, then summer and a day of great anticipation. After a year in service our sister was coming home for her annual holiday. We didn't know what time. Dad was in the back-kitchen shaving and Mam was polishing over the black-leaded grate for the umpteenth time when a neighbour came puffing down our garden path to tell us she couldn't be sure, but somebody was comin' up the village that might be her!

Dad wiped the lather off his face and ran through the

door – his face naked with love for this treasured homecomer. I saw him take her into his arms through the window. How could this glamorous, beautiful young woman be our sister?

I thought she had been dressed up to the nines when she left home in a new navy serge dress and black shoes off the packman topped with a second-hand straw boater, her long brown hair hanging down her back. Now, taller, plumped out, with shiny, short, marcel-waved hair, dressed in a smart brown suit, a cream silk blouse, with dainty brown shoes and pink silk stockings – no wonder Father looked beside himself with pride as he brought her in through the door. Short-sighted Mam blinked her tears away behind her glasses. The warm, scented hug my sister gave me made me feel I was polluting her.

'Quick, goo upstairs and fetch the best spoons and knives down,' Mam whispered urgently to me. Mam kept our best bits of cutlery well polished with brick dust in a cardboard shoe-box on the wash-stand table. There was a mirror over it. The reflection of my very plain face, straight dull hair, steel-rimmed glasses and old frock was too awful: I burst into tears. The strongest emotion was shame that such a beautiful sister had to own such as me.

We all felt a bit shy at the tea table. After tea, too shy to take her arm, I followed a worshipful distance behind my sister as she walked around the top of the village – marvelling at her magnanimity for talking and laughing with the local young chaps. How I bragged about her to my friends at school the next day! About her beauty, her clothes, and the proper night-dress trimmed with lace she wore to bed.

My little brother and I hurried home from school. Mam told us our sister had walked to town to buy us some fancy cakes for tea; with our adoration increased, we ran through the woodland path to meet her. Her eyes lit up at the sight of us but she looked as though she had been crying.

We walked each side of her in subdued silence for a bit. I couldn't stand it. 'Wot be the matter?' I asked.

She burst into tears. ''Tis Kezzie Larkin. I seen her in town today. She was dressed in long old rags carrying pegs around in a basket wi' a gypsy 'oman. Poor Kezzie, her's nothing but a gypsy now.'

Our Scott

I don't remember when we got him; he was just there, part of the family, a small black and white mongrel, our Scott.

His appetite was very catholic, but the scraps he wheedled from our poor-man's table gave him a prodigious amount of energy. He was a master scrounger. I can still see the swollen veins on the butcher's face when Scott stole a string of sausages from his basket and ran off for safety in the narrow gap between our garden shed and nextdoor's thorny hedge. Poking sticks, well-aimed stones, curses and threats did not deter him from his stolen feast.

The wails from a short-sighted neighbour still ring in my ears. She had put two slices of fish she had fried for tea to keep warm on her steel fender. She found only a well-licked plate and Scott sitting by her open cottage door, contentedly smacking his chops.

He landed me in some scrapes with Mam before she started to shut him up in the back-kitchen at meal-times. Before that, he would sneak under the table, pushing his head persistently against the legs of us children, begging us to pass him down scraps from our plates. Even ever-hungry Scott turned up his nose at the little dollops of cabbage I dropped down to him from my Sunday dinner-plate. There they still were, soiling the scrubbed stone flags under my chair when Mam cleared up.

He constantly dropped me in trouble at school, too. It was difficult for Mam to keep our cottage door shut with my toddler siblings about. I rarely progressed more than half-way through the long wooded walk to school before he was there, trotting behind my heels, tail wagging madly, ready for school.

'Goo on wum, you naughty dog!' I would scold him. Down went his tail between his legs, his body made an about-turn but his head turned to me, his eyes two brown pools of hurt betrayal.

I couldn't bear it. 'No, no, you be a good dog. I do love you,' and back he would rush at me, all reproach gone.

Keeping this up all the way to the schoolyard gate was a dreadful hindrance and gave me no option but to leave him looking the picture of misery outside, made worse by his put-on bout of the shivers.

Assembly and scripture lesson would be over and sums begun before I poked my head round the classroom door. A terrible duffer at arithmetic, I copped it from my long-suffering teacher.

'Ah! Miss Sloth has arrived at last! Now we must all wait until she gets to her desk; no need for her to arrive at lessons early, because she never gets a sum right. Oh well, she can have a black mark in her book, and stay in during playtime for an extra arithmetic lesson.'

No good telling Teacher about Scott. My burdens were heavy, but his suffering, left scolded and abandoned outside, was much worse.

Though he wasn't allowed to attend school, we considered our Scott a genius. How else could he be clever enough to know when the dog-licence man was coming round the village? When this happened, on his own initiative, Scott hid in the coal-hole in the back-kitchen with never a sniff or a whine to betray his presence, so that Mam could look the man straight in the eye and deny we kept a dog. The licence was seven-and-six per annum; we just didn't have that sort of money, and Scott knew it.

Our small living-room and back-kitchen-cum-coal-house were always overcrowded with a crawling baby, toddlers' feet, old Great-Auntie's corn-calloused rheumaticky ones, Mam's busy feet, Dad's heavy boots and the fidgety feet of us bigger ones. But if Scott couldn't find a lap to sit on, he was adept at finding a corner to curl up in out of everybody's way. Ever ready to defend us all, he would growl only when the rare strange footstep – bar the dog-licence man's – approached the door.

Nearly every child's father in our area was a miner, and it was the hungry twenties. Unsurprisingly, when the men went on strike rather than submit to even more inhuman conditions, food scraps became too precious even for well-loved dogs.

Father explained to us why he had found another home for Scott. It was with a kindly old pit butty of his, whose children had grown up and left home for work, and were now able to help their parents out.

Father walked over three miles to take Scott to his new home, where he was given a bellyful of food as the initial bribe to stay. He had returned, almost to our garden gate, when the dog came panting up behind him, and the tear smudges were still on our faces as we welcomed him back.

Father had to be firm. The next day he walked Scott back to his new home. 'Kip'n shut up f'r a couple o' days to settle 'un in,' he advised his old friend.

Three days later Scott bounded joyously back through our door.

Father sighed. 'All right then, old bwoy, if thee'st rather starve wi' us lot than live wi' a vull belly zomewhere else, thee shal'st stop 'ere.'

Scott was getting on a bit, but still very agile, when I left home at fourteen to go into domestic service. The strike was over, but not for Father.

Pit-owners and management had black-listed him for his courage in speaking up against their demands. Mine was one less mouth for Mam to feed but, dreadfully homesick, I lived for the day when I could go home for the holidays.

Not knowing what chores my mistress might want done before I started out, I could not let my family know what time to meet me. When I had walked from the railway-halt to the edge of the forest where a woodland path led to our village, I would call, 'Scott, Scott, come on, Scott.'

In a matter of minutes, a small black and white bundle would come bounding through the ferns, impelled like a small rocket by his own enthusiasm, right up into my arms; my herald, to welcome me home. Sensing what his urgent departure meant, my little brother and sisters would come running in his wake, turning my heart over a little as they pulled up shyly in front of the big sister who had become a bit of a stranger after a year from home.

I was seventeen when I went home for my annual summer holiday from my job in London. At the woodland path I called out for Scott. No Scott came, despite repeated callings. Disappointed, I walked home through the forest.

Disappointment turned to heartache when I stepped indoors; matters had turned from bad to worse. Father still had no job; his loyal butties helped out from their own meagre resources, but sad-eyed and grey-faced, he seemed to have shrunk. So had Mam, and the pot-bellies and skinny legs of the little ones told their own story.

After the hugs and kisses, I sat down to a good meal that, by hook or by crook, Mam had mustered for my homecoming. 'Where's our Scott?' I asked.

Father took a time to answer. 'I be afeared, my wench, that we 'an't'n any more. The poor old bwoy was in bad shape. No doubt 'im could 'a' gone on a bit longer if we could 'a' give 'im the right sort o' victuals, but 'twas cruel to let'n goo on. 'Is poor legs was givin' out, an' 'im was sufferin'.'

Our way of life had not included such luxuries as the services of a vet. I sensed that it had been Dad's job to put Scott out of his misery. I knew that Father, intelligent and utterly humane, would have thought of the most merciful way. Just then I could not harass him further to find out.

Mam pushed my plate of food towards me, but it was not easy to swallow with no warm head pushing my knees under the table.

FULL HEARTS
AND
EMPTY BELLIES

A 1920s Childhood from the Forest of Dean
to the Streets of London

Winifred Foley

The *Sunday Times* bestseller

Winifred Foley grew up in the 1920s – a bright, determined miner's daughter – in a world of unspoilt beauty and desperate hardship. Living hand-to-mouth in a tumbledown cottage in the Forest of Dean, Foley – 'our Poll' – had a loving family and the woods and streams of a forest 'better than Heaven' as a playground. But a brother and sister had died in infancy, bread had to be begged from kindly neighbours and she never had a new pair of shoes or a shop-bought doll. And most terrible of all, like her sister before her, at fourteen little Poll had to leave her beloved forest for the city, bound for a life in service among London's grey terraces.

Now you can order superb titles directly from Abacus

☐ Full Hearts and Empty Bellies   Winifred Foley   £6.99

The prices shown above are correct at time of going to press. However, the publishers reserve the right to increase prices on covers from those previously advertised, without further notice.

────────── ⬭ABACUS ──────────

Please allow for postage and packing: **Free UK delivery.**
Europe: add 25% of retail price; Rest of World: 45% of retail price.

To order any of the above or any other Abacus titles, please call our credit card orderline or fill in this coupon and send/fax it to:

Abacus, PO Box 121, Kettering, Northants NN14 4ZQ
Fax: 01832 733076   Tel: 01832 737526
Email: aspenhouse@FSBDial.co.uk

☐ I enclose a UK bank cheque made payable to Abacus for £ . . . .
☐ Please charge £ . . . . . . to my Visa/Delta/Maestro

☐☐☐☐☐☐☐☐☐☐☐☐☐☐☐☐☐☐

Expiry Date ☐☐☐☐   Maestro Issue No. ☐☐

NAME (BLOCK LETTERS please) . . . .

ADDRESS . . . .

. . . .

. . . .

Postcode . . . . Telephone . . . .

Signature . . . .

Please allow 28 days for delivery within the UK. Offer subject to price and availability.